Water
Regulations
Guide

First edition published in December 2000, re-printed June 2001 by Water Regulations Advisory Scheme, Unit 13, Willow Road, Pen-y-Fan Industrial Estate, Crumlin, Gwent, NP11 4EG

ISBN 0-9539708-0-9

Second Edition: Third Impression

*Designed and produced by Isca Graphics,
9 Highfield Close, Caerleon, Newport NP18 3DW.
Illustrations by William Padden & Co, Fair View,
Much Birch, Hereford HR2 8HL.*

Printed in the UK by the Westdale Press, Cardiff

*Typeset in Leawood and Meta typefaces on an environmentally considered
paper 'Greencoat' that is totally chlorine free and with an 80% recycled content.*

Water Regulations Guide

Acknowledgements

The Authors wish to acknowledge the help and guidance given in the preparation of the various aspects of this Guide by the many Water Supply Industry personnel (including the Technical Committee and regional Technical Support Groups of the Water Regulations Advisory Scheme); staff of the Scheme including Simon Warburton, David Hodges and the Manager Dr Stephen Tuckwell; representatives of manufacturers' associations; individual plumbing industry and manufacturing representatives; representatives of the plumbing installers; DETR staff members present and retired; and a number of un-allied individual contributors including Victor King. Their help has been of inestimable value in ensuring that, as far as possible the needs and interests of all users of this Guide have been recognised and satisfied.

Water Regulations Guide

*Incorporating the Water Supply (Water Fittings) Regulations 1999
and the Water Byelaws 2000, Scotland*

Contents

Abbreviations and Symbols

GL   *Ground level*

WC   *Water closet*

WB   *Washbasin*

SL   *Spill-over level*

WP   *Warning/overflow pipe*

SV   *Stopvalve*

SgV   *Servicing valve*

CV   *Appliance control valve or tap*

DT   *Drain tap*

T   *Tundish with air gap*

SCV   *Single check valve*

DCV   *Double check valve*

FC   *Siphonic or non-siphonic flushing cistern*

PFC   *Pressure flushing cistern*

FV   *Pressure flushing valve*

PRV   *Pressure reducing valve*

TRV   *Temperature relief valve*

TPRV   *Combined temperature and pressure relief valve*

EV   *Expansion valve*

ExVl   *Expansion vessel*

S   *Strainer*

AVV   *Anti-vacuum valve*

PIDC   *Pipe interrupter with permanent atmospheric vent*

PIDB   *Pipe interrupter with atmospheric vent and moving element*

Foreword

▷ On 1 July 1999 each of the Water Suppliers in England and Wales ceased to enforce their own Water Byelaws and instead, began enforcing the new Regulations of the Secretaries of State of England and Wales – or the 'Regulator' as referred to in the Regulations. The three Water Authorities in Scotland commenced enforcing new Byelaws on 4 April 2000 and these, for the most part, mirror the Regulations for England and Wales. The Department of the Environment in Northern Ireland intends to review its Regulations in due course and it is likely that they will also mirror the Regulations in England and Wales.

▷ Because of the Water Supply Industry's new responsibilities, the offices of the Department of the Environment, Transport and the Regions (DETR), will monitor the Industry's enforcement regime of notifications, inspection and control and the Water Supplier's 'housekeeping' is likely to be more rigorous than previously. However, as indicated in a Code of Practice available from any Water Supplier, enforcement will be more transparent but customers will no longer be able to rely, necessarily, upon the local discretion of the Water Inspector – as in the past.

▷ For the most part, the Regulations are a repeat of some of the former Byelaws which were applied in England and Wales and were applied in Scotland. Installers and users of water fittings must not cause or permit waste, misuse, undue consumption or contamination of the supply of wholesome water. The differences in the Regulations are noticeable in the sections on notification, backflow prevention and flushing of WCs. There is also a general move towards conservation of water.

▷ The Regulations and the Schedules to the Regulations are published with the permission of the DETR. The DETR formal Guidance to the Regulations and the Schedules, the 'G' clauses, are also published in this Guide and also with the permission of the DETR.

▷ Much will be found to be familiar about the Water Supply Industry 'Recommendations and Comments' ('R' clauses) as many have been extracted from the earlier publication, the 'Water Supply Byelaws Guide'. New guidance will be found mostly in the sections on backflow prevention and flushing of WCs.

▷ The predecessor 'Water Byelaws Guide' proved to be of inestimable value to those designing fittings, making fittings and the installing and the controlling of the installation of water fittings. In the light of enhanced enforcement procedures this new Guide, produced by Laurie Young, a consulting engineer specialising in water services and Graham Mays, the former manager of the Water Regulations Advisory Scheme on behalf of, and to the requirements and approval of, the Water Supply Industry, should prove, with its improved illustrations and layout, of even more use and help to its readers than the earlier book.

▷ References are made in the Guide to European Standards (ENs), and British Standards (BSs). Readers should be aware that a European Standard is in preparation, EN 806 , Parts 1 to 5 which refers to plumbing installations in buildings.

▷ References to approved fittings and appliances and any specific installation instructions may be found in the 'Water Fittings and Materials Directory' published by the Water Regulations Advisory Scheme, Fern Close, Pen-y-Fan Industrial Estate, Oakdale, Gwent, NP11 3EH. E-mail: info@wras.co.uk

Notes on the Use of the Water Regulations Guide

The text of the Water Regulations Guide is divided into three sections:–

1. The text of Regulations (Byelaws) and the Schedules to the Regulations (Byelaws) –

2. The formal, legal, DETR Guidance to the Regulations (Byelaws) – Referred to as **'G'** clauses.

3. The Water Supply Industry 'Recommendations and Comments' – Referred to as **'R'** clauses.

The formal DETR Guidance includes illustrations which will be found with the **'G'** clauses. Illustrations provided by the Water Supply Industry will be found with the relevant **'R'** clauses.

Water Supply (Water Fittings) Regulations 1999

Summary of the Water Supply (Water Fittings) Regulations 1999

General

The Regulations make provision for preventing contamination, waste, misuse, undue consumption and erroneous measurement of water supplied by a water undertaker. The Regulations consist of three Parts and three Schedules as follows.

Part I of the Regulations deals with the preliminaries

REGULATION 1 states the title of the Regulations and interpretations of terms used within the Regulations, including a definition of the Regulator.

REGULATION 2 defines the application of the Regulations whereby they do not apply to certain water fittings in connection with water supplied for non-domestic purposes, or to water fittings lawfully installed before 1 July 1999.

Part II of the Regulations deals with the principal requirements

REGULATIONS 3 AND 4 impose general requirements in relation to water fittings. Water fittings must not be installed, connected, arranged or used in such a manner that they are likely to cause waste, misuse, undue consumption or contamination, or erroneous measurement, of the water supplied. They must be of an appropriate quality or standard, and be suitable for the circumstances in which they are used; and they must be installed, connected or disconnected in a workmanlike manner.

REGULATION 5 requires a person who proposes to install certain water fittings to notify the water undertaker, and not to commence installation without the undertaker's consent. The undertaker may withhold consent or grant it on certain conditions. This requirement does not apply to some fittings which are installed by a contractor who is approved by the undertaker or certified by an organization specified by the Regulator.

REGULATION 6 Where an approved contractor installs, alters, connects or disconnects a water fitting, he must provide a certificate that it complies with these Regulations.

Part III of the Regulations deals with enforcement etc.

REGULATIONS 7 AND 8 provide for a fine not exceeding level 3 on the standard scale for contravening the Regulations. It is a defence to show that the work on a water fitting was done by or under the direction of an approved contractor, and that the contractor certified that it complied with the Regulations. This defence is extended to the offences of contaminating, wasting and misusing water under section 73 of the Water Industry Act 1991. (Regulation 8).

REGULATION 9 enables water undertakers and local authorities who enter premises to carry out inspections, measurements and tests for the purposes of the Regulations.

REGULATION 10 requires the water undertaker to enforce the requirements of the Regulations; this duty is enforceable by the Regulator or the Director General of Water Services.

REGULATION 11 enables the Regulator to relax the requirements of these Regulations on the application of the Water Undertaker.

REGULATION 12 requires the Regulator to consult water undertakers and organizations representing water users before giving an approval for the purpose of the Regulations, and to publicise approvals.

REGULATION 13 provides for disputes arising under the Regulations between a Water Undertaker and a person who has installed or proposes to instal a water fitting to be referred to arbitration.

REGULATION 14 revokes the existing Water Byelaws made by water undertakers under section 17 of the Water Act 1945.

Schedule 1 – Fluid categories

Schedule 1 defines categories of fluids which may exist, both within and downstream, of water supply pipework.

Schedule 2 – Requirements for water fittings

Schedule 2 consists of 31 'Paragraphs' which are part of the Regulations.

Note: For convenience of referencing these Paragraphs, which refer to the technical content of the Regulations, each of the twelve sub-headings within the Schedule is shown as a 'Section'. Each Section shows the statutory 'Paragraphs' included in that Section with 'Statutory Guidance clauses' ('G' clauses) and the Water Supply Industry's Recommendations and Comments clauses' ('R' clauses).

Schedule 3 – Byelaws revoked

Schedule 3 consists of a list of Water Companies whose Byelaws have been revoked (Schedule 3 is not shown in this document).

The Water Supply (Water Fittings) Regulations 1999

Statutory Instruments

SI 1999 No. 1148 and incorporating amendment SI 1999 No. 1506

WATER INDUSTRY, ENGLAND AND WALES
The Water Supply (Water Fittings) Regulations 1999

Made	1 April 1999
Laid before Parliament	14 April 1999
Coming into force	1 July 1999

The Secretary of State for the Environment, Transport and the Regions and the Secretary of State for Wales acting jointly, in exercise of their powers under sections 74, 84 and 213(2) of the Water Industry Act 1991[a], hereby make the following Regulations:

PART I
PRELIMINARY

CITATION, COMMENCEMENT AND INTERPRETATION

(1) These Regulations may be cited as the Water Supply (Water Fittings) Regulations 1999 and shall come into force on 1 July 1999.

(2) In these Regulations –

'the Act' means the Water Industry Act 1991;

'approved contractor' means a person who

(a) has been approved by the water undertaker for the area where a water fitting is installed or used, or

(b) has been certified as an approved contractor by an organisation specified in writing by the regulator;

'the Directive' means Council Directive 89/106/EEC on the approximation of laws, regulations and administrative provisions of the member States relating to construction products [b];

'EEA Agreement' means the agreement on the European Economic Area signed at Oporto on 2 May 1992 [c] as adjusted by the Protocol signed at Brussels on 17 March 1993 [d];

'EEA State' means a State which is a contracting party to the EEA Agreement;

'European technical approval' means a favourable technical assessment of the fitness for use of a construction product for an intended use, issued for the purposes of the Directive by a body authorised by an EEA State to issue European technical approvals for those purposes and notified by that State to the European Commission;

'fluid category' means a category of fluid described in Schedule 1 to these Regulations;

'harmonized standard' means a standard established as mentioned in the Directive by the European standards organisation on the basis of a mandate given by the Commission of the European Economic Community and published by the Commission in the Official Journal of the European Communities;

'material change of use' means a change in the purpose for which, or the circumstances in which, premises are used, such that after that change the premises are used (where previously they were not so used) –

(i) as a dwelling;

(ii) as an institution;

(iii) as a public building; or

(iv) for the purposes of the storage or use of substances which if mixed with water result in a fluid which is classified as either fluid category 4 or 5;

[a] 1991 c.56
[b] OJ No. L40, 11.2.89, p12.
[c] Cmnd 2073.
[d] Cmnd 2183

'**regulator**' means –

(a) in relation to any water undertakers whose area of appointment is wholly or mainly in Wales and their area of appointment, the National Assembly of Wales;

(b) in relation to all other water undertakers and their area of appointment, the Secretary of State;

'**supply pipe**' means so much of any service pipe as is not vested in the water undertaker;

and paragraph 1 of Schedule 2 has effect for the purposes of that Schedule.

APPLICATION OF REGULATIONS

2

(1) Subject to the following provisions of this regulation, these Regulations apply to any water fitting installed or used, or to be installed or used, in premises to which water is or is to be supplied by a water undertaker.

(2) These Regulations do not apply to a water fitting installed or used, or to be installed or used, in connection with water supplied for purposes other than domestic or food production purposes, provided that –

(a) the water is metered;

(b) the supply of the water is for a period not exceeding one month, or, with the written consent of the water undertaker, three months; and

(c) no water can return through the meter to any pipe vested in a water undertaker.

(3) Except for the purposes of paragraph 14 of Schedule 2 (prevention of cross connection to unwholesome water), these Regulations do not apply to water fittings which are not connected or to be connected to water supplied by a water undertaker.

(4) Nothing in these Regulations shall require any person to remove, replace, alter, disconnect or cease to use any water fitting which was lawfully installed or used, or capable of being used, before 1 July 1999.

PART II
REQUIREMENTS

RESTRICTION ON INSTALLATION ETC. OF WATER FITTINGS

3

(1) No person shall –

(a) install a water fitting to convey or receive water supplied by a water undertaker, or alter, disconnect or use such a water fitting; or

(b) cause or permit such a water fitting to be installed, altered, disconnected or used,

in contravention of the following provisions of this Part.

(2) No water fitting shall be installed, connected, arranged or used in such a manner that it causes or is likely to cause –

(i) waste, misuse, undue consumption or contamination of water supplied by a water undertaker; or

(ii) the erroneous measurement of water supplied by a water undertaker.

(3) No water fitting shall be installed, connected, arranged or used which by reason of being damaged, worn or otherwise faulty, causes or is likely to cause –

(i) waste, misuse, undue consumption or contamination of water supplied by a water undertaker; or

(ii) the erroneous measurement of water supplied by a water undertaker.

REQUIREMENTS FOR WATER FITTINGS ETC

4

(1) Every water fitting shall –

(a) be of an appropriate quality and standard; and

(b) be suitable for the circumstances in which it is used.

(2) For the purposes of this regulation, a water fitting is of an appropriate quality or standard only if –

(a) it bears an appropriate CE marking in accordance with the Directive;

(b) it conforms to an appropriate harmonized standard or European technical approval;

(c) it conforms to an appropriate British Standard or some other national specification of an EEA State which provides an equivalent level of protection and performance; or

(d) it conforms to a specification approved by the regulator.

(3) Every water fitting shall comply with the requirements of Schedule 2 to these Regulations as it applies to that fitting.

(4) Where any requirement of Schedule 2 relates to a water system, every water fitting which forms part of that system shall be fitted or, as the case may be, altered or replaced so as to comply with that requirement.

(5) Every water fitting shall be installed, connected, altered, repaired or disconnected in a workmanlike manner.

(6) For the purposes of this regulation, a water fitting is installed, connected, altered, repaired or disconnected in a workmanlike manner only if the work is carried out so as to conform –

(a) to an appropriate British Standard, a European technical approval or some other national specification of an EEA State which provides an equivalent level of protection and performance;

(b) to a specification approved by the regulator; or

(c) to a method of installation approved by the water undertaker.

NOTIFICATION

5

(1) Subject to paragraph (2), any person who proposes to install a water fitting in connection with any of the operations listed in the Table below –

(a) shall give notice to the water undertaker that he proposes to begin work;

(b) shall not begin that work without the consent of that undertaker which shall not be withheld unreasonably; and

(c) shall comply with any conditions to which the undertaker's consent is subject.

TABLE

1. The erection of a building or other structure, not being a pond or swimming pool.

2. The extension or alteration of a water system on any premises other than a house.

3. A material change of use of any premises.

4. The installation of –

(a) a bath having a capacity, as measured to the centre line of overflow, of more than 230 litres;

(b) a bidet with an ascending spray or flexible hose;

(c) a single shower unit (which may consist of one or more shower heads within a single unit), not being a drench shower installed for reasons of safety or health, connected directly or indirectly to a supply pipe which is of a type specified by the regulator;

(d) a pump or booster drawing more than 12 litres per minute, connected directly or indirectly to a supply pipe;

(e) a unit which incorporates reverse osmosis;

(f) a water treatment unit which produces a waste water discharge or which requires the use of water for regeneration or cleaning;

(g) a reduced pressure zone valve assembly or other mechanical device for protection against a fluid which is in fluid category 4 or 5;

(h) a garden watering system unless designed to be operated by hand; or

(i) any water system laid outside a building and either less than 750mm or more than 1350mm below ground level.

5. The construction of a pond or swimming pool with a capacity greater than 10,000 litres which is designed to be replenished by automatic means and is to be filled with water supplied by a water undertaker.

(2) This regulation does not apply to the installation by an approved contractor of a water fitting falling within paragraph 2, 4(b) or 4(g) in the Table.

(3) The notice required by paragraph (1) shall include or be accompanied by –

   (a) the name and address of the person giving the notice, and (if different) the name and address of the person on whom notice may be served under paragraph (4) below;

   (b) a description of the proposed work or material change of use, and

   (c) particulars of the location of the premises to which the proposal relates, and the use or intended use of those premises;

   (d) except in the case of a fitting falling within paragraph 4(a), (c), (h) or 5 in the Table above –

      (i) a plan of those parts of the premises to which the proposal relates, and

      (ii) a diagram showing the pipework and fitting to be installed; and

   (e) where the work is to be carried out by an approved contractor, the name of the contractor.

(4) The water undertaker may withhold consent required under paragraph (1), or grant it subject to conditions, by a notice given before the expiry of the period of ten working days commencing with the day on which notice under that paragraph was given.

(5) If no notice is given by the water undertaker within the period mentioned in paragraph (4), the consent required under paragraph (1) shall be deemed to have been granted unconditionally.

CONTRACTOR'S CERTIFICATE

6

(1) Where a water fitting is installed, altered, connected or disconnected by an approved contractor, the contractor shall upon completion of the work furnish a signed certificate stating whether the water fitting complies with the requirements of these Regulations to the person who commissioned the work.

(2) In the case of a fitting for which notice is required under Regulation 5 (1) above, the contractor shall send a copy of the certificate to the water undertaker.

PART III
ENFORCEMENT ETC.

PENALTY FOR CONTRAVENING REGULATIONS

7

(1) Subject to the following provisions of this regulation, a person who –

   (a) contravenes any of the provisions of regulation 3(1), (2) or (3) or 6(1) or (2);

   (b) commences an operation listed in the Table in regulation 5(1) without giving the notice required by that paragraph;

   (c) commences an operation listed in the Table in regulation 5(1) without the consent required by that paragraph; or

   (d) carries out an operation listed in the Table in regulation 5(1) in breach of a condition imposed under regulation 5(4);

is guilty of an offence and liable on summary conviction to a fine not exceeding level 3 on the standard scale.

(2) In any proceedings against an owner or occupier for an offence under paragraph (1) which is based on the installation, alteration, repair, connection or disconnection of a water fitting, it shall be a defence to prove –

   (a) that the work in question was carried out by or under the direction of an approved contractor, and

   (b) that the contractor certified to the person who commissioned that work that the water fitting complied with the requirements of these Regulations.

MODIFICATION OF SECTION 73 OF THE ACT

In section 73 of the Act (offences of contaminating, wasting and misusing water etc.), after subsection (1) there shall be inserted:–

(1A) In any proceedings under subsection (1) above it shall be a defence to prove –

   (a) that the contamination or likely contamination, or the wastage, misuse or undue consumption, was caused (wholly or mainly) by the installation, alteration, repair or connection of the water fitting on or after 1 July 1999;

(b) that the works were carried out by or under the direction of an approved contractor within the meaning of the Water Supply (Water Fittings) Regulations 1999; and

(c) that the contractor certified to the person who commissioned those works that the water fitting complied with the requirements of those regulations.

INSPECTIONS, MEASUREMENTS AND TESTS

9

Any person designated in writing –

(a) for the purposes of section 74(4) or 170(3), by a water undertaker, or

(b) for the purposes of section 84(2), by any local authority,

may carry out such inspections, measurements and tests on premises entered by that person or on water fittings or other articles found on any such premises, and take away such samples of water or of any land, and such water fittings and other articles, as that person may consider necessary for the purposes for which those premises were entered.

ENFORCEMENT

10

(1) A water undertaker shall enforce the requirements of these Regulations in relation to the area for which it holds an appointment under Part II of the Act.

(2) The duty of a water undertaker under this regulation shall be enforceable under section 18 of the Act –

(a) by the regulator; or

(b) with the consent of or in accordance with a general authorisation given by the regulator, by the Director.

RELAXATION OF REQUIREMENTS

11

(1) Where a water undertaker considers that any requirement of Schedule 2 to these Regulations would be inappropriate in relation to a particular case, the undertaker may apply to the regulator to authorise a relaxation of that requirement.

(2) The water undertaker shall give notice of any proposed relaxation in such manner and to such persons as the regulator may direct.

(3) The regulator may grant the authorisation applied for with such modifications and subject to such conditions as he thinks fit.

(4) The regulator shall not grant an authorisation before the expiration of one month from the giving of the notice, and shall take into consideration any objection which may have been received by him.

(5) A water undertaker to whom an authorisation is granted under paragraph (3) in a particular case may relax the requirements of Schedule 2 in that case in accordance with the terms of that authorisation.

APPROVAL BY THE REGULATOR OR THE WATER UNDERTAKER

12

(1) Before approving a specification under regulation 4 or under Schedule 2, the regulator shall consult –

(a) every water undertaker;

(b) such trade associations as he considers appropriate; and

(c) such organisations appearing to him to be concerned with the interests of water users as he considers appropriate.

(2) Where the regulator approves a specification under regulation 4 or under Schedule 2, he shall give notice of the approval to all persons who were consulted under paragraph (1) and shall publish it in such manner as he considers appropriate.

(3) Where the water undertaker approves a method of installation under regulation 4, the undertaker shall give notice of the approval to the regulator and shall publish it in such manner as the undertaker considers appropriate.

(4) This regulation applies to the revocation or modification of an approval as it applies to the giving of that approval.

DISPUTES

Any dispute between a water undertaker and a person who has installed or proposes to install a water fitting –

(a) as to whether the water undertaker has unreasonably withheld consent, or attached unreasonable conditions, under regulation 5 above; or

(b) as to whether the water undertaker has unreasonably refused to apply to the regulator for a relaxation of the requirements of these Regulations,

shall be referred to arbitration by a single arbitrator to be appointed by agreement between the parties or, in default of agreement, by the regulator.

REVOCATION OF BYELAWS

The byelaws referred to in column (2) of Schedule 3, being made or having effect as if made by the water undertakers referred to in column (1) of Schedule 3 under section 17 of the Water Act 1945 [a], are hereby revoked.

Signed by authority of the Secretary of State for Environment, Transport and the Regions

Michael Meacher

31 March 1999

Minister of State,
Department of the Environment,
Transport and the Regions

Signed by authority of the Secretary of State for Wales

Jon Owen Jones

1 April 1999

Parliamentary Under-Secretary of State,
Welsh Office

[a] 1945 c.42.

Water Byelaws 2000, Scotland

Summary of the
Water Byelaws 2000, Scotland

General

The Byelaws make provision for preventing contamination, waste, misuse, undue consumption and erroneous measurement of water supplied by a water undertaker.

The Byelaws mirror the requirements of the Water Supply (Water Fittings) Regulations 1999 which apply in England and Wales.

Part I of the Byelaws deals with the preliminaries

BYELAW 1 states the title of the Byelaws and interpretations of terms used.

BYELAW 2 defines the application of the Byelaws whereby they do not apply to certain water fittings in connection with water supplied for non-domestic purposes, or to water fittings lawfully installed before 4 April 2000.

Part II of the Byelaws deals with the principal requirements

BYELAWS 3 AND 4 impose general requirements in relation to water fittings. Water fittings must not be installed, connected, arranged or used in such a manner that they are likely to cause waste, misuse, undue consumption or contamination, or erroneous measurement, of the water supplied. They must be of an appropriate quality or standard, and be suitable for the circumstances in which they are used; and they must be installed, connected or disconnected in a workmanlike manner.

BYELAW 5 requires a person who proposes to install certain water fittings to notify the undertaker, and not to commence installation without the undertaker's consent. The undertaker may withhold consent or grant it on certain conditions. This requirement does not apply to some fittings which are installed by a contractor who is approved by the undertaker or certified by an organisation approved under the Water Supply (Water Fittings) Regulations 1999.

BYELAW 6 requires that where an approved contractor installs, alters, connects or disconnects a water fitting, he must provide a certificate that it complies with the Byelaws.

Part III of the Byelaws deals with enforcement etc

BYELAW 7 provides a fine not exceeding level 3 on the standard scale for contravening the Byelaws. It is a defence to show that the work on a water fitting was done by or under the direction of an approved contractor, and that the contractor certified that it complied with the Byelaws.

BYELAWS 8 AND 10 have not been allocated as the content of the similarly numbered Regulations in England and Wales refer to legislation not applicable in Scotland. However, the numbering of subsequent Byelaws has been retained to provide consistency of numbering with the Regulations in England and Wales.

BYELAW 9 enables the undertaker to enter premises to carry out inspections, measurements and tests for the purposes of the Byelaws.

BYELAW 11 enables Scottish Ministers to relax the requirements of these Byelaws on the application of the undertaker.

BYELAW 12 requires undertakers to publicise any method of installation that they may approve under the Byelaws.

BYELAW 13 provides for disputes arising under the Byelaws between the undertaker and a person who has installed or proposes to install a water fitting to be referred to arbitration.

BYELAW 14 revokes the existing Byelaws.

Schedule 1 – Fluid categories

Schedule 1 defines categories of fluids which may exist, both within and downstream, of water supply pipework.

Schedule 2 – Requirements for water fittings

Schedule 2 consists of 31 'Paragraphs' which are part of the Water Byelaws.

(Note: For convenience of referencing these Paragraphs, which refer to the technical content of the Byelaws, each of the twelve sub-headings within Schedule 2 is shown as a 'Section'. Each Section shows the statutory 'Paragraphs' included in that Section with 'Statutory Guidance clauses' ['G' clauses] and 'Recommendation and Comments clauses' ['R' clauses]).

Water Byelaws 2000, Scotland

Water Byelaws 2000, Scotland

Made by the ____ Scotland Water Authority, as water authority in terms of section 62 of the Local Government etc. (Scotland) Act 1994 [a], (hereinafter referred to as the 'the undertaker') under section 70 of the Water (Scotland) Act 1980 [b] for preventing waste, undue consumption, misuse or contamination of water supplied by them.

PART I
PRELIMINARY

CITATION, COMMENCEMENT AND INTERPRETATION

(1) These Byelaws may be cited as the _____ of Scotland Water Authority Byelaws 2000 and shall come into force on 4 April 2000.

(2) In these Byelaws

'the Act' means the Water (Scotland) Act 1980;

'approved contractor' means a person who

(a) has been approved by the undertaker for the area where a water fitting is installed or used, or

(b) has been certified as an approved contractor by an organisation specified under the Water Supply (Water Fittings) Regulations 1999[c];

'the Directive' means Council Directive 89/106/EEC on the approximation of laws, regulations and administrative provisions of the member States relating to construction products[d];

'EEA Agreement' means the agreement on the European Economic Area signed at Oporto on 2 May 1992 [e] as adjusted by the Protocol signed at Brussels on 17 March 1993 [f];

'EEA State' means a State which is a contracting party to the EEA Agreement;

'European technical approval' means a favourable technical assessment of the fitness for use of a construction product for an intended use, issued for the purposes of the Directive by a body authorised by an EEA State to issue European technical approvals for those purposes and notified by that State to the European Commission;

'fluid category' means a category of fluid described in Schedule 1 to these Byelaws;

'harmonised standard' means a standard established as mentioned in the Directive by the European standards organisation on the basis of a mandate given by the Commission of the European Economic Community and published by the Commission in the Official Journal of the European Communities;

'material change of use' means a change in the purpose for which, or the circumstances in which, premises are used, such that after that change the premises are used (where previously they were not so used)

(i) as a dwelling;

(ii) as an institution;

(iii) as a public building; or

(iv) for the purposes of the storage or use of substances which if mixed with water result in a fluid which is classified as either fluid category 4 or 5;

'supply pipe' means so much of any service pipe as is not vested in the undertaker;

and paragraph 1 of Schedule 2 has effect for the purposes of that Schedule.

APPLICATION OF BYELAWS

2

(1) Subject to the following provisions of this Byelaw, these Byelaws apply to any water fitting installed or used, or to be installed or used, in premises to which water is or is to be supplied by the undertaker.

(2) These Byelaws do not apply to a water fitting installed or used, or to be installed or used, in connection with water supplied for purposes other than domestic or food production purposes, provided that –

[a]   Chapter 39, 1994
[b]   Chapter 45, 1980
[c]   SI 1999/1148
[d]   OJ No. L40, 11.2.89, p12.
[e]   Cmnd 2073.
[f]   Cmnd 2183.

(a) the water is metered;

(b) the supply of the water is for a period not exceeding one month, or, with the written consent of the undertaker, three months; and

(c) no water can return through the meter to any pipe vested in the undertaker.

(3) Except for the purposes of paragraph 14 of Schedule 2 (prevention of cross connection to unwholesome water), these Byelaws do not apply to water fittings which are not connected or to be connected to water supplied by the undertaker.

(4) Nothing in these Byelaws shall require any person to remove, replace, alter, disconnect or cease to use any water fitting which was lawfully installed or used, or capable of being used, before 4 April 2000.

PART II
REQUIREMENTS

RESTRICTION ON INSTALLATION ETC. OF WATER FITTINGS
3

(1) No person shall –

(a) install a water fitting to convey or receive water supplied by the undertaker, or alter, disconnect or use such a water fitting; or

(b) cause or permit such a water fitting to be installed, altered, disconnected or used,

in contravention of the following provisions of this Part.

(2) No water fitting shall be installed, connected, arranged or used in such a manner that it causes or is likely to cause –

(i) waste, misuse, undue consumption or contamination of water supplied by the undertaker; or

(ii) the erroneous measurement of water supplied by the undertaker.

(3) No water fitting shall be installed, connected, arranged or used which by reason of being damaged, worn or otherwise faulty, causes or is likely to cause –

(i) waste, misuse, undue consumption or contamination of water supplied by the undertaker; or

(ii) the erroneous measurement of water supplied by the undertaker.

(4) In this Byelaw, 'use' excludes use as a water fitting in such a way as constitutes an offence under paragraph 30(1) of Schedule 4 to the Water (Scotland) Act 1980; and 'used' shall be construed accordingly.

REQUIREMENTS FOR WATER FITTINGS ETC.
4

(1) Every water fitting shall –

(a) be of an appropriate quality and standard; and

(b) be suitable for the circumstances in which it is used.

(2) For the purposes of this Byelaw, a water fitting is of an appropriate quality or standard only if –

(a) it bears an appropriate CE marking in accordance with the Directive;

(b) it conforms to an appropriate harmonised standard or European technical approval;

(c) it conforms to an appropriate British Standard or some other national specification of an EEA State which provides an equivalent level of protection and performance; or

(d) it conforms with the terms of a specification approved under The Water Supply (Water Fittings) Regulations 1999.

(3) Every water fitting shall comply with the requirements of Schedule 2 to these Byelaws as it applies to that fitting.

(4) Where any requirement of Schedule 2 relates to a water system, every water fitting which forms part of that system shall be fitted or, as the case may be, altered or replaced so as to comply with that requirement.

(5) Every water fitting shall be installed, connected, altered, repaired or disconnected in a workmanlike manner.

(6) For the purposes of this Byelaw, a water fitting is installed, connected, altered, repaired or disconnected in a workmanlike

manner only if the work is carried out so as to conform –

(a) to an appropriate British Standard, a European technical approval or some other national specification of an EEA State which provides an equivalent level of protection and performance;

(b) it conforms with the terms of a specification approved The Water Supply (Water Fittings) Regulations 1999; or

(c) to a method of installation approved by the undertaker.

NOTIFICATION

5

(1) Subject to paragraph (2), any person who proposes to install a water fitting in connection with any of the operations listed in the Table below

(a) shall give notice to the undertaker that he proposes to begin work;

(b) shall not begin that work without the consent of the undertaker which shall not be withheld unreasonably; and

(c) shall comply with any conditions to which the undertaker's consent is subject.

TABLE

1. The erection of a building or other structure, not being a pond or swimming pool.

2. The extension or alteration of a water system on any premises other than a house.

3. A material change of use of any premises.

4. The installation of

(a) a bath having a capacity, as measured to the centre line of overflow, of more than 230 litres;

(b) a bidet with an ascending spray or flexible hose;

(c) a single shower unit (which may consist of one or more shower heads within a single unit), not being a drench shower installed for reasons of safety or health, connected directly or indirectly to a supply pipe which is of a type which conforms with terms of a specification approved under The Water Supply (Water Fittings) Regulations 1999;

(d) a pump or booster drawing more than 12 litres per minute, connected directly or indirectly to a supply pipe;

(e) a unit which incorporates reverse osmosis;

(f) a water treatment unit which produces a waste water discharge or which requires the use of water for regeneration or cleaning;

(g) a reduced pressure zone valve assembly or other mechanical device for protection against a fluid which is in fluid category 4 or 5;

(h) a garden watering system unless designed to be operated by hand; or

(i) any water system laid outside a building and either less than 750mm or more than 1350mm below ground level.

5. The construction of a pond or swimming pool with a capacity greater than 10,000 litres which is designed to be replenished by automatic means and is to be filled with water supplied by the undertaker.

(2) This Byelaw does not apply to the installation by an approved contractor of a water fitting falling within paragraph 2, 4(b) or 4(g) in the Table.

(3) The notice required by paragraph (1) shall include or be accompanied by

(a) the name and address of the person giving the notice, and (if different) the name and address of the person on whom notice may be served under paragraph (4) below;

(b) a description of the proposed work or material change of use, and

(c) particulars of the location of the premises to which the proposal relates, and the use or intended use of those premises;

(d) except in the case of a fitting falling within paragraph 4(a),(c), (h) or 5 in the table above –

(i) a plan of those parts of the premises to which the proposal relates, and

(ii) a diagram showing the pipework and fitting to be installed; and

(e) where the work is to be carried out by an approved contractor, the name of the contractor.

(4) The undertaker may withhold consent required under paragraph (1), or grant it subject to conditions, by a notice given before the expiry of the period of ten working days commencing with the day on which notice under that paragraph was given.

(5) If no notice is given by the undertaker within the period mentioned in paragraph (4), the consent required under paragraph (1) shall be deemed to have been granted unconditionally.

CONTRACTOR'S CERTIFICATE

6

(1) Where a water fitting is installed, altered, connected or disconnected by an approved contractor, the contractor shall upon completion of the work furnish a signed certificate stating whether the water fitting complies with the requirements of these Byelaws to the person who commissioned the work.

(2) In the case of a fitting for which notice is required under Byelaw 5 above, the contractor shall send a copy of the certificate to the undertaker.

PART III
ENFORCEMENT ETC.

CONTRAVENTION OF BYELAWS AND DEFENCES

7

(1) Subject to the following provisions of this Byelaw, a person who –

(a) contravenes any of the provisions of Byelaw 3(1), (2) or (3) or 6(1) or (2);

(b) commences an operation listed in the Table in Byelaw 5(1) without giving the notice required by that paragraph;

(c) commences an operation listed in the Table in Byelaw 5(1) without the consent required by that paragraph; or

(d) carries out an operation listed in the Table in Byelaw 5(1) in breach of a condition imposed under Byelaw 5(4);

is guilty of an offence and liable on summary conviction to a fine not exceeding level 3 on the standard scale.

(2) In any proceedings against an owner or occupier for an offence under paragraph (1) which is based on the installation, alteration, repair, connection or disconnection of a water fitting, it shall be a defence to prove

(a) that the work in question was carried out by or under the direction of an approved contractor, and

(b) that the contractor certified to the person who commissioned that work that the water fitting complied with the requirements of these Byelaws.

8   NOT ALLOCATED

INSPECTIONS, MEASUREMENTS AND TESTS

9

Any person designated in writing for the purposes of section 38 of the Act, by the undertaker may carry out such inspections, measurements and tests on premises entered by that person or on water fittings or other articles found on any such premises, and take away such samples of water or of any land,

and such water fittings and other articles, as that person may consider necessary for the purposes for which those premises were entered.

---

10   NOT ALLOCATED

RELAXATION OF REQUIREMENTS
11

Where the undertaker considers that any requirement of these Byelaws would be inappropriate in relation to a particular case or class of cases, the undertaker may apply to Scottish Ministers to authorise a relaxation of that requirement in accordance with Section 70 (4) of the Water (Scotland) Act 1980.

APPROVAL BY THE UNDERTAKER
12

Regulations 12(1) and 12(2) deleted from Byelaws

(1) Where the undertaker approves a method of installation under Byelaw 4, the undertaker shall give notice of the approval to Scottish Ministers and shall publish it in such manner as the undertaker considers appropriate.

(2) This Byelaw applies to the revocation or modification of an approval as it applies to the giving of that approval.

DISPUTES
13

Any dispute between the undertaker and a person who has installed or proposes to install a water fitting –

(a) as to whether the undertaker has unreasonably withheld consent, or attached unreasonable conditions, under Byelaw 5 above; or

(b) as to whether the undertaker has unreasonably refused to apply to Scottish Ministers for a relaxation of the requirements of these Byelaws,

shall be referred to arbitration by a single arbiter to be appointed by agreement between the parties or, in default of agreement, by Scottish Ministers.

REVOCATION OF BYELAWS
14

The Byelaws made by;

the _____ Regional Council under section 70 of the Water (Scotland) Act 1980 on _____and confirmed by the Secretary of State for Scotland on _____;

The foregoing Byelaws, which come into operation on 4 April 2000 were made by _____ of Scotland Water Authority on _____ and sealed with their Common Seal and signed for them by _____their Chief Executive and confirmed by the Scottish Ministers on _____.

General Guidance on the Water Supply (Water Fittings) Regulations 1999 and the Water Byelaws 2000, Scotland

Requirements for water fittings (Regulation (Byelaw) 4)

Wholesome water fittings must be of an appropriate quality or standard and be suitable for the circumstances in which they are used (Regulation (*Byelaw*) 4(2)). Fittings or materials which conform to the Regulators' Specifications are acceptable. Where fittings or materials have been successfully submitted to the WRAS Scheme for approval against the specifications, they will be listed in the Water Fittings and Materials Directory, which is published six-monthly by WRAS.

If listed products are installed and used in accordance with any installation requirements listed in the Directory, and with any other particular provisions of the Regulations (*Byelaws*), they will satisfy the requirements of Regulation (*Byelaw*) 4(1). Certain types of fittings and materials with the British Standard Kitemark or other certification bodies' approvals are deemed to satisfy the Regulations (*Byelaws*) without further testing. The Standards, the product types and their manufacturers are also listed in the WRAS Water Fittings and Materials Directory.

For a fitting to bear an *appropriate* CE mark, a harmonised standard for that product must exist but there are none in the potable water sector at the time of publication. Similarly there are no current European Technical Approvals (ETAs) for any potable water fitting at present. Appropriate British Standards are available only for a limited range of fittings and these are detailed in the Directory. For other national specifications of an EEA state to be accepted they would have to show that they provide an equivalent level of protection or performance by comparison with the regulators' specifications. These specifications are listed in the WRAS website (www.wras.co.uk).

Where other products are claimed to comply with the regulators' specification, harmonised or other standards, it shall be the responsibility of **the installer, owner or occupier** to provide evidence to demonstrate compliance to the reasonable satisfaction of the water supplier.

Commentary on Notification (Regulations (Byelaws) 5 and 6)

In most circumstances, before work starts on the installation of any water fittings (which includes water system pipes, above or below ground), the water supplier must be notified of the proposed installation. Work must not start without the water supplier's consent and any conditions attached to the consent must be followed. If, within ten working days of the correctly documented notification being received at the water supplier's address designated for the purpose, the water supplier has neither granted consent subject to conditions nor refused consent, the consent is deemed to have been granted unconditionally and installation may proceed.

If notification plans contain non-compliant fittings or installation details, consent, whether deemed or granted, does not remove the obligation on **the installer, owner and occupier** to ensure that the water system as installed nonetheless complies with the Regulations (*Byelaws*).

There are a few circumstances where prior notification does not have to be made. One is the extension or alteration of an existing water system in a house. However, if the extension or alteration includes the installation of any items in connection with the operations listed in paragraphs 1, 3, 4 or 5 of the Table in Regulation (*Byelaw*) 5, prior notification and consent is still required for them. Another circumstance is certain types of installation work by an Approved Contractor (see Regulation (*Byelaw*) 5(2), 6 and 7 and Approved Contractors, below). Prior notification is not required where an existing fitting is repaired or replaced with a similar suitable item, provided there is no material change of use of premises or increased backflow risk.

Regulation (*Byelaw*) 5(3) sets out the information which is required for notification. Some water suppliers provide a form for notification by applicants. This may be part of a standard application pack for new water supplies. Where Regulation 5(3)(d)(ii) refers to diagrams showing pipework and fittings to be installed, for many proposed installations in dwellings and simple commercial premises with only domestic use of water, a straightforward schematic diagram may suffice, providing it shows the relative positions and layout of the system and details of the fittings and appliances which it is intended to install.

Builders of housing developments can seek the water supplier's 'type approval' of their standard designs of plumbing systems. This enables the notification of future developments which are to be constructed to one of the approved designs to be made without submission of further detailed diagrams.

Approved Contractors

Approved Contractors (see Regulation (*Byelaw*) 1(2)) include those approved by the water suppliers. Some water suppliers operate their own approval schemes. Others have adopted the national Water Industry Approved Plumbers' Scheme (WIAPS) which is operated by WRAS on their behalf. Organisations other than water suppliers can seek approval by the regulator to operate Approved Contractors' Schemes.

An approved contractor can issue a certificate to a customer which certifies that the installation work carried out complies with the Regulations (*Byelaws*). If the installation is shown in due course not to have complied with the Regulations (*Byelaws*), the owner or occupier of the premises can use as a defence in any prosecution the fact that an approved contractor issued the certificate.

In the WIAPS Scheme, approved contractor status can be held by an individual installer or a firm of plumbing contractors. In the latter case, at least one employee of the plumbing contracting firm must be an approved contractor in his or her own right for each five plumbers' employed. The approved contractor must supervise all installation work that is covered by the certificates, which must be signed by the approved contractor in person.

Prior consent is not required for Approved Contractors for the following work:

- the installation of water fittings as part of the alteration or extension of a water system in any premises. However, if the extension or alteration includes the installation of any items in connection with the operations listed in paragraphs 1, 3, 4(a), 4(c) to (f), 4(h) and (i) or 5 of the Table in Regulation (*Byelaw*) 5, then prior notification and consent is still required for them.

- the installation of a bidet with ascending spray or flexible hose.

- the installation of a mechanical device, other than a reduced pressure zone (RPZ) valve, for protection against a fluid which is in fluid category 4 or 5.

It is a water industry requirement that prior notice shall be given of the installation of a reduced pressure zone (RPZ) valve. This enables, amongst other things, a check that the device will operate with the available water pressure. Further information is given in the water supply industry's code of practice for the installation of RPZ valves (Water Regulations Advisory Scheme Information and Guidance Note No. 9-03-02: **Type BA – Verifiable Backflow Preventer with Reduced Pressure Zone** (RPZ Valve) Requirements for Installation, On-Site Testing and Maintenance).

Schedule 1
Fluid categories

Water Supply (Water Fittings) Regulations 1999

FLUID CATEGORY 1

Wholesome water supplied by a water undertaker and complying with the requirements of regulations made under section 67 of the Water Industry Act 1991[a].

FLUID CATEGORY 2

Water in fluid category 1 whose aesthetic quality is impaired owing to –

(a) a change in its temperature, or

(b) the presence of substances or organisms causing a change in its taste, odour or appearance, including water in a hot water distribution system.

FLUID CATEGORY 3

Fluid which represents a slight health hazard because of the concentration of substances of low toxicity, including any fluid which contains –

(a) ethylene glycol, copper sulphate solution or similar chemical additives, or

(b) sodium hypochlorite (chloros and common disinfectants).

FLUID CATEGORY 4

Fluid which represents a significant health hazard because of the concentration of toxic substances, including any fluid which contains –

(a) chemical, carcinogenic substances or pesticides (including insecticides and herbicides), or

(b) environmental organisms of potential health significance.

FLUID CATEGORY 5

Fluid representing a serious health hazard because of the concentration of pathogenic organisms, radioactive or very toxic substances, including any fluid which contains –

(a) faecal material or other human waste;

(b) butchery or other animal waste; or

(c) pathogens from any other source.

[a] 1991 c. 56.

Water Byelaws 2000 Scotland

FLUID CATEGORY 1

Wholesome water supplied by the undertaker and complying with the requirements of The Water Supply (Water Quality) (Scotland) Regulations 1990[a] and any amendment[b].

FLUID CATEGORY 2

Water in fluid category 1 whose aesthetic quality is impaired owing to –

(a) a change in its temperature, or

(b) the presence of substances or organisms causing a change in its taste, odour or appearance, including water in a hot water distribution system.

FLUID CATEGORY 3

Fluid which represents a slight health hazard because of the concentration of substances of low toxicity, including any fluid which contains –

(a) ethylene glycol, copper sulphate solution or similar chemical additives, or

(b) sodium hypochlorite (chloros and common disinfectants).

FLUID CATEGORY 4

Fluid which represents a significant health hazard because of the concentration of toxic substances, including any fluid which contains –

(a) chemical, carcinogenic substances or pesticides (including insecticides and herbicides), or

(b) environmental organisms of potential health significance.

FLUID CATEGORY 5

Fluid representing a serious health hazard because of the concentration of pathogenic organisms, radioactive or very toxic substances, including any fluid which contains –

(a) faecal material or other human waste;

(b) butchery or other animal waste; or

(c) pathogens from any other source.

[a] 1991 c. 56.
[b] 1991/1333 (S.129), SI 1992/575, SI 1996/3047 & SI 1998/994

For examples and interpretations, see Section 6.1

Schedule 2
Section 1:
Paragraph 1:
Interpretations

Notes

Schedule 2

1.

In this Schedule –

'backflow' means flow upstream, that is in a direction contrary to the intended normal direction of flow, within or from a water fitting;

'cistern' means a fixed container for holding water at atmospheric pressure;

'combined feed and expansion cistern' means a cistern for supplying cold water to a hot water system without a separate expansion cistern;

'contamination' includes any reduction in chemical or biological quality of water due to a change in temperature or the introduction of polluting substances;

'distributing pipe' means any pipe (other than a warning, overflow or flushing pipe) conveying water from a storage cistern, or from hot water apparatus supplied from a cistern and under pressure from that cistern;

'expansion valve' means a pressure-activated valve designed to release expansion water from an unvented water heating system;

'flushing cistern' means a cistern provided with valve or device for controlling the discharge of the stored water into a water closet pan or urinal;

'overflow pipe' means a pipe from a cistern in which water flows only when the water level in the cistern exceeds a predetermined level;

'pressure relief valve' means a pressure-activated valve which opens automatically at a specified pressure to discharge fluid;

'primary circuit' means an assembly of water fittings in which water circulates between a boiler or other source of heat and a primary heat exchange inside a hot water storage vessel, and includes any space heating system;

'secondary circuit' means an assembly of water fittings in which water circulates in supply pipes or distributing pipes of a hot water storage system;

'secondary system' means an assembly of water fittings comprising the cold feed pipe, any hot water storage vessel, water heater and pipework from which hot water is conveyed to all points of draw-off;

'servicing valve' means a valve for shutting off for the purpose of maintenance or service the flow of water in a pipe connected to a water fitting;

'stopvalve' means a valve, other than a servicing valve, used for shutting off the flow of water in a pipe;

'storage cistern' means a cistern for storing water for subsequent use, not being a flushing cistern;

'temperature relief valve' means a valve which opens automatically at a specified temperature to discharge fluid;

'terminal fitting' means a water outlet device; and

'vent pipe' means a pipe open to the atmosphere which exposes the system to atmospheric pressure at its boundary.

Interpretations

Guidance

Recommendations

Interpretations

G1.1

The interpretations shown in Paragraph 1 of the Schedule are all used in the Regulations and Guidance clauses within this Guidance Document.

R1.1.1

Several terms used in the Regulations and in the Regulators' Guidance Clauses are not found in Schedule 2; Paragraph 1 to the Regulations. Definitions of some fittings or devices can be found in the relevant paragraphs of Schedule 2. Some terms are already defined in primary legislation, chiefly the Water Industry Act 1991; these definitions are not repeated in the Regulations. However, for ease of reference, these meanings are included in the 'R' clauses.

R1.1.2

Regulations 3(2) and 3(3) refer to waste, misuse, undue consumption, contamination or erroneous measurement of water supplied by a Water Supplier. Guidance on the meaning of these terms is given below:

Waste – This may be defined as water supplied by a Water Supplier which is allowed to run to waste through faulty installation, a faulty appliance or poor maintenance, that is, a leaking fitting or a dripping tap or through any other fault.

Misuse – This may be regarded as the use of water supplied by a Water Supplier for any purpose other than that for which it is supplied. This includes the use of the energy in the mains water supply as a means of providing motive power or for the generation of electricity.

Undue consumption – This refers to the operation of fittings and appliances that use more water for the purpose for which they were designed than that established by the performance criteria of the Water Regulations Advisory Committee of the Department of the Environment, Transport and the Regions, or more than is reasonable in comparison with other fittings or appliances serving similar purposes.

Contamination of water supplied by a Water Supplier
This is defined as any reduction in aesthetic, chemical or biological quality of water due to raising its temperature or the introduction of polluting substances.
See Schedule 1 of the Regulations, 'Fluid categories'.

Erroneous measurement – This relates to the by-passing of a water meter, the taking-off of a supply upstream of a water meter and tampering with a water meter resulting in interference with the measurement of water passing through the meter.

Backflow prevention arrangements and devices – The general requirements are shown in Schedule 2: Paragraph 15. The Regulators' guidance on this paragraph and the Regulator's Specification for the Prevention of Backflow lists the various arrangements and devices, and describes them and their applicability for use in different situations.

Recommendations

R1.1.3
Other terms used within the Regulations, the Regulators' Guidance and the Water Industry recommendations relating to backflow prevention are defined in Schedule 2: Paragraph 15 and explanations of others, with suggested abbreviations used in this document, are given below:

Wholesome water – Water supplied by a Water Supplier and complying with the requirements of Regulations made under Section 67 of the Water Industry Act 1991 (the Water Supply (Water Quality) Regulations 1989 (the Water Supply (Water Quality) (Scotland) Regulations 1990) as from time to time amended or replaced). The term 'wholesome water' is equivalent to potable water (ie. fit to drink), but potable is a term no longer used in regulations.

Water fittings – The term water fittings includes all pipes, pipe fittings, joints, all types of valves, backflow prevention devices, cisterns, hot water storage vessels and all other components within a cold and hot water installation that are necessary for the function and operation of a water supply system. Water fittings may, if not installed or maintained correctly, contravene the requirements of the Regulations and give rise to waste, misuse, undue consumption or contamination.

Service pipe – So much of a pipe which is, or is to be, connected with a water main for supplying water from that main to any premises as:
a. is or is to be subject to water pressure from that main; or
b. would be so subject but for the closing of some valve.
(Water Industry Act 1991 s.219[1]). See Section 4: Diagram R10.3.

Supply pipes – So much of any service pipe as is not vested in the Water Supplier (Regulation 1[2]). It is normally the length of the service pipe between the boundary of the part of the street in which the water main is laid, and any terminal fitting directly connected to it and under mains pressure (such as a tap, float operated valve or inlet to an appliance), (see Section 4: Diagram R10.3).

Hot water pipes which convey water directly from a hot water storage vessel, instantaneous heater or combination boiler, which are supplied directly, or through a pressure reducing valve, from a cold water supply pipe are also referred to as supply pipes.

Diagram
R1.1.3a:
Illustration of supply pipes and distributing pipes

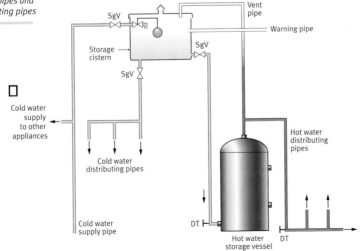

Interpretations

Communication pipes – That part of a service pipe which is vested in the Water Supplier (see Section 4: Diagram R10.3).

Distributing pipes – Any cold water pipe or hot water pipe that conveys water from a storage cistern, either directly or through a hot water storage vessel or other device, and is under pressure from that cistern (see Diagram R1.1.3a).

Distributing pipes may be 'common' where the distributing pipe serves several appliances, or 'independent' where a distributing pipe serves only one appliance or device, for example, a distributing pipe serving a hot water storage vessel (commonly called a cold feed pipe) or a bidet with a submerged inlet.

Cisterns – Examples of cisterns:

Storage cisterns where water is stored for subsequent use. Storage cisterns may also be 'dedicated', that is, where they serve a single appliance or system; for example, a storage cistern serving a hot water storage vessel only (see Diagram R1.1.3b).

Feed and expansion cisterns which are used to supply water, and store expanded water, to primary and other heating systems (see Diagram R1.1.3c).

Flushing cisterns which are used for flushing WCs or urinals.

Interposed cisterns, these are backflow prevention arrangements and are described in Section 6: Clause S15.2.

Diagram
R1.1.3b:
Example of dedicated storage cistern

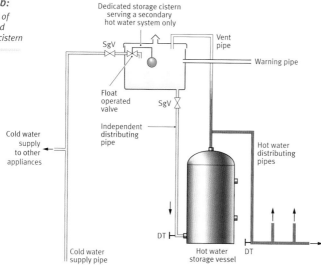

Recommendations

Diagram
R1.1.3c:
*Example of feed and
expansion cistern*

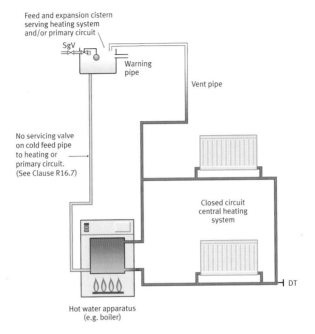

Feed and expansion cistern
serving heating system
and/or primary circuit

SgV

Warning
pipe

Vent pipe

No servicing valve
on cold feed pipe
to heating or
primary circuit.
(See Clause R16.7)

Closed circuit
central heating
system

DT

Hot water apparatus
(e.g. boiler)

Water treatment apparatus

Water softener – Equipment which reduces the hardness mineral (calcium,
magnesium) concentrations to less than 50 mg/l (ppm) as $CaCO_3$ or $MgCO_3$.
The commonly used processes are:

a. Ion exchange, where the ions of the hardness minerals in the water are
replaced by ions of sodium. The process involves the regeneration of an
'ion exchange' resin using common salt.

b. Reverse osmosis, where the total dissolved solids in the water are reduced
by passing the water through a semi-permeable membrane.

c. Distillation, where the water is boiled and the steam produced is condensed
and collected, the salts giving rise to hardness remaining in the boiling vessel.

Chemical water conditioner – Instead of replacing or removing the calcium
and magnesium salts, it is possible to make the calcium and magnesium less
available for formation of deposits. This can be effected by adding 'polyphosphates'
in a liquid or solid form to the water. This causes the water to behave in some ways
as if it had been softened, although the water has not been softened by the accepted
definition with respect to the reduction in the levels of calcium and magnesium.

Physical water conditioner – Equipment which uses a physical process, such
as electronic, electrolytic, magnetic or electromagnetic, to reduce scale formation
caused by hard water without permanently changing its chemical composition
or softening it.

Guidance   **R**ecommendations

Abbreviations and symbols

G1.2

A list of abbreviations and symbols is shown in the Contents List (see page vi or at the last leaf of the book) and Diagrams G8.2a, b and c, show their application as typical water supply systems in houses.

R1.2

As far as possible the list of abbreviations and symbols shown after the Contents List has been based on those contained in British Standard Specifications, European Standards and ISO Documents. None of these Standards cover all of the many fittings used in plumbing installations. Wherever possible, the abbreviations and symbols shown in the CEN Document prEN 806-1, which is based on ISO 14617, are used together with some based on CEN Product Standards, where these are applicable. However, these Standards may not include symbols for some of the fittings used for the United Kingdom traditional plumbing systems; in these cases an appropriate abbreviation or symbol is shown in this Guide.

Schedule 2
Section 2:
Paragraph 2:
Materials and substances in contact with water

Notes

Schedule 2

2.

(1) Subject to sub-paragraph (2) below, no material or substance, either alone or in combination with any other material or substance or with the contents of any water fitting of which it forms a part, which causes or is likely to cause contamination of water shall be used in the construction, installation, renewal, repair or replacement of any water fitting which conveys or receives, or may convey or receive, water supplied for domestic or food production purposes.

(2) This requirement does not apply to a water fitting downstream of a terminal fitting supplying wholesome water where –

    (a) the use to which the water downstream is put does not require wholesome water; and

    (b) a suitable arrangement or device to prevent backflow is installed.

Materials and substances in contact with water

Guidance

Recommendations

General

G2.1

Materials or substances, either alone or in combination, which cause, or are likely to cause, contamination of water should not be used in the construction, installation, renewal, repair or replacement of any water fitting which conveys or receives water supplied for domestic or food production purposes. Particular materials unsuitable for use in contact with water intended for domestic or food production purposes include lead and bitumastic coatings derived from coal tar.

R2.1   PIPES, PIPE FITTINGS AND JOINTS
R2.1.1

The following provides details of pipes, fittings and methods of jointing which generally conform with the requirements of paragraph 2(1) of this Schedule. They may be used in water supply installations subject to the approval of individual water suppliers who may not permit certain materials where the quality of the water in a particular area may have a corrosive or deleterious interaction with the material used for the manufacture or installation of the pipe, pipe fitting or joints.

R2.1.2   STEEL PIPES

BS 1387: Specification for screwed and socketed steel tubes and tubulars and for plain end steel tubes suitable for welding or for screwing to BS 21 pipe threads.

Steel tubes with screwed threads may be jointed using wrought steel pipe fittings to BS 1740: Part 1: Specification for wrought steel pipe fittings (screwed BS 21 R-series thread), or fittings to BS 143 and 1256: Specification for malleable cast iron and cast copper alloy threaded pipe fittings.

Steel tube to this standard is manufactured in nominal sizes DN8 to DN150 in light, medium and heavy wall thicknesses.

a. If laid in the ground, pipes, joints and fittings are to be:
   (i) heavy gauge galvanised tube; and
   (ii) protected by the methods set out in BS 534:
        Section 26 External protection, and Section 27 to 29 'Internal protection'.

b. If installed above ground, pipes, joints and fittings are to be:
   (i) heavy or medium gauge tube. Where installed as part of a fire sprinkler system from which no water is drawn or used for other purposes, light gauge tube may be used; and
   (ii) coated externally and internally in accordance with BS 534: Sections 24 and 25 or galvanised in accordance with BS 1387: Section 4.3. In some geographical areas where water is aggressive to zinc alternative materials should be considered. Installers should seek advice from the Water Suppliers on the areas concerned.

Pipes to BS 1387 are identified at each end by a ring of paint giving the class colour, that is, light gauge is brown, medium gauge is blue, and heavy gauge is red. Diagram R2.1.2 illustrates the application of each gauge.

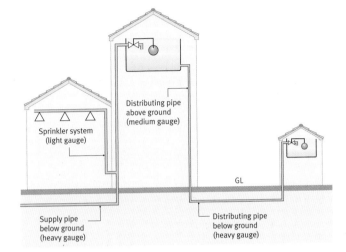

Diagram
R2.1.2:

*Illustration of
use of different
classes of
steel pipes*

BS 534: Specification for steel pipes, joints and specials for water and sewage

Steel tube to this standard is manufactured in sizes 60.3mm to 2,235mm outside diameters. The specification requires that materials shall conform to BS 3601 and dimensions selected from Table 1 of BS 3600.

a. If laid in the ground, pipes and fittings are to be protected by the methods set out in BS 534: Section 26 External protection and Sections 27 to 29 Internal protection.

b. If installed above ground, pipes and fittings are to be coated externally and internally in accordance with Sections 24 and 25 of BS 534.

c. Acceptable standards for pipe joints include:

   (i)   BS 21: Specification for pipe threads for tubes and fittings where pressure-tight joints are made on the threads (metric dimensions).

   (ii) BS 1965: Specification for butt-welding pipe fittings for pressure purposes. Part 1: Carbon steel.

   (iii) BS 4504: Part 3: Section 3.1: Circular flanges for pipes, valves and fittings – specification for steel flanges.

   (iv) BS 2494: Specification for elastomeric seals for joints in pipework and pipelines.

   (v)   BS 143 & 1246: Specification for malleable cast iron and cast copper alloy threaded pipe fittings.

Elastomeric joint rings for pipework and pipelines should also conform with BS EN681-1: Elastomeric seals. Material requirements and BS 7874: Method of test for microbiological seals for joints in pipework and pipelines.

R2.1.3 IRON PIPES

BS EN 545: Ductile iron pipes, fittings, accessories and their joints for water pipelines

Ductile iron pipes to this standard are manufactured in sizes DN40 to DN2000.

a. If laid in the ground, pipes and fittings are to be coated externally and lined internally with cement mortar or epoxy resin in accordance with an appropriate standard. In some areas the water suppliers may require that, additionally, the pipes should be laid in a protective sleeve.

b. If installed above ground, pipes and fittings are to be coated internally and externally (and if required, cement mortar lined) in accordance with the standard.

Ductile iron pipes up to 300mm diameter are tested at works to 50 bar but should not be tested, when installed, to more than 45 bar. The complete installation should be considered as being suitable for working pressures of at least 12 bar.

Elastomeric materials for use in joints should conform with BS 2494: Specification for elastomeric seals for joints in pipework and pipelines. Elastomeric joint rings for pipework and pipelines should also conform with BS EN681-1: Elastomeric seals. Material requirements and BS 7874: Method of test for microbiological seals for joints in pipework and pipelines.

Joints are of a proprietory nature, as only flanged joints are covered by a British Standard. Diagram R2.1.3a illustrates a push-in joint incorporating a specially shaped rubber gasket for pipelines conveying liquids. It can be deflected by several degrees in any direction and is capable of axial movement. It is used in ductile spun iron pipes and fittings in nominal sizes DN80 to DN600.

Diagram
R2.1.3a:
Push-in type joint

Gasket

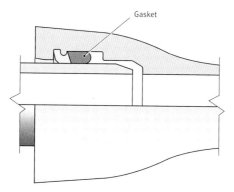

Diagram R2.1.3b illustrates a self-anchor joint which uses standard production ductile spun iron pipes and fittings in conjunction with a modified version of the gasket. The gasket is of standard design in respect of dimensions and shape but stainless steel toothed inserts are moulded into the gasket and grip into the pipe surface on attempted withdrawal.

Diagram
R2.1.3b:
Push-in type joint with self-anchoring gasket

Gasket with locking ring

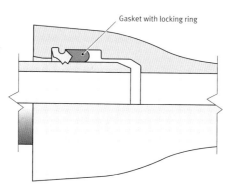

Recommendations

A typical mechanical joint is shown in Diagram R2.1.3c in which the seal is effected by compressing a wedge shaped gasket on to the jointing surface in the pipe socket and the outside of the pipe spigot by means of a pressure gland and a series of bolts and nuts. The joint may be deflected to a limited degree in any direction and is capable of axial movement.

Diagram
R2.1.3c:
*Typical
mechanical joint*

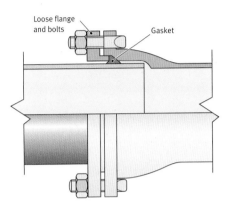

Flanged joints are self-anchoring and therefore external anchorages are not required at changes of direction and at blank ends. This joint is used mainly in pumping stations, industrial pipework and for other installations where the pipework is not buried in the ground. It is also commonly used to facilitate the installation and removal of valves in spigot and socket pipelines below ground and for valve bypass arrangements. A typical flange joint is illustrated in Diagram R2.1.3d.

Flanges for flange joints should conform to BS 4504: Part 3: Section 3.1: Circular flanges for pipes, valves and fittings – specification for steel flanges.

Diagram
R2.1.3d:
*Typical flange
joint*

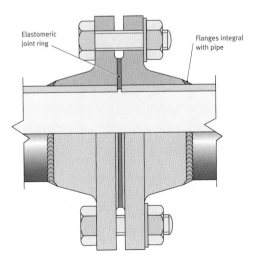

Materials and substances in contact with water

R2.1.4 COPPER TUBES

BS EN 1057: Copper and copper alloys. Seamless, round copper tubes for water and gas in sanitary and heating applications

Copper tube to this standard is designed to be jointed by compression or capillary fittings, brazing or welding. Copper tube shall either bear a certification mark or certification in a form acceptable to the undertakers which states that it has been effectively cleaned of deleterious matter during, or subsequent to, manufacture.

a. The excessive use of flux when soldering copper joints or the failure to properly flush out debris, swarf or flux residues can cause damage to copper pipe.

b. Soft solder containing lead must not be used for joining copper pipes and fittings on wholesome water systems (see Clause R2.12).

c. All underground pipework should be coloured blue for identification purposes. Blue plastic coated copper is available for this purpose.

d. In some areas where pipes are laid in the ground the Water Supplier may advise that copper tubes and fittings are externally coated with a works applied protective coating.

e. Joints and fittings for use with copper tube to BS EN 1057 are:

   (i)   BS 4504: Part 3: Section 3.3: Circular flanges for pipes, valves and fittings – specification for copper alloy and composite flanges.

   (ii) BS 1724: Specification for bronze welding by gas.

   (iii) BS EN 1254-1: Fittings with ends for capillary soldering or capillary brazing to copper tubes or BS EN 1254-2: Fittings with compression ends for use with copper tubes.

   (iv) If laid in the ground, compression fittings shall conform to BS EN 1254-2: Type B.

   (v) Where dezincification resistance is required (see Section 3: Clause R7.5) for copper alloy fittings they shall be made from gunmetal to BS EN 12165, BS EN 12163, BS EN 12164 or BS EN 12167 material CZ 132 (resistant to dezincification) or tested for dezincification resistance in accordance with ISO 6509 (See Clause G7.6).

   (vi) No pipe joint in the ground shall be made using adhesives.

Capillary and compression joints for use with copper tube are illustrated in Diagrams R2.1.4a, R2.1.4b and R2.1.4c.

Recommendations

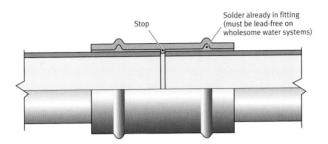

Stop

Solder already in fitting
(must be lead-free on
wholesome water systems)

**Diagram
R2.1.4a:**

*Capillary fittings
for use with copper
tube suitable for
joints above or
below ground*

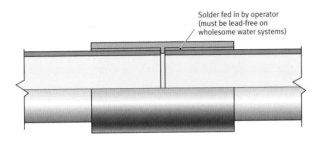

Solder fed in by operator
(must be lead-free on
wholesome water systems)

**Diagram
R2.1.4b:**

*Manipulative
compression fittings
for use with copper
tube for joints above
or below ground*

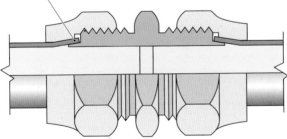

Copper tube end flared outwards

**Diagram
R2.1.4c:**

*Non-manipulative
compression fittings
for use with copper
tube for joints above
ground only*

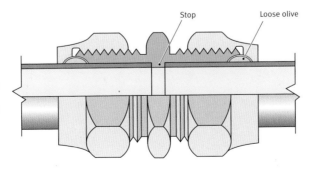

Stop

Loose olive

Recommendations

R2.1.5 UNPLASTICISED PVC PIPES

BS 3505: Specification for unplasticised polyvinyl chloride (PVC-U) pressure pipes for cold potable water

Pipes to this standard are manufactured in imperial sizes up to DN24 for use at pressures up to 15 bar at 20°C.

a. If laid in the ground PVC-U pipe shall be of the appropriate class for the maximum working pressure but not less than 12 bar for sizes up to and including size DN 2.

b. Pipes of nominal size below DN3 are not recommended for service installations.

c. Joints and fittings for use with unplasticised PVC pressure pipes should conform with BS 4346:

>   Part 1: Injection moulded unplasticised PVC fittings for solvent welding for use with pressure pipes, including potable water supply.

>   Part 2: Mechanical joints and fittings principally of unplasticised PVC (see Diagram R2.1.5a).

>   Part 3: Solvent cement welded joints (see Diagram R 2.1.5b).

d. Compression fittings similar to those used for polyethylene pipes may also be used on PVC-U. If used on pipes laid below ground they must be made of dezincification resistant or immune material.

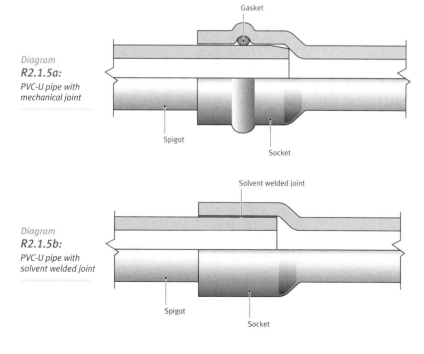

Gasket

Diagram
R2.1.5a:
PVC-U pipe with mechanical joint

Spigot

Socket

Solvent welded joint

Diagram
R2.1.5b:
PVC-U pipe with solvent welded joint

Spigot

Socket

Recommendations

R2.1.6 POLYETHYLENE PIPES

BS 6572: Blue polyethylene pipes up to nominal size 63 for below ground use for potable water.

Blue polyethylene pipe to this standard conforms to metric series dimensions. This pipe is specially developed for services laid in the ground. It is pigmented blue and there is one class designed for a working pressure of 12 bar at 20°C in sizes up to nominal size 63. It may be used above ground in situations where it is not exposed to direct sunlight.

BS 6730: Black polyethylene pipes up to nominal size 63 for above ground use for cold potable water

This pipe conforms to metric series dimensions and has been specially developed for above ground use for optimum resistance to ultra-violet light in situations where pipes are exposed to direct sunlight.

BS EN 1254-3: Fittings with compression ends for use with plastics pipes.

These fittings conform to metric series dimensions and are suitable for use with BS 6572 (blue) or BS 6730 (black) polyethylene pipe.

a. If laid in the ground it is essential that the method of jointing and the material used in the joint are suitable for use underground.

b. Copper alloy fittings shall be made from gunmetal to BS EN 12165, BS EN 12163, BS EN 12164 or BS EN 12167 materials CZ 132 (resistant to dezincification).

WAA-SWMC IGN 4-32-04 ISSN 0267-0305 Polyethylene socket and spigot joints and fittings, saddles and drawn bends for fusion jointing for use with cold potable water polyethylene pressure pipes.

This covers fusion fittings for pipes with outside diameters in the nominal size range DN 20 to DN 1000, in both blue and black pigmented polyethylene, for use in cold potable water services at pressures up to 10 bar or 12 bar at 20°C according to size.

WAA-SWMC IGN 4-32-06 ISSN 0267-0305 Specification for polyethylene electrofusion couplers and fittings for cold potable water supply for nominal sizes up to and including DN 180.

This covers electrofusion joints and fittings in the nominal range DN 20 to DN 180, in both blue pigmented and black pigmented polyethylene (PE) electrofusion couplers and fittings for the conveyance of cold potable water at temperatures up to 20°C at a nominal pressure rating of 12 bar (for sizes up to and including DN 63) and 10 bar (for sizes greater than DN 63).

PE pipe fusion welding should be performed in accordance with WAA-SWMC IGN No. 4-32-08 Specification for site fusion jointing of MDPE pipe and fittings.

BS 4991: Propylene copolymer pressure pipe (Series 1)

This pipe in Series 1 form conforms to size 1/4 to 24 and should only be used where the normal sustained working temperature does not exceed 20°C.

a. If laid in the ground should be size 1 to 18 and designed for a working pressure of 9.0 bar and to avoid confusion with other services it must be identifiable by the colour blue.

b. If installed above ground the pipe should be of the appropriate class to withstand the required test pressure.

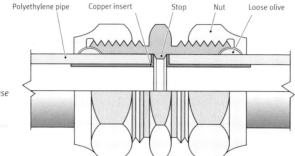

Diagram
R2.1.6:
Typical joint for use on polyethylene and PVC-U pipes

Labels on diagram: Polyethylene pipe · Copper insert · Stop · Nut · Loose olive

R2.1.7 PLASTICS PLUMBING PIPES FOR HOT AND COLD USE

BS 7291: Part 2: Specification for polybutylene (PB) pipes and associated fittings

Specifies requirements and test conditions for polybutylene materials and pipes of 10mm to 35mm outside diameter in alternative metric sizes standardised for plastics pipes or copper tubes.

BS 7291: Part 3: Specification for cross-linked polyethylene (PE-X) pipes and associated fittings

Specifies requirements and test conditions for cross-linked polyethylene materials and pipes of 10mm to 35mm outside diameter in alternative metric sizes standardised for plastics pipes or copper tubes.

BS 7291: Part 4: Specification for chlorinated polyvinyl chloride (PVC-C) pipes and associated fittings and solvent cement

Specifies requirements and test conditions for chlorinated polyvinyl chloride materials and pipes of 12mm to 63mm outside diameter in metric sizes standardised for plastics pipes.

R2.1.8 STAINLESS STEEL PIPES

BS 4127: Light gauge stainless steel tubes, primarily for water applications.

Specifies requirements for stainless steel tubes, suitable for connection by capillary fittings, compression fittings, by inert gas welding or by adhesive bonding. The standard covers the size range from 6mm to 159mm outside diameter.

No pipe joint laid in the ground shall be made using adhesives.

Guidance   *Recommendations*

G2.2
For non-metallic materials, this requirement is deemed to be met by compliance with the appropriate British Standard, BS 6920: Suitability of non-metallic products for use in contact with water intended for human consumption with regard to their effect on the quality of water. No standard of any other EEA State provides an equivalent level of performance in all attributes, though certain attributes of several such standards are deemed equivalent. Further advice on the equivalence of foreign standards is available from the Water Regulations Advisory Scheme.

R2.2
Information on approved products can be found in the Water Fittings and Materials Directory published by the Water Regulations Advisory Scheme. See Information Guidance Note – IGN 9-01-02 Requirements for the testing of non-metallic products for use in contact with potable water.

G2.3
Water fittings and materials for water fittings complying with paragraph 2(1) of Schedule 2 should be tested by an approved test house and the results published in approved lists.

R2.3
See recommendations in Clause R2.2 above.

G2.4
When water fittings or materials are specified to a British Standard or other document, the reference is to the latest available edition of the document referred to.

R2.4
When referring to standards or other documents it is essential that the latest available edition of the document is consulted.

G2.5
The following factors should be considered when determining the suitability of materials and fittings which are, or will be, in contact with the water supplied:

a. *internal and external temperatures to which they will be subjected;*

b. *the effect of internal and external corrosion;*

c. *compatibility of different materials;*

d. *the effect of ageing, fatigue, durability and other mechanical factors; and*

e. *permeability.*

R2.5
Local circumstances can affect the use of materials. Seek the advice of the Water Supplier, which may have specific requirements.

Materials and substances in contact with water

G2.6

Providing a suitable backflow prevention device is installed, sub-paragraph 2(1) of Schedule 2 does not apply to water fittings downstream of a terminal fitting supplying wholesome water, where the recipient use does not need to be wholesome, for example:

a. *a hosepipe, used in connection with a clothes washing machine or dishwasher, or for watering a garden, or washing a vehicle, where the fitting to which the hosepipe is, or may be connected to, or incorporate, a suitable device to prevent backflow through the hosepipe; or*

b. *a flushing cistern; or*

c. *a feed cistern connected to a primary heating circuit; or*

d. *a closed circuit; or*

e. *an overflow or warning pipe.*

R2.6

This proviso allows hoses not complying with Paragraph 2(1) of this Schedule to be connected to a supply or distributing pipe in certain cases. It also exempts flushing cisterns where it is common practice to use additives, etc. This proviso also exempts cisterns and pipes connected to closed circuits where inhibitors can be used without risk of contamination of drinking water providing adequate precautions are taken to prevent backflow as set out in Section 6.

Stopvalves, servicing valves and drain taps

G2.7

Draw-off taps, stopvalves, servicing valves and draining taps should be designed so that, where applicable, their seals can be readily renewed or replaced; do not incorporate a loose washer plate; be designed and manufactured so that they may be easily closed to shut off the supply of water; and be capable of operating at the appropriate water temperature and pressure.

R2.7

The requirement for the renewal or replacement of seals includes valve washers and ceramic discs.

G2.8

Stopvalves of 15mm to 50mm nominal size laid underground should be screwdown valves complying with BS 5433 or plug cocks conforming with BS 2580. Stopvalves for use above ground should be screwdown valves complying with BS 1010 or as for below ground use. Stopvalves of nominal size 50mm may, and larger sizes should be cast iron gate valves complying with BS 5163. Spherical type valves may also be used in all sizes for above and below ground.

R2.8

Other types of stopvalves and servicing valves may be used providing that they conform to an appropriate British or European Standard, or the Regulations, and are suitable for the purpose.

Guidance   Recommendations

Terminal fittings

G2.9
Taps and combination assemblies used in water supply installations should be appropriate for the residual pressure available and the flow required at a particular appliance.

G2.10
Low resistance taps and combination tap assemblies suitable for minimum inlet pressures of 0.1 bar (0.01 MPa) should comply with BS 5412, or BS 1010 where appropriate, and high resistance taps and combination fittings suitable for minimum inlet pressures of 0.5 bar (0.05 MPa) with BS EN 200 and BS 6920.

R2.10
Low resistance draw-off taps conforming to BS 5412 and BS 1010 have been the standard taps used in the United Kingdom. They are suitable for residual pressures at the inlet of 0.1 bar (1 metre head) to 10 bar (100 metres head) and are made of materials that satisfy the requirements of BS 6920.

High resistance draw-off taps and combination tap assemblies conforming to BS EN 200 are suitable for residual pressures at the inlet of 0.5 bar (5 metres head) to 10 bar (100 metres head). As BS EN 200 does not contain any reference to materials it is essential that the tap and fittings, additionally, comply with the requirements of BS 6920 and this should be ascertained at the time of specification and installation.

It should be noted that high resistance draw-off taps require a minimum residual inlet pressure of 0.5 bar (5 metres head) and are often unsuitable for use where the water pressure is derived from a storage cistern, particularly in a house. Unless the minimum inlet pressures can be provided within the water system, an insufficient flow rate may be experienced.

Joining of different types of materials

G2.11
Except for plastics pipes, new pipework should not be connected to existing lead or other pipework without appropriate protection being provided against galvanic corrosion.

R2.11
See Section 3: Clause R3.2.

Materials and substances in contact with water

Jointing materials and compounds

G2.12
Soft solder for capillary jointing of copper or copper alloy water fittings should consist of Tin/Copper, Alloy No. 23 or 24, or Tin/Silver, Alloy No. 28 or 29, complying with BS EN 29453.

R2.12
Except where water is not required to be wholesome and for space heating systems, soft solders containing lead must not be used for joining pipes or other fittings within a water supply installation. The packaging of the solder shall indicate that the solder is lead free.

Only the minimum amount of flux required to make a successful joint shall be used and the residue removed by flushing.

G2.13
Silver solder or silver brazing filler metals and copper-phosphorus brazing filler metals for capillary jointing of copper or copper alloy pipes should conform to BS 1845, Table 2: Group AG (AG14 or AG20) or Table 3: Group CP (CP1 to CP6), respectively.

R2.13
To protect the quality of the water passing through an installation it is essential that only filler metals specified in G2.13 are used.

G2.14
Silver solder or silver brazing material for capillary jointing of stainless steel pipes should be cadmium free.

R2.14
Soft solder should not be used for jointing stainless steel pipes. Where capillary type joints are used they should be jointed by silver solder or silver brazing.

G2.15
Jointing compounds used for sealing screwed water fittings should comply with BS 6956: Part 5.

R2.15
Only jointing compounds that comply with G2.15 are to be used for jointing screwed pipes and fittings. Other proprietary compounds and hemp are not acceptable as they may promote microbial growth.

G2.16
Unsintered polytetrafluoroethylene (PTFE) tape for thread sealing applications should comply with BS 6974 and the material should also satisfy the requirements of BS 6920: Part 1.

R2.16
Only approved jointing materials are to be used for jointing screwed pipes and fittings. Hemp or gaskin are not to be used for any types of joints in any circumstances.

Schedule 2
Section 3:
Paragraphs
3, 4, 5, 6 & 7:
Requirements for
water fittings

Notes

Schedule 2

3.

Every water fitting shall –

(a) be immune to or protected from corrosion by galvanic action or by any other process which is likely to result in contamination or waste of water; and

(b) be constructed of materials of such strength and thickness as to resist damage from any external load, vibration, stress or settlement, pressure surges, or temperature fluctuation to which it is likely to be subjected.

4.

Every water fitting shall –

(a) be watertight;

(b) be so constructed and installed as to –

   (i) prevent ingress by contaminants, and

   (ii) inhibit damage by freezing or any other cause;

(c) be so installed as to minimise the risk of permeation by, or deterioration from contact with, any substance which may cause contamination; and

(d) be adequately supported.

5.

Every water fitting shall be capable of withstanding an internal water pressure not less than $1^1/_2$ times the maximum pressure to which that fitting is designed to be subjected in operation.

6.

No water fitting shall be installed, connected or used which is likely to have a detrimental effect on the quality or pressure of water in a water main or other pipe of a water undertaker.

7.

(1) No water fitting shall be embedded in any wall or solid floor.

(2) No fitting which is designed to be operated or maintained, whether manually or electronically, or which consists of a joint, shall be a concealed water fitting.

(3) Any concealed water fitting or mechanical backflow prevention device, not being a terminal fitting, shall be made of gunmetal, or another material resistant to dezincification.

(4) Any water fitting laid below ground level shall have a depth of cover sufficient to prevent water freezing in the fitting.

(5) In this paragraph 'concealed water fitting' means a water fitting which –

(a) is installed below ground;

(b) passes through or under any wall, footing or foundation;

(c) is enclosed in any chase or duct; or

(d) is in any other position which is inaccessible or renders access difficult.

Requirements for water fittings

Guidance   **Recommendations**

General

G3.1
Water fittings should be
adequate for the purpose
and satisfy the appropriate
British Standard, or
acceptable equivalent.

G3.2
Pipes of different metallic
materials are not to be
connected unless suitable
precautions are taken to
ensure that corrosion
through galvanic action
cannot take place.

R3.2
Lead pipe is prohibited for use in new installations and
for replacement in any part of an existing water supply
installation, therefore where a defective length of lead pipe
needs replacing an alternative acceptable material should
be used. Apart from the harmful effects of lead pipes and
fittings and some other materials on the water passing
through them, problems of corrosion due to galvanic action
can occur where pipes of different materials are directly
connected together.

Galvanic action can cause severe corrosion of pipes and fittings and can occur
between pipes made of dissimilar materials in two ways:

a. Direct galvanic action takes place where two dissimilar metals are in contact; and

b. Indirect galvanic action occurs where dissolution of one metal upstream of
another causes accelerated corrosion of the downstream material, the water
acting as the electrolyte.

A simple explanation of what occurs when dissimilar metals are joined or connected
together (direct galvanic corrosion) is that an electric cell is set up across the joint. This
is basically the same as a wet cell battery except that in this case the water acts as the
electrolyte (ie. a liquid capable of carrying electricity). The resultant current flow, though
minute, causes one metal to corrode, and eventually perforation of the fitting occurs.

Indirect galvanic action occurs when particles of one metal are taken into solution and
the resultant solution attacks a pipe or fitting of a different metal further along the
pipework system. An example of this is when the water, having passed through copper
pipe to a galvanised cistern, remains in the cistern for some time and an attack on the
galvanising takes place; eventually perforation will occur.

Even though the use of an intervening non-conductive material will prevent direct
galvanic action at the point of contact of two different metals, this will not prevent the
occurrence of indirect galvanic corrosion. The relative positions of metals in the pipework
system then becomes most important. The obvious answer is to use only one metal in
the system but as this is often impracticable, precautions can be taken by using
non-conductive plastics materials.

The Regulations would normally be satisfied if the sequence of metals in any water
fitting (pipe, cistern, hot water storage vessel, etc) in relation to the normal direction
of flow were as shown below in Diagram R3.2.

Diagram
R3.2:

*Correct sequence
of metals in relation
to normal direction
of flow*

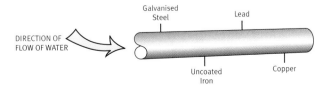

DIRECTION OF
FLOW OF WATER

Galvanised
Steel

Lead

Uncoated
Iron

Copper

Guidance

Recommendations

Care should be taken in the use of metallic jointing methods which, if manufactured of several different materials, should in general conform with the above sequence.

Plastics pipes may be used in conjunction with any material. Although copper pipe should not be used in the replacement of a section of lead pipe, the use of one or two short copper liners in repairs should not result in water picking up a significant concentration of copper. Problems can arise in cases where copper flow and return pipes are connected to galvanised hot water tanks or to galvanised storage cisterns used in conjunction with copper cylinders.

Where pipe systems include pipes with high electrical insulation value (for example, plastics pipes) it is essential that all lengths of metal pipes and other fittings are adequately electrically bonded and earthed in accordance with relevant statutory requirements.

G3.3
All water fittings including supply pipes, distributing pipes and discharge pipes connected to operational and safety devices in cold and hot water systems should be capable of withstanding temperatures to allow for malfunctions within the system and should comply with the requirements of BS 6700: 1997

R3.3
BS 6700: 1997: Clause 1.4.1 requires that all water fittings are capable of withstanding, without damage or deterioration, and at the maximum working pressure, sustained temperatures of 40°C for cold water installations and 95°C for heated water installations with occasional short-term excursions in excess of 100°C to allow for malfunctions. It also requires discharge pipes connected to temperature or expansion relief valves to be capable of withstanding any continuous hot water or steam discharge at temperatures up to 125°C.

G3.4
The suitability and thickness of copper hot water storage vessels and other apparatus should not be determined exclusively on the basis of pressure considerations. A greater thickness of the walls of the vessel, together with the need or otherwise of protector rods or internal coating, should take into consideration the type of water supplied in the area and its possible effect in combination with other factors.

R3.4
In some circumstances cathodic protection can give protection against galvanic action. This involves using sacrificial anodes which are fitted inside cisterns, cylinders or tanks and on pipelines so that the anode will corrode instead of the fitting it protects until a protective coating is formed on the latter. Fittings made from galvanised steel are frequently protected in this way. In some instances cathodic protection may have an adverse effect on water quality. Corrosion of the anode can give rise to concentrations of metals exceeding the limits for drinking water. Where this method is proposed it is recommended that expert advice be sought.

The sacrificial anodes are usually made from magnesium alloy and are fixed to the fittings to be protected so that they are immersed in the water. When used in copper storage vessels anodes are usually made of aluminum rod. Guidance, relating to the geographical area concerned, should be sought from the Water Supplier (see Diagram R3.4 overleaf).

Requirements for water fittings

Diagram
R3.4:
Examples of providing cathodic protection against galvanic corrosion by using sacrificial anodes

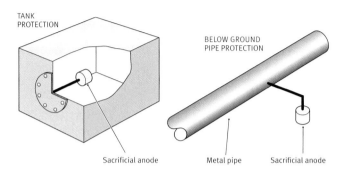

TANK PROTECTION

BELOW GROUND PIPE PROTECTION

Sacrificial anode   Metal pipe   Sacrificial anode

Watertightness of fittings and prevention of ingress by contaminants

G4.1
Water fittings are to be watertight and suitable for the default pressures and temperatures likely to be encountered within the installation.

R4.1
Water fittings should be checked before installation to ensure that they are suitable for the default pressures and temperatures likely to be encountered during use. They should be approved by an accepted test-house. Fittings that are not so approved may not be able to satisfy the requirements for pressure and temperature.

Water fittings should be constructed so that the entry of contaminants, such as chemicals, vermin, insects or others, is prevented. The most vulnerable fittings are those incorporating air gaps, that is, where the water itself is open to the atmosphere, such as water in cisterns and reference to this is given in Schedule 2: Section 7: Paragraph 16.

Protection against freezing

G4.2
All cold water fittings located within the building but outside the thermal envelope, or those outside the building must be protected against damage by freezing.

R4.2
It is also recommended that the thickness of insulation provided on hot water supply and distributing pipes, and those used in space heating systems, should be adequate to prevent freezing.

The thermal envelope may be defined as that part of a building which is enclosed within walls, floor and roof and which is thermally insulated in accordance with the requirements of the Building Regulations.

G4.3
If the frost protection provided is insufficient for exceptional freezing conditions, or the premises are left unoccupied or without adequate heating, damage and leakage can often be avoided by shutting off the water supply and draining the system before the onset of freezing.

R4.3
Wherever possible, all water pipes should be located within the thermal envelope of the building where heating is provided for some part of the day. In rooms devoid of heating, even if the pipes are located within the thermal envelope, water fittings should be provided with facilities for isolating and draining. They should also be insulated against frost as 'normal conditions' in accordance with Table G4.11.

Guidance

Recommendations

G4.4

Where low temperatures persist insulation will only delay the onset of freezing. Its efficiency is dependant upon its thickness and thermal conductivity in relation to the size of pipe, the time of exposure, the location and possibly the wind-chill factor.

R4.4

The common understanding that insulation to prevent freezing of water in pipes is provided to 'keep the cold out' is incorrect. Insulation is provided to retain the 'heat energy' in the water in the pipe. This is illustrated in Diagram R4.4 where it is apparent that for a given thermal conductivity of insulation material the smaller diameter of pipe requires a greater minimum thickness of insulation than is required for a larger diameter pipe.

In some cases therefore, and as illustrated in the right hand column of Table G4.11, where there is only a short length of pipe, say in a roof space or the vertical pipe to a standpipe or cattle trough, it may be acceptable to use a 22mm diameter pipe instead of a 15mm pipe, thus reducing the insulation thickness required from an 'unacceptable' 91mm to an 'acceptable' 24mm.

Diagram
R4.4:

Illustration showing the relative thicknesses of insulation required for a particular size of pipe for an ambient temperature of -3°C with water at +3°C

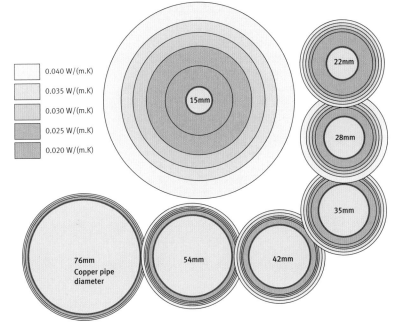

0.040 W/(m.K)

0.035 W/(m.K)

0.030 W/(m.K)

0.025 W/(m.K)

0.020 W/(m.K)

22mm

28mm

35mm

15mm

76mm
Copper pipe
diameter

54mm

42mm

G4.5

In exceptional circumstances, and in those parts of the United Kingdom where very low temperatures are sustained during both day and night, unless the system is isolated and drained before the onset of freezing, additional measures may be required to ensure that freezing of water fittings does not occur. Other methods of preventing damage to water fittings that may be considered are the;

a. provision of froststats to activate the heating system when the air temperature drops to a preselected value; and

b. provision of strategically placed thermostatically controlled shut-off and draining valves for isolating and draining sections of pipework.

Guidance

G4.6

Thermal insulating materials should be of the closed cell type complying with BS 5422 and be installed in accordance with BS 5970.

G4.7

Some of the types of insulation materials relating to the thermal conductivities shown in Table G4.11 are as follows:

Less than 0.020 W/(m.K)	*Rigid phenolic foam*
0.020 to 0.025 W/(m.K)	*Polisocyanurate foam and rigid polyurethane foam*
0.025 to 0.030 W/(m.K)	*PVC foam*
0.030 to 0.035 W/(m.K)	*Expanded polystyrene, extruded polystyrene, cross-linked polyethylene foam, expanded nitrile rubber and improved polyethylene foam*
0.035 to 0.040 W/(m.K)	*Standard polyethylene foam, expanded synthetic rubber and cellular glass.*

G4.8

It is essential that:

a. *there is no gap in the insulation at bends, valves, etc. as heat loss due to these conditions could freeze local pockets of the pipe system in less than one hour; and*

b. *an external vapour barrier is provided and protected against mechanical or other damage; and*

c. *where water pipes are located directly below ceiling or roof void insulation;*

   (i) *the full calculated thickness; or*

   (ii) *a minimum thickness of 9mm, high emissivity surfaced, closed cell insulation, whichever is the greater, is installed around the water pipe to prevent condensation, saturation and subsequent failure of the ceiling insulation.*

G4.9

Hot water fittings outside the thermal envelope, where water is likely to be static for a period, should be protected against freezing. The thickness of insulation applied to hot water pipes for energy conservation purposes is usually of insufficient thickness to protect against low temperature conditions.

G4.10

Stop valves, servicing valves and drain taps should be labelled so that the parts of the system which they control can be determined for maintenance purposes; also for isolation and draining when buildings are unoccupied during cold weather.

G4.11

For the purpose of protection against freezing of pipes two conditions are assumed:

A. *NORMAL CONDITIONS*

In domestic accommodation, and in other types of premises where applicable, where habitable rooms are normally heated for up to 12 hours each day; water fittings in unheated rooms need to be protected against freezing, particularly overnight, even though they are within the envelope of the heated accommodation. For example, water fittings in cloakrooms, store rooms, utility rooms, in roof spaces but located below the ceiling insulation, etc.

Guidance

Recommendations

The recommended commercial thicknesses of insulation for minimum and practical protection against freezing in the unheated parts of normally occupied buildings when the heating is turned off in the remainder of the building, such as overnight, is shown in Table G4.11. Except where indicated otherwise, the insulation thicknesses shown under the respective thermal conductivity values are considered reasonable to provide a nominal minimum of 12 hours protection. An absence of more than 24 hours is not considered normal occupation.

R4.11

The guidance relates to protective measures that need to be taken to prevent damage to cold and hot water pipes by low ambient temperature conditions and sets out sound advice with recommendations for the thickness of insulation required to protect water fittings from freezing given in Table G4.11.

The thicknesses of thermal insulation recommended in Table G4.11 is calculated on the design method given in BS 5422. However, sustained periods of low air temperatures can vary throughout the United Kingdom and each installation should be considered according to its geographic location.

Water pipes that are located;

a. above ground level external to buildings or less than 750mm depth of cover; or

b. under suspended ground floors; or

c. in unheated communal staircases, corridors, garages or roof spaces,

will need to be protected with a thickness of insulation much greater than that recommended in Table G4.11.

B. *EXTREME CONDITIONS*

Extreme conditions apply to water fittings installed outside a building, or inside any building or part of a building which is unheated, or only marginally heated for less than 12 hours each day; or water fittings inside a building but located outside the thermal envelope. For example, water fittings located under suspended ground floors, above the level of ceiling insulation in a roof space, in a communal staircase or corridor in flats, domestic garages or other buildings, or externally above ground level.

It is recommended that for water fittings in these locations the thickness of insulation should be substantially increased and the advice of insulation specialists or manufacturers be obtained. Guidance on design methods can be obtained from BS 5422.

It should be noted that the principal criteria used in BS 5422 (water temperature, ambient temperature, time of exposure, percentage ice formation, thermal conductivity and thickness of insulation) cannot represent all circumstances or permutations, so that where it is necessary to avoid excessive ice formation it would be prudent to consult insulation suppliers or manufacturers.

Requirements for water fittings

Guidance   *Recommendations*

Table G4.11: *Recommended minimum commercial thicknesses of thermal insulation for copper water pipes of minimum wall thickness complying with BS EN 1057 in normal conditions of exposure*

THERMAL CONDUCTIVITY OF INSULATION MATERIAL AT 0°C IN W/(m.K)						
	0.02	0.025	0.03	0.035	0.04	
mm	*mm*	*mm*	*mm*	*mm*	*mm*	**Notes**
15	20 (20)	30 (30)	25*(45)	25*(70)	32*(91)	1 Except for 15mm pipes with thermal conductivities of 0.030,
22	15 (9)	15 (12)	19 (15)	19 (19)	25 (24)	0.035 and 0.040 W/(m.K), shown with a *, which are limited to
28	15 (6)	15 (8)	13 (10)	19 (12)	22 (14)	50% ice formation after 9, 8 and 7 hours respectively, the above
35	15 (4)	15 (6)	9 (7)	9 (8)	13 (10)	recommended commercially available minimum thicknesses
42 and over	15 (3)	15 (5)	9 (5)	9 (5)	9 (8)	

of insulation should limit ice formation to under 50% after 12 hours for the remainder of the pipe sizes, when based on an air temperature of -6°C and a water temperature of +7°C. The minimum calculated insulation thicknesses for 12 hours protection under the above conditions are shown in the appropriate location in brackets.

2 Commercial thicknesses of insulation with the higher thermal conductivities are generally limited to a minimum of 9mm. Materials with a lower thermal conductivity, such as rigid phenolic foam, polisocyanurate foam and rigid polyurethane foam are installed by specialist firms and are usually limited to a minimum thickness of about 15mm.

3 Normal conditions to frost exposure are considered to be when water fittings are installed inside buildings within the thermal envelope, but within rooms or voids which are not heated for a minimum period of 12 hours each day for the whole of the winter period. Examples could include the following:

a. Unheated cloakrooms, store rooms, utility rooms, etc.
b. Below the ceiling insulation in a roof space

Equivalent of Table 3.1 in DETR guidance document

G4.12
Self-regulating trace heating conforming to BS 6351, in conjunction with a nominal thickness of thermal insulation, is an acceptable method of protection against freezing.

R4.12
Geographical location, altitude and the wind chill factor can have a direct bearing on the thickness and type of protection required to reduce the likelihood of water freezing in pipes. From Table G4.11 and Diagram R4.4 it can be seen that for extreme conditions the thickness of insulation required for smaller diameter pipes can be out of all proportion to the diameter of the pipe and impractical to provide. In such instances it can be economical to provide a form of trace heating with an additional nominal thickness of insulation.

Further information is given in Information and Guidance Note IGN 9-02-02: 'Precautions against freezing in plumbing systems' published by the Water Regulations Advisory Scheme.

G4.13
The thickness of insulation for the protection of cold water cisterns in roof spaces and other exposed locations should be calculated in accordance with BS EN 1057. Water fittings connecting to and from cold water cisterns are particularly vulnerable and all insulation should be closely sealed, except for the air vent to the cistern.

Guidance   *Recommendations*

Plastics and permeable materials

G4.14
Water fittings should be installed to minimise any risk of contamination by permeation of fluids through the material or materials used.

G4.15
Water fittings that are made of a material which is susceptible to permeation by any fluid that causes, or is likely to cause, contamination of water passing through the fitting, should not be laid or installed in such a location, in relation to other services or contaminated ground, that permeation occurs.

R4.15
Because plastics pipes may also be permeated by some fluids, such as natural gas, care should be taken regarding the circumstances in which they are used. Diagram R4.15 shows a recommendation by the National Joint Utilities Group (NJUG) Report 6 for relative positions of utility services in a service trench. It provides in effect a space of about 350mm between gas and water services.

Protective measures will be required where the dimensions and depths cannot be achieved.

Diagram
R4.15:
Relative positions of utility services

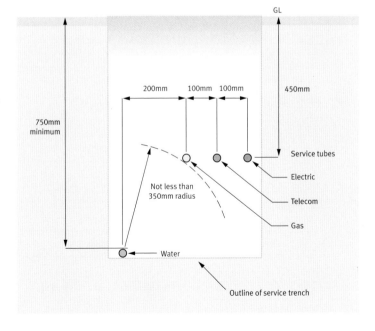

Requirements for water fittings

G4.16

Water fittings made of plastics, or other material which are likely to be damaged by exposure to oil, petrol or any other contaminant, should not be laid in contaminated ground, or should be protected.

R4.16

Pipes of plastics must not be laid in ground subject to spillage of hydrocarbons such as oil, petrol or creosote which can cause deterioration of the pipe and consequent contamination and waste of water (see Diagram R4.16). In addition to the case illustrated, taste problems have also arisen where plastics pipes have been laid in close contact with damp proofing materials. For further information and advice see 'Pipe Materials Selection Manual' published by WRc.

Diagram
R4.16:

Damage to plastics pipework by permeation

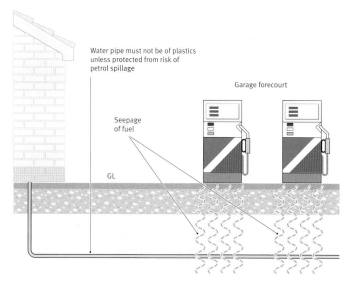

Water pipe must not be of plastics unless protected from risk of petrol spillage

Garage forecourt

Seepage of fuel

GL

Fixing of water fittings

G4.17

Water fittings should be adequately protected against damage from any cause, including the environment through which they pass.

G4.18

Water fittings should be adequately supported, the spacing for support being dependent on the material of the pipes. Allowance should be made to accommodate any reasonable foreseeable movement, including thermal movement, in accordance with Clause 3.1.7 of BS 6700: 1997.

R4.18

Schedule 2: Paragraph 4(d) requires water fittings to be adequately supported and it is recommended that spacings for fixing internally located piping should be in accordance with Table R4.18.

Piping that is to be insulated shall be secured on clips or brackets that allow sufficient space between the pipe and supporting wall surface to which the pipe is fixed for the insulation to be properly installed.

Allowance should be made for expansion and contraction of pipes by forming expansion loops or introducing changes of direction in pipe systems where there are long straight runs and few bends and offsets, depending on the type of pipe materials and joints used.

Guidance

Recommendations

This is particularly important where temperature changes are considered (e.g. hot water distribution pipework) and where the pipe material has a relatively large coefficient of thermal expansion (e.g. plastics). In installations with limited straight runs and many bends and offsets, thermal movement is accommodated automatically.

Table R4.18: *Maximum spacing of fixing brackets for internal piping*

TYPE OF PIPING	NOMINAL DIAMETER OF PIPE		SPACING ON HORIZONTAL RUN	SPACING ON VERTICAL RUN
	mm		m	m
Copper complying with R250 (Half hard) and R290 (Hard) of BS EN1057: 1996 and stainless steel complying with BS 4127: Part 2:1972	15		1.2	1.8
	22		1.8	2.4
	28		1.8	2.4
	35		2.4	3.0
	42		2.4	3.0
	54		2.7	3.0
	67		3.0	3.6
	76		3.0	3.6
	108		3.0	3.6
	133		3.0	3.6
	159		3.6	4.2
	Copper	Steel		
Copper complying with R220 (Annealed) of BS EN 1057: 1996 and steel complying with BS 1387:1985	15	15	1.8	2.4
	22	20	2.4	3.0
	28	25	2.4	3.0
	35	32	2.7	3.0
	42	40	3.0	3.6
	54	50	3.0	3.6
	67	65	3.0	3.6
	75	80	3.6	4.5
	108	100	3.9	4.5
Ductile iron complying with BS EN 545.	75		2.7	2.7
	100		2.7	2.7
	150		3.6	3.6
Unplasticised PVC[1] complying with BS 3505:1986	1/4		0.6	1.1
	1/2		0.7	1.3
	3/4		0.7	1.4
	1		0.8	1.6
	1 1/4		0.9	1.7
	1 1/2		1.0	1.9
	2		1.1	2.2
	3		1.4	2.8
	4		1.6	3.1
	6		1.9	3.7
Black MDPE pipe complying with BS 6730: 1986 (1998)	25		0.6	1.2
	32		0.6	1.2
	50		0.8	1.5
	63		0.8	1.6
Chlorinated PVC-C[2] complying with BS 7291: Parts 1 & 4	12 to 25		0.5	1.0
	32 to 63		0.8	2.2
Polybutylene (PB) and cross-linked polyethylene (PE-X)[2] complying with BS 7291: Parts 1, 2 & 3	Up to 16		0.3	0.5
	18 to 25		0.5	0.8
	28		0.8	1.0
	32		0.9	1.2
	35		0.9	1.2

Notes

[1]
Figures are for normal ambient temperatures below 20°C. For temperatures above 20°C the pipe manufacturer should be consulted.

[2]
Based on water temperature up to 80°C.

Requirements for water fittings

Pressure requirements

G5.1
All water fittings should be capable of withstanding an internal water pressure of not less than 1.5 times the maximum operating pressure

G5.2
In determining the maximum operating pressure to which the system is subjected, the increase in static pressure in the following instances should be taken into consideration:

a. the supply pipe during night periods when there may be little demand on the system; and

b. in any water supply installation where pumps are installed.

R5.2
While some water fittings are classified for lower pressures only, many of the pipes, joints, stopvalves, float operated valves, mechanical backflow preventers and other types of valves conforming to a British or European Standard are suitable for operating pressures up to 10 bar and all are tested up to a test pressure of at least 15 bar.

In most mains distribution systems operated by Water Suppliers, pressure increases during periods of very low demand, such as during the night period. The amount of increase in pressure will vary, depending on the size of main, the numbers of consumers supplied and the sophistication of the pumping and pressure control system. The amount of increase in pressure in a water main may be ascertained by the use of an automatic pressure recorder operating over a period. This pressure variation can also occur in pumped water supply installations in buildings where constant running pumps are used. In most cases this increase in pressure is nominal and can easily be absorbed within the margin of the test pressure.

Surge pressures

G5.3
The internal test pressure does not take into consideration any transient or surge pressures which may be generated within the system and the designer or installer should take the effect of any surge into consideration in determining the test pressure applied to an installation.

R5.3
Surge pressures are usually evident from noise generated within the system as 'water hammer' emanating from pipes as a result of the rapid closure of a draw-off tap or from a rapidly oscillating float-operated valve.

G5.4
Transient pressure increases or surge (water hammer) may be generated by the rapid closure of a valve; for example, float-operated valves, spherical valves or disc valves. When installed, attenuation devices or water hammer arresters may reduce the effects of surge.

R5.4
Except where water has been distributed under a high mains pressure, the problem of surge in building water supply installations is not normally a significant problem. This is partly due to appliances being served with water from storage cisterns, as distinct to being supplied directly from the supply pipe, as has been the practice in mainland Europe for many years.

With the increasing use in the UK of appliances served directly from the supply pipe, together with the use of draw-off taps incorporating ceramic discs and the use of solenoid operated valves in appliances such as washing machines, both of which have a rapid rate of shut-off, an increasing number of problems of surge are arising.

Guidance **Recommendations**

The increase in pressure caused by surge takes place over a very short period and can be many times the static pressure existing normally within the pipe. As this pressure rise is momentary, and is dependent on the time taken to stop the flow of water, it is often insufficient to damage the water fittings, but measures may need to be taken to absorb the pressure rise and reduce noise. One method of keeping surge within reasonable limits is to incorporate hydro-pneumatic accumulators or surge arresters at suitable points within the system.

Pumps or boosters

G6.1

Written approval should be obtained from the Water Undertaker before any pump or booster is connected to a supply pipe, unless the pump or booster is incapable of drawing more than 0.2 litres per second.

R6.1

Where a pump draws water directly from a supply pipe or a water main there is a possibility of the pump attempting to draw more water than the main can provide; in this situation the pressure in the main may be reduced and vacuum conditions arise, thus creating conditions in which backflow may occur and could lead to a reduction in the quality of the water in the main.

While there is likely to be little increased demand on a supply pipe if a pump or booster is connected 'indirectly' to a supply pipe, that is, connected from the outlet of a cistern supplied with water from a supply pipe; under Regulation 5(1) 'Table', sub-clause 4 (d), the written consent of the Water Supplier is required before installation of a pump or booster drawing more than 0.2 litres per second (12 litres per minute), connected either directly or indirectly to a supply pipe (see Diagrams R6.1a and R6.1b).

Diagram
R6.1a:
Pump connected directly to a supply pipe

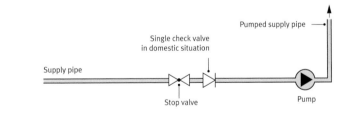

Diagram
R6.1b:
Pump connected indirectly to a supply pipe

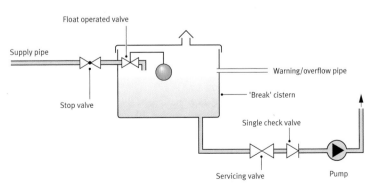

Requirements for water fittings

The written consent of the Water Supplier will be deemed to have been given in the case of pumps incapable of drawing more than 0.2 litres per second (12 litres per minute) installed in drink vending and dispensing machines, domestic water softeners or pumped showers which in all other respects fully comply with the Regulations. In the case of pumped (power) showers, the written consent of the Water Supplier is also required if the shower is of a type specified by the Regulator, irrespective of the flow through the shower.

It should be noted that the requirement to notify the Water Supplier where it is proposed to install a pump or booster of a discharge capacity greater than 0.2 litres per second does not apply to a pump installed in a:

a. hot water primary or secondary circulation circuit; or

b. a drinking water or a cooling system circuit,

where the pump is installed to overcome friction within the circulation pipe (circulator) and does not contribute, or only marginally contributes, to the flow capacity of the pipe.

Pumped showers

G6.2
Showers, and other appliances, which are supplied with water through a pump located either upstream or downstream of the mixing valve, and capable of delivering more than 0.2 litres/second, may not be supplied with water direct from a supply pipe unless written approval has been obtained from the water supplier (see Regulation 5).

R6.2
Under Regulation 5(1) 'Table', sub-clause 4(d), an installer will need to obtain the Water Supplier's written permission before any pumped shower drawing more than 0.2 litres a second may be supplied with water either directly or indirectly from a supply pipe.

G6.3
Irrespective of whether the water supply to a shower is pumped or the shower incorporates a pump, whether supplied with water from either a supply pipe or a distributing pipe, and is of a type specified by the regulator, consent to install the shower should be obtained from the Water Undertaker (see Regulation 5).

R6.3
Under Regulation 5(1), 'Table', sub-clause 4(c), an installer will need to obtain the Water Supplier's written permission before any shower connected directly or indirectly to a supply pipe, and which is of a type specified by the Regulator, can be installed.

Care should be taken at the point of connection of a branch pipe serving a pumped shower, or similar pumped appliance. For instance, negative pressures can be developed within the pipe system if the draw-off is high and pipes are insufficiently sized, thus increasing velocities within the pipework upstream of the pump. This could have an adverse effect on the functioning of backflow prevention measures, depending on the types of backflow prevention devices or arrangements within the system. It is essential therefore, that pipework is properly sized and inlets to pumps are taken from independent distributing pipes or common vented distributing pipes.

Guidance   *Recommendations*

Location of water fittings

G7.1

Unless they are located in an internal wall which is not a solid wall, a chase or duct which may be readily exposed, or under a suspended floor which may, if necessary, be readily removed and replaced, or to which there is access, water fittings should not be:

a. located in the cavity of a cavity wall; or

b. embedded in any wall or solid floor; or

c. installed below a suspended or solid floor at ground level.

See Diagrams G7.1a to G7.1f for typical details of acceptable arrangements in floors and Diagrams G7.1g to G7.1m for locations in walls and behind panels.

(Note: Any notching or holes made within floor or roof joists should be within the limits shown in Building Regulations, Approved Document A, Section 1B6.)

R7.1

Detailed guidance on concealed fittings cannot be given for every circumstance likely to be encountered. Several illustrative examples are shown in Diagrams G7.1a to G7.1f and G7.1g to G7.1m. These are based on the principles:

a. That enclosure within chases and ducts can be permitted as long as leaks would become apparent and the section of pipe could be exposed by the removal of covers or superficial surface finishes (tiles or screeded finish, etc), or the pipe could be withdrawn for repair.

b. That particular care should be taken where continuous flooring such as chipboard is laid. Properly formed openings with removable covers should be provided to give adequate access for inspection and dismantling of pipe joints and for removal of sections of pipe.

The bedding of any pipe and associated pipe joints forming part of a closed circuit system of underfloor space heating in screed or in a properly formed chase in a wall or solid floor which is subsequently plastered or screeded is generally acceptable if the pipe and joints can be exposed for repair or replacement by removing the surface layers of plaster or screed.

Where pipes are located in a chase within a solid wall or floor, adequate room for expansion and contraction should be included and only a minimum number of fittings should be located within the chase (see Diagrams G7.1c and G7.1k). Pipes located in a chase within a solid floor are generally only permissible for heating pipes and should not be concreted in or the chase filled with screeding material (see Diagram G7.1c). Always seek the advice of the local water supplier before locating pipes in chases.

Where pipes are installed within a purpose made duct (see Diagram G7.1b) the pipe should be capable of being withdrawn for inspection and therefore no self anchoring fittings such as bends or branches can be incorporated unless the duct has a removable cover which will allow the pipes to be inspected and replaced if necessary.

Where pipes are located beneath continuous chipboard floors (see Diagram G7.1d), provision for access to the pipework should be provided at the time of installation as to cut sections of the floor out at a later date could result in damage to the pipework. The pipework below a chipboard floor or behind a plasterboard wall will also be susceptible to damage from nails or screws (see Diagrams G7.1d, G7.1h and G7.1l).

All pipes located in areas where subsequent inspection will be difficult or impracticable should be pressure tested before being concealed.

Where the pipe is installed within the internal leaf of an external wall, frost protection measures may be required (see Diagrams G7.1g, G7.1h, G7.1i and G7.1k).

Requirements for water fittings

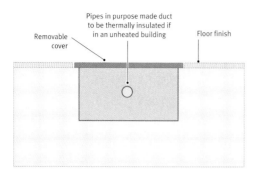

Removable cover

Pipes in purpose made duct to be thermally insulated if in an unheated building

Floor finish

Diagram
G7.1a:
Pipe in purpose made duct with removable cover

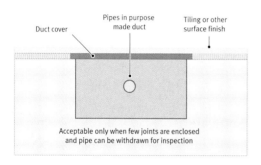

Duct cover

Pipes in purpose made duct

Tiling or other surface finish

Acceptable only when few joints are enclosed and pipe can be withdrawn for inspection

Diagram
G7.1b:
Pipe in purpose made duct with no access

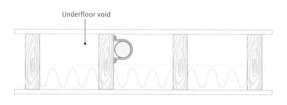

Underfloor void

Diagram
G7.1e:
Pipe located under insulated ground floor

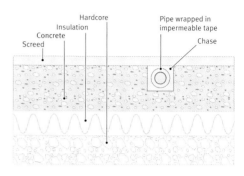

Screed
Concrete
Insulation
Hardcore
Pipe wrapped in impermeable tape
Chase

Diagram
G7.1c:
Pipe located in chase in ground supported concrete floor

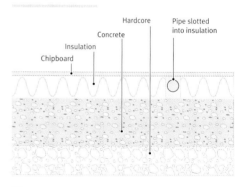

Chipboard
Insulation
Concrete
Hardcore
Pipe slotted into insulation

Diagram
G7.1d:
Pipe located between insulation in ground supported concrete floor

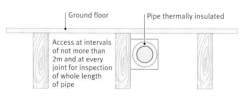

Ground floor
Pipe thermally insulated
Access at intervals of not more than 2m and at every joint for inspection of whole length of pipe

Diagram
G7.1f:
Pipe located under non-insulated ground floor

Guidance

Diagram G7.1i:

Pipe in duct with non-removable cover in internal leaf of external wall

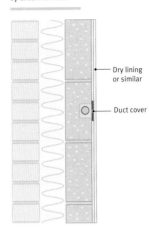

Dry lining or similar

Duct cover

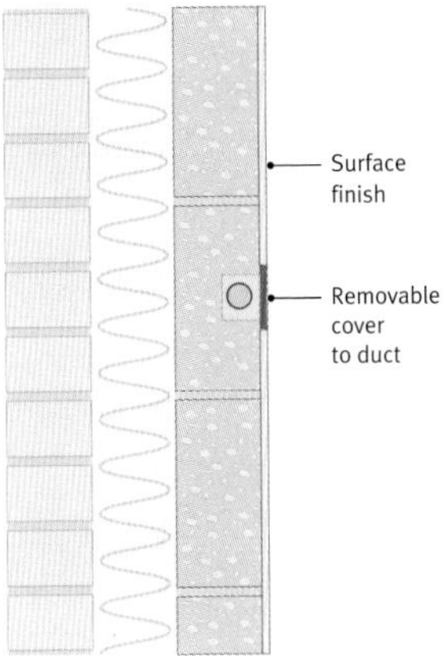

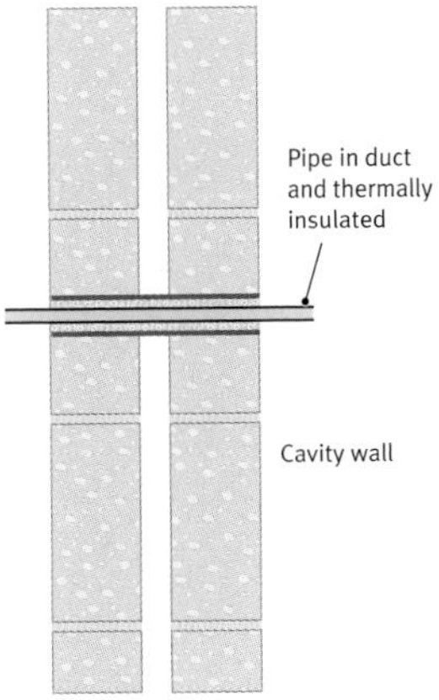

Diagram G7.1h:

Pipe clipped to nogging or stud in timber framed internal leaf of external wall

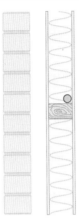

Diagram G7.1g:

Pipe in duct with removable cover in internal leaf of external wall

Surface finish

Removable cover to duct

Plaster board and studding wall (internal)

Pipe located within wall

Diagram G7.1l:

Pipe located in an internal studded wall

Pipe in duct and thermally insulated

Cavity wall

Pipe bedded in chase to be wrapped in impermeable tape

Diagram G7.1k:

Pipe bedded in chase in internal leaf of external wall

Diagram G7.1j:

Pipe passing through cavity wall

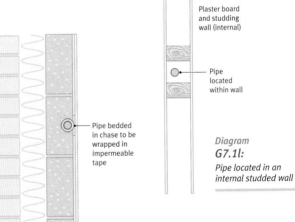

Removable panel

Preferred position for pipes. Access will be difficult if laid on the side of the bath remote from the removable panel

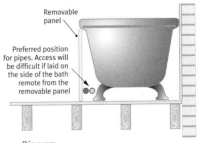

Diagram G7.1m:

Accessibility of pipes behind bath panels

G7.2

Pipes entering buildings at the approved depth should be passed through a duct and the ends of the duct sealed as shown in Diagrams G7.2a, G7.2b and G7.2c to prevent the ingress of gas or vermin into the building.

R7.2

It is essential that pipes entering buildings below ground level are sealed against the entry of fluids, vermin and insects, as Diagrams G7.2a, G7.2b and G7.2c.

Where the incoming pipe:

a. has less than 750mm of ground cover above the pipe, or the pipe enters the building at a distance of less than 750mm from the external face of the wall, the annular space between the outside of the pipe and the inside of the duct should be provided with insulating material; or

b. passes through an airspace below an internal suspended lower floor, the pipe should be fully insulated in that air space.

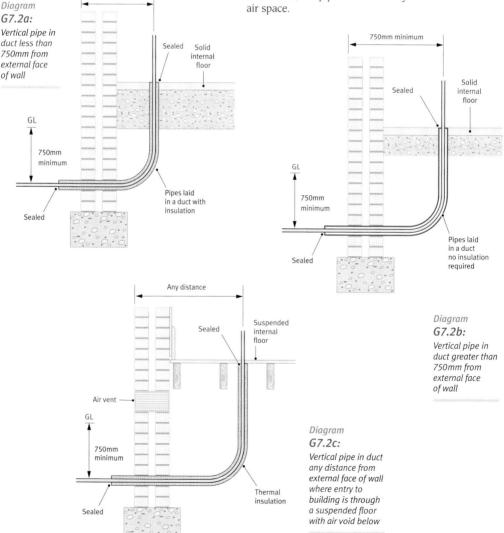

Diagram
G7.2a:

Vertical pipe in duct less than 750mm from external face of wall

Diagram
G7.2b:

Vertical pipe in duct greater than 750mm from external face of wall

Diagram
G7.2c:

Vertical pipe in duct any distance from external face of wall where entry to building is through a suspended floor with air void below

Guidance   *Recommendations*

Concealed fittings

G7.3
A concealed pipe may be installed in a pipe sleeve or duct located under or within a solid floor provided that the pipe can be readily removed and replaced.

R7.3
Any pipe located within a pipe sleeve, under or within the construction of a solid floor, should be capable of being withdrawn for repair from one, or either, end of the pipe sleeve.

Where single cold or hot water pipes are located within vertical pipe sleeves, used as vertical pipe ducts, the pipes should be wrapped, either continuously or at intervals to prevent lateral movement of the pipe within the pipe duct. Where both cold and hot water pipes are located in this type of duct the pipes should be separately insulated over their full length.

Dezincification resistant materials

G7.4
Water fittings are to be resistant to corrosion and, where specified, to dezincification.

R7.4
Some waters can cause a form of corrosion whereby a meringue-like product grows in or on certain brass fittings; this is known as dezincification. This process may not only choke the pipe or fitting but ultimately cause leakages and fittings to become inoperable.

G7.5
All concealed water fittings, except terminal fittings, (including those buried underground), together with backflow prevention devices, are required to be manufactured of gunmetal or other dezincification resistant materials.

R7.5
All water fittings that are concealed under floors, in walls, buried underground or in any other inaccessible location, are to be manufactured of dezincification resistant material. The only exclusions to this requirement are terminal fittings, for example, draw-off taps and shower mixer fittings. Mechanical backflow prevention devices and safety devices (eg. temperature or pressure relief valves) are also to be manufactured of dezincification resistant material.

G7.6
Dezincification resistant fittings should be of DRA quality, the depth of dezincification being not less than 200 microns in any direction. Each fitting should be marked with the symbol CR or DRA and should be tested in accordance with ISO 6509.

R7.6
Paragraph 7(3) of the Schedule relates to dezincification and will normally be satisfied if a water fitting, or any part made of copper alloy containing zinc, is made of gunmetal or of a brass resistant to dezincification.

All gunmetals and certain types of brasses are immune and, suitable brasses are now available for hot stamping which are also resistant to dezincification. Suitable fittings are marked with the CEN agreed symbol DRA, that is, dezincification resistant and grade A. Within the United Kingdom the symbol shown in Diagram R7.6 is used for marking of dezincification resistant fittings.

Diagram
R7.6:
Symbol for dezincification resistant materials

Guidance   **Recommendations**

Water fittings laid underground

G7.7
Wherever practicable and except for pipes laid under a building, the vertical distance between the top of every water pipe installed below ground and the finished ground level should be:

a. not less than 750mm; and

b. not more than 1,350mm.

R7.7
The depths of cover shown in Diagram G7.7 are the normally accepted minimum and maximum depths of cover required.

Diagram
G7.7:
Cover requirements for pipes laid underground

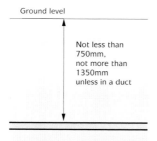

Ground level

Not less than 750mm, not more than 1350mm unless in a duct

G7.8
Where compliance with the minimum cover of 750mm is impracticable, and with the written approval of the Water Undertaker, the water fittings should be installed as deep as is practicable below the finished ground level and be adequately protected against damage from freezing and from any other cause.

R7.8
Where it is impracticable to lay pipes within the minimum and maximum limits of cover shown in Diagram G7.7 the requirement may be satisfied if the pipe is laid as illustrated in Diagrams G7.8a and G7.8b providing written approval is obtained from the Water Supplier.

The thickness of insulation required for underground pipes laid with less than the normal minimum required depth of cover and all pipes above ground, should be determined for extreme conditions in accordance with recommendations in Clause R4.11. The external surface of the insulation should be watertight and be protected against mechanical damage by a load relieving slab located above the insulated pipe as shown in Diagram G7.8a.

The ideal method of supplying water to a building below street level (eg. basement flat) is illustrated in Diagram R7.8a. Where this is impracticable and with the written approval of the Water Supplier, the method illustrated in Diagram R7.8b may be used as an alternative, with trace heating in addition to insulation if necessary.

Diagram R7.8c on page 3.24 illustrates a method of laying service pipes below a stream.

Guidance   **R**ecommendations

Diagram
G7.8a:

*Pipes laid over
an underground
obstruction*

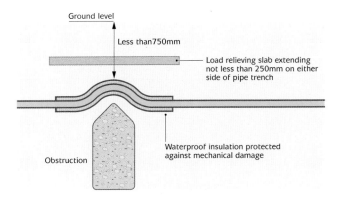

Ground level

Less than 750mm

Load relieving slab extending
not less than 250mm on either
side of pipe trench

Obstruction

Waterproof insulation protected
against mechanical damage

Diagram
G7.8b:

*Pipes laid
under an
underground
obstruction*

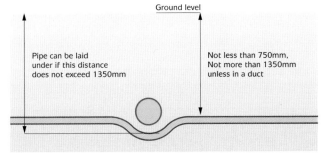

Ground level

Pipe can be laid
under if this distance
does not exceed 1350mm

Not less than 750mm,
Not more than 1350mm
unless in a duct

Diagram
R7.8a:

*Preferred method
of supplying
water to a
building below
street level*

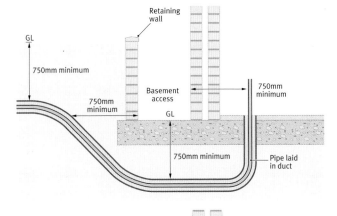

GL

750mm minimum

Retaining
wall

750mm
minimum

Basement
access

GL

750mm
minimum

750mm minimum

Pipe laid
in duct

Diagram
R7.8b:

*Alternative
method of
supplying water
to a building
below street
level*

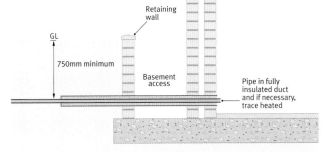

GL

750mm minimum

Retaining
wall

Basement
access

Pipe in fully
insulated duct
and if necessary,
trace heated

Requirements for water fittings

Diagram
R7.8c:
*Suggested method
of stream crossing of
service pipes*

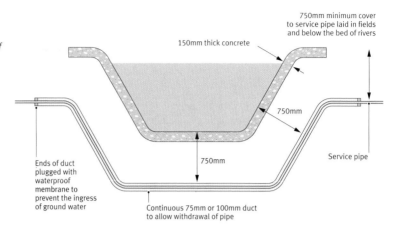

750mm minimum cover
to service pipe laid in fields
and below the bed of rivers

150mm thick concrete

750mm

Service pipe

750mm

Ends of duct
plugged with
waterproof
membrane to
prevent the ingress
of ground water

750mm

Continuous 75mm or 100mm duct
to allow withdrawal of pipe

G7.9
*Water fittings laid
underground should be
resistant to dezincification
and be installed to
accommodate any
movement.*

R7.9
Water fittings laid underground should be
resistant to dezincification in accordance with
clause G7.6. Underground pipes should be laid with
even support and care should be taken that the
ground immediately surrounding the pipe is
free of sharp stones.

G7.10
*Water fittings installed
underground should not be
jointed or connected to any
other water fitting by
adhesives.*

R7.10
This guidance prevents any metal or other fittings
which are jointed by means of adhesives from being
used below ground level or where passing through a
foundation, wall, footing, duct or any other place or
position to which access is difficult.

Schedule 2
Section 4:
Paragraphs
8, 9, 10, 11, 12 & 13:
Water system design
and installation

Notes

Schedule 2

8.

No water fitting shall be installed in such a position, or pass through such surroundings, that it is likely to cause contamination or damage to the material of the fitting or the contamination of water supplied by the water undertaker.

9.

Any pipe supplying cold water for domestic purposes to any tap shall be so installed that, so far as is reasonably practicable, the water is not warmed above 25°C.

10.

(1) Every supply pipe or distributing pipe providing water to separate premises shall be fitted with a stopvalve conveniently located to enable the supply to those premises to be shut off without shutting off the supply to any other premises.

(2) Where a supply pipe or distributing pipe provides water in common to two or more premises, it shall be fitted with a stopvalve to which each occupier of those premises has access.

11.

Water supply systems shall be capable of being drained down and be fitted with an adequate number of servicing valves and drain taps so as to minimise the discharge of water when water fittings are maintained or replaced. A sufficient number of stopvalves shall be installed for isolating parts of the pipework.

12.

(1) The water system shall be capable of withstanding an internal water pressure not less than $1^1/2$ times the maximum pressure to which the installation or relevant part is designed to be subjected in operation ('the test pressure').

(2) This requirement shall be deemed to be satisfied –

    (a) in the case of a water system that does not include a pipe made of plastics, where –

        (i) the whole system is subjected to the test pressure by pumping, after which the test continues for one hour without further pumping;

        (ii) the pressure in the system is maintained for one hour; and

        (iii) there is no visible leakage throughout the test;

    (b) in any other case, where either of the following tests is satisfied –

TEST A

        (i) the whole system is subjected to the test pressure by pumping for 30 minutes, after which the test continues for 90 minutes without further pumping;

        (ii) the pressure is reduced to one third of the test pressure after 30 minutes;

        (iii) the pressure does not drop below one third of the test pressure over the following 90 minutes; and

        (iv) there is no visible leakage throughout the test.

TEST B

        (i) the whole system is subjected to the test pressure by pumping for 30 minutes, after which the pressure is noted and the test continues for 150 minutes without further pumping;

        (ii) the drop in pressure is less than 0.6 bar (60kPa) after the following 30 minutes, or 0.8 bar (80kPa) after the following 150 minutes; and

        (iii) there is no visible leakage throughout the test.

13.

Every water system shall be tested, flushed and where necessary disinfected before it is first used.

Water system design and installation

General

G8.1
The following factors should be taken into consideration in the design of a water supply system:

a. the estimated daily consumption and the maximum and average flows required, together with the estimated peak flow; and

b. the location of the available supply main and minimum and maximum pressures available; and

c. the quality, quantity and pressure required at outlets and the available pressures at various times during a typical day; and

d. the cold water storage capacity required, if any; and

e. the likelihood of ground subsidence due to mining activities or any other reason if it will have a detrimental effect on the supply; and

f. the likelihood of existing contamination of the site; and

g. transient or surge pressures that may arise during the operation of the system.

R8.1
Before determining any aspect of the type or size of a water supply installation, a full assessment must be made of the following.

a. The estimated daily consumption of water, when and over what period the total quantity of water is required and the maximum peak flow, such as may be required during periods of low mains pressure. These factors will vary and will be dependent on the type of establishment being served, and in the case of industrial or other non-household premises, on the type of processes undertaken within the premises.

b. The location of the nearest water main in relation to the site will need to be ascertained, together with its size and the minimum and maximum pressures that are available, or likely to be available, both at the time of the work to be carried out and in the future. This information is normally available from the Water Supplier.

c. All the information in 'a' and 'b' above needs to be established at an early stage in the planning of the building services, as the information will be required before any decision can be taken, for example as to;

   (i) whether sufficient quantity of water will be available to supply all appliances direct from the supply pipe or whether water storage will be required; or,

   (ii) whether there is sufficient pressure to serve appliances on the top floor of the building or whether pumping or boosting will be required.

d. The Water Supplier should be consulted as there may be local requirements for the provision of storage. Whether storage will be required is also dependent on the rate of flow and minimum pressures required at sanitary appliances for their efficient operation. Also, whether water storage can be safely accommodated at the top of a building, or whether it will be necessary to provide the major volume of the storage at low level and pump to minimal size storage cisterns at roof level. The quality of stored water can deteriorate with minimal rises in temperature and this should be taken into account in determining the location of storage cisterns.

e. There is a need to know whether there have been, or are, any mining activities below the site or whether the type of sub-strata is such that ground subsidence could occur.

f. It is necessary to establish what the site may have been used for previously. Surface measures may have been taken to overcome the effects of contaminated land, but there may still be contaminated material at the depth at which supply pipes are laid.

g. With the increasing use of taps and valves that close rapidly and give rise to pressure surge and the practice of serving all appliances with water directly off the supply pipe, there is an increasing problem with transient surge problems throughout the water system during their operation. This may be apparent from noise problems, arising from so called water hammer.

Types of distribution systems

G8.2

Subject to specific requirements of the local Water Undertaker, water may be supplied to appliances and draw-off points as follows:

a. from a distributing pipe deriving its supply from a storage cistern; or

b. directly from and under pressure from a supply pipe; or

c. a combination of 'a' and 'b' subject to necessary precautions being taken to prevent cross-connections and backflow; or

d. from a pumped supply or distributing pipe, where this is necessary due to lack of pressure.

See Diagrams G8.2a, G8.2b and G8.2c for examples of typical installations of distribution methods used in houses.

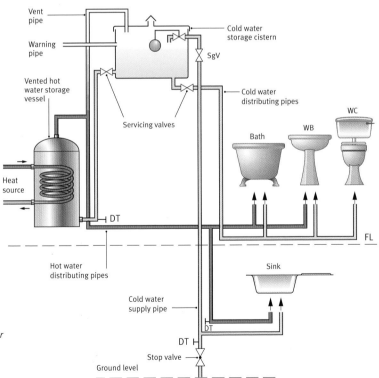

Diagram
G8.2a:

System with cold water draw-off point over kitchen sink taken from supply pipe and all other cold and hot water supplies to sanitary appliances supplied with water through a cold water cistern.

Diagrams G8.2b and G8.2c overleaf ▶

G u i d a n c e

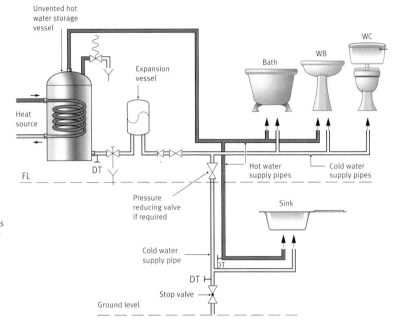

**Diagram
G8.2b:**

*System with all cold
and hot water supplies
to sanitary appliances
taken directly off the
supply pipe.*

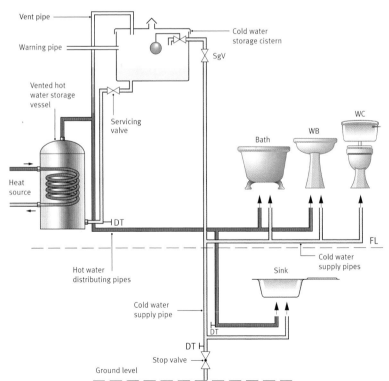

**Diagram
G8.2c:**

*System with cold water
to sanitary appliances
taken directly from a
supply pipe and hot
water supplied through
a cold water cistern.*

Recommendations

R8.2

Guidance Clause G8.2 refers to four different methods of supplying water within a building and three of these methods are illustrated for typical systems within a house.

a. Diagram G8.2a shows a system where the cold water draw-off point over the kitchen sink is taken from the supply pipe and all other cold and hot water supplies to sanitary appliances are supplied with water from a cold water storage cistern. This method of water supply is used in houses and other premises in a large part of the United Kingdom.

   The method provides a reserve of water in the unlikely event of a mains failure. It also provides:

   (i) additional protection to the mains from contamination; and

   (ii) constant low pressures with reduced risk of leakage; and

   (iii) balanced pressures to serve cold and hot water mixer fittings.

   This method of distribution involves the risk of contamination of the storage cistern, frost damage where a cistern is located in the roof space of a building, the physical space required by the cistern, the cost of structural support and additional pipework.

b. The method of water supply illustrated in Diagram G8.2b shows all sanitary appliances and hot water apparatus supplied with water directly off the supply pipe as described in Guidance Clause G8.2b. The method has been used in mainland Europe and many other parts of the world for many years and is being increasingly used for new housing in the UK. Water is normally distributed under a higher pressure than in cistern fed systems and smaller pipes may be used within the system, together with high resistance draw-off taps. There are no storage cisterns at high level which require structural support and that need protection against frost where they are sited in unheated locations. However, such systems require a larger incoming supply pipe and premises do not have a reserve of water if a mains failure occurs.

c. Guidance Clause G8.2c together with Diagram G8.2c, refer to water systems which are installed in many parts of the United Kingdom and are a compromise between the systems described in Clauses G8.2a and G8.2b, in that all cold water supplies to sanitary appliances are taken directly off the supply pipe but hot water apparatus is supplied through a cold water storage cistern. Except for the incoming supply pipe, smaller pipes may be used within this system as the cold water pipework will be under higher pressure and although a cold water cistern is still required to serve the hot water system the quantity of water stored will be less than where cold water supplies to the sanitary appliances are derived from storage. With this system there is no cold water storage in the event of a mains failure. Also, there can be unbalanced pressures at some draw-off points.

d. Diagram R8.2 overleaf, shows a typical method of cold water supply often used in a multi-storey building for supplying water to floors where the pressure within the supply pipe is insufficient for water to be delivered at the highest point of the installation. The method utilises a cistern located at low level and a pneumatic pressure boosting system which ensures water availability at all floors. Where the Water Supplier has given written consent the low level cistern may be dispensed with, in which case the pumps may draw water directly from the supply pipe. Other methods of supply using constantly running pumps, and systems where all the water is stored at low or high level are available. The limitations on the use of pumps on both supply pipes and distributing pipes are referred to in Clauses G6.1 and R6.1.

Diagram R8.2 overleaf ▶

Diagram
R8.2:

Pneumatic pumping installation

Distributing pipe

Warning/ overflow pipe

Drinking water supplies taken from boosted supply pipe

Air vessel with membrane and pressure sensor to control pump

Incoming supply pipe

Warning/overflow pipe

Drinking water taken from unboosted supply where mains pressure is sufficient

Type AG air gap

'Break' cistern

Duplicate pumps

Boosted supply

Unboosted supply

Design flow rates and pipesizing

G8.3

Generally, installations incorporating cold water systems and hot water storage systems should be designed and installed so that the design flow rates given in Table G8.3, which is based on Table 3 of BS 6700: 1997, will be available at each outlet, and any group of outlets where the total demand does not exceed 0.3 litre/second, when only that outlet or group of outlets is discharging. When simultaneous discharge occurs the rate of flow of water at any outlet in use should not be less than the minimum rate shown.

R8.3

Wherever practicable the water demands shown for individual appliances in Table G8.3 should be rigorously followed.

As all appliances are not in use at the same time and to avoid pipes of excessive size a method of determining the simultaneous demand in each length of pipe should be used. The simultaneous demand will vary according to the type of building, for example, hotels, schools, factories, flats etc.

Many ways of pipesizing water systems are available and are based on both manual and computer calculation methods. One method which is suitable for sizing pipework in houses and flats, together with examples, is included in Clause 2.5 and Annex D of British Standard 6700: 1997.

Guidance

G8.4
Where hot water systems are installed that incorporate instantaneous heaters or combination boilers the rates of flow shown in Table G8.3 may not be achievable and the system should be designed accordingly.

Recommendations

R8.4
In instantaneous hot water systems where the flow of hot water may be limited by the capacity of the heater, it is unlikely that the flow rates suggested in Table G8.3 will be achieved. In these cases, although the flow rates may be less, the same method of sizing the pipes can be used.

Table G8.3: *Recommended design flow rates of cold and hot water to sanitary appliances*

OUTLET FITTING OR APPLIANCE	RATE OF FLOW – LITRES/SECOND		NOTES
	DESIGN RATE	MIN. RATE	
WC cistern (to fill in 2 minutes)	0.13	0.05	1. Flow rates required for washing and dish-washing machines for other than single dwellings should be obtained from the manufacturer.
WC pressure flushing valve (DN 20)	1.5	1.0	
WC flushing trough (per WC served)	0.15	0.1	
Urinal cistern (each position served)	0.004	0.002	2. Mixer fittings or combination tap assemblies deliver less flow than two separate taps; it is suggested that 70% of the above flow rates may be sufficient.
Urinal flushing valve	0.3	0.15	
Washbasin (pillar or mixer taps)	0.15	0.1	
Handbasin (pillar or mixer taps)	0.1	0.07	3. The rate of flow required to shower heads will depend on the type fitted; the advice of the shower manufacturer should be sought.
Handbasin (spray or spray mixer taps)	0.05	0.03	
Bidet	0.2	0.1	
Bath (G 3/4)	0.3	0.2	
Bath (G 1)	0.6	0.4	4 The above rates of flow to appliances are applicable where hot water centralised storage systems are installed. Where hot water systems incorporate instantaneous heaters or combination boilers the rates of flow shown in the Table may not be achievable and the system should be designed accordingly.
Shower head	0.2	0.1	
Kitchen sink (G 1/2)	0.2	0.1	
Kitchen sink (G 3/4)	0.3	0.2	
Kitchen sink (G 1)	0.6	0.4	
Washing machine	0.2	0.15	
Dish-washing machine	0.15	0.1	

Equivalent of Table 4.1 in DETR guidance document

Contamination of water fittings and water contained within them

G8.5
Water fittings should not be laid or installed in, on, or pass through any contaminated environment; for example, foul soil, refuse or a refuse chute, ashpit, sewer, drain, cesspool, manhole or inspection chamber.

R8.5
This prohibition is made regardless of any protection to the pipe or other fittings. Diagram R8.5 illustrates the correct method of laying pipes in the vicinity of manholes.

Diagram R8.5 overleaf ▶

G u i d a n c e   *R e c o m m e n d a t i o n s*

Diagram
R8.5:
*Location of
underground pipes
relative to manholes*

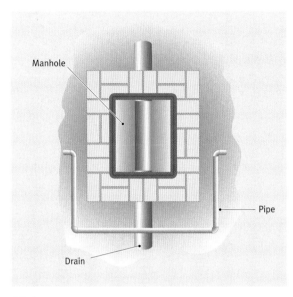

G8.6
*Storage cisterns holding
water for domestic
purposes and other water
fittings are not to be
installed in such positions
that surface, ground or
foul water, or any
other water that is
unwholesome, may enter
the cistern or fitting.*

R8.6
See Section 7: Clause R16.13.2 for further information

Distribution temperature of cold water

G9.1
*So far as is reasonably
practical the temperature
of water within cold water
pipes should not exceed
20°C and adequate
measures should be taken
to ensure that this
temperature is not
exceeded.*

R9.1
The temperature of water derived from Water Suppliers
mains can vary from approximately 4°C in winter to 25°C
during extended periods of hot weather. This wide variation
is also dependant on the type of water source, ground water
sources averaging 10°C throughout the year, mains water
derived from surface water sources varying more widely.

It is important to avoid those temperature ranges within a
water system which may promote the growth of legionella.
The Health and Safety Executive's publication HS(G)70 –
'The control of Legionellosis including Legionaires' Disease'
– includes recommendations to prevent the proliferation of
legionella and its recommendations should be followed.

It has been determined that water temperatures in the
range of 20°C to 45°C favour the growth of legionella; it is
uncommon to find proliferation of growth below 20°C and it
does not survive above 60°C. The presence of sediment,

Recommendations

sludge, scale and organic material can act as a source of nutrients for legionella and the use of materials in the system that can harbour or provide nutrients for bacteria and other organisms should be avoided. All non-metallic materials should satisfy the requirements of BS 6920 or equivalent, and be listed in the Water Regulations Advisory Scheme's 'Water Fittings and Materials Directory'.

It is recommended that cold and hot water supply systems operate at the following temperatures:
a. hot water to be stored at not less than 60°C; and,
b. hot water to be distributed at not less than 50°C; and,
c. cold water storage and distribution not to exceed 20°C.

Pipe work serving cold water taps should be as short and direct as possible and any length of pipe serving single cold water taps should be insulated to prevent heat gain from any adjacent hot water pipes or other sources of heat. The relative positions of cold water pipes to hot water pipes should be such that the cold water pipes are not warmed. Wherever possible horizontal cold and hot water pipes should be fixed so that the hot water pipe is at a higher elevation than the cold water pipe (see Diagram R9.1 below).

In the case of hot water distributing and primary and secondary circulating pipes, insulation should be provided to prevent heat loss, leading to waste of water through excessive draw-off, and in extreme cases it may be necessary to use trace heating to maintain suitable water temperatures within hot water pipes serving small numbers of appliances. Attention is also drawn to Section 8: Table G18.7 which shows maximum recommended lengths of uninsulated hot water pipes.

Diagram
R9.1:

Relative positions of horizontal cold and hot water pipes

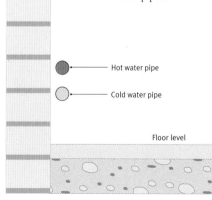

Hot water pipe

Cold water pipe

Floor level

Water system design and installation

Operational fittings and accessibility

G10.1

Operational fittings such as stopvalves, servicing valves and drain taps should be readily accessible for operation and maintenance.

R10.1

Examples of operational fittings are stopvalves, servicing valves, float-operated valves or devices, drain taps, backflow prevention devices, pressure reducing valves, strainers, some forms of safety devices, temporary connections to heating systems and WC and urinal flushing devices.

G10.2

Operational fittings may be located in a duct, access chamber or cupboard provided with a hinged door or removable cover which is visible at all times. The door or cover should not be covered with any decorative material, such as carpet, wall or floor tiling or wallpaper, which requires removal to access the door or cover.

R10.2

It is essential that all operational water fittings are located in such a position that they are readily and easily accessible so that they can be readily maintained and operated without having recourse to removing permanent enclosures or decorative materials.

Stopvalves to premises

G10.3

Every supply and distributing pipe providing water to premises should be fitted with a stopvalve to control the supply to those premises only (see Diagrams G10.4a, b and c).

R10.3

Every supply and distributing pipe providing water to premises should be fitted with a stopvalve located at the boundary of the premises, or elsewhere, to enable the supply to be shut off without shutting off the supply to any other premises (see Diagram R10.3).

Diagram
R10.3:
Typical water service connection showing supply pipe and location of stopvalves

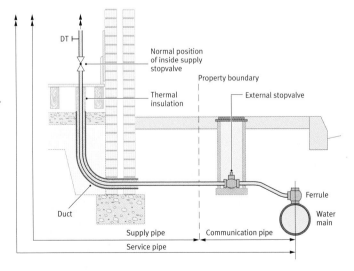

Guidance

G10.4

Every supply and distributing pipe providing water in common to two or more premises is to be fitted with a stopvalve (whether inside or outside premises) to which each occupier of the premises has access (see Diagrams G10.4b and G10.4c).

Note: Whole site backflow protection in accordance with Clause G15.24 should be provided to each of the separately occupied premises shown in Diagrams G10.4b and G10.4c.

Diagram
G10.4a:

Location of stopvalves in block of flats with separate supply pipes to each flat

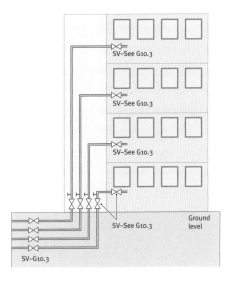

Diagram
G10.4b:

Location of stopvalves in block of flats supplied from a common supply pipe

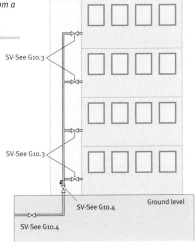

Diagram
G10.4c:

Location of stopvalves in block of flats with common distributing pipe supply

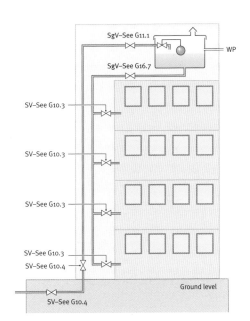

Water system design and installation

R10.4

The Water Acts normally require premises to have separate supply pipes wherever this is possible. Where a supply or distributing pipe provides water in common to two or more premises a stopvalve should be provided, either inside or outside the premises, to which each occupier has access. The principle is that if any occupiers are suffering damage or nuisance to their premises due to a leaking or defective fitting whether on their own premises or on a common pipe they should have ready access to a stopvalve which controls the supply to those premises or fittings.

Attention is drawn to the need for the provision of whole site backflow protection where two or more premises are served by a common supply pipe (see Section 6: Clause G15.24).

Location of stopvalves in buildings

G10.5

Stopvalves should, so far as reasonably practical, be installed inside the premises above floor level, near where the supply pipe enters the building and so installed that closure of the stopvalve will prevent the supply of water to all points of use.

R10.5

As far as is reasonably practicable:

a. a stopvalve should be located inside the building; and,

b. be located above floor level; and,

c. as near as possible to the point where the supply first enters the building; and,

d. so installed that its closure will prevent the supply of water to any point within the premises.

Diagram R10.3 illustrates the preferred location of the internal stopvalve on an incoming supply pipe.

Provision of servicing valves

G11.1

Inlets to all float-operated valves, cisterns, clothes washing machines, dishwashing machines, water heaters, water softeners and other similar appliances should be provided with a servicing valve to facilitate maintenance.

R11.1

The provision of servicing valves also applies to any mechanical backflow prevention devices where the backflow risk being protected against is fluid category 4 and 5 (see Clause G15.7e and R15.7).

G11.2

Servicing valves should be fitted as close as is reasonably practical to float operated valves or other inlet devices of an appliance.

R11.2

Servicing valves should be located adjacent to the appliances they are required to serve and they should be readily accessible.

G11.3

Servicing valves may be of the screwdown or spherical type.

R11.3

While there are many suitable and compact spherical screwdriver operated valves available for use as servicing valves, there is no objection to using a screwdown type of valve of the type which is normally used as a stopvalve.

G u i d a n c e   **R e c o m m e n d a t i o n s**

Provision of draining taps

G11.4

Sufficient draining taps should be provided to facilitate the draining of all supply and distributing pipes within the building.

R11.4

Wherever practicable, all cold and hot water pipes and pipework in central heating systems should be installed in such a manner that the whole installation can be drained. While much of the system will be emptied through draw-off taps and other terminal points there will be locations where drain taps will need to be provided to drain low points. The draining taps should be located in such a position that they can be readily accessed for operation and connection of a drain hose but should not be located below ground or such that there is any possibility of becoming submerged (see Diagram R11.6 below).

G11.5

Draining taps should be of the screwdown type conforming to BS 2879 or, where located in a frost free location, of an approved spherical type.

R11.5

Care needs to be taken in the use of spherical pattern draining taps. Cases have been reported where these have been used in frost susceptible locations and, after draining, have been left in the closed position; this has resulted in the tap being damaged during subsequent freezing temperatures. If these types of drain tap are used it is advisable to leave the drain tap in the open position after draining, remembering to close the taps before restoring the water supply. Other suitable drain taps are listed in the WRAS Water Fittings & Materials Directory.

G11.6

Draining taps should not be buried or covered with soil, or installed so that they are submerged, or likely to be submerged.

R11.6

Care is required in the location of draining taps to avoid contamination and to eliminate backflow of contaminated water during a drainage operation. An example is given in Diagram R11.6 where a draining tap is situated in a sump which may be flooded. Test points should also not be permitted in locations where they can be submerged. This applies to test points in water meter chambers.

Diagram
R11.6:

Example of a draining tap in a prohibited location

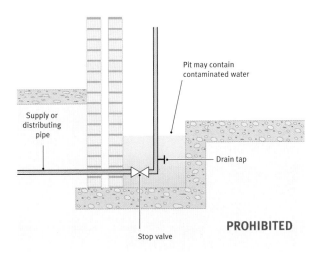

Pit may contain contaminated water

Supply or distributing pipe

Drain tap

PROHIBITED

Stop valve

Guidance   **R**ecommendations

Redundant fittings and dead legs

G11.7

Any draw-off fitting that is permanently removed from the installation should have the branch pipe serving the fitting disconnected at its source.

R11.7

This requirement is to prevent contamination due to water in any unused pipework becoming stagnant.

It is not acceptable to lay branch pipes which terminate with blank ends to facilitate connection of future appliances unless there is a physical break at the junction with the supply pipe.

A fitting or appliance may however, remain unconnected for a period not exceeding 60 days to allow a reasonable amount of time for installers to obtain replacements for broken or damaged fittings or appliances.

An example of the meaning of this guidance is shown in Diagram R11.7. Assuming that the house shown in the diagram has been modernised and that the outside WC will no longer be required it would not be permissible to seal off the supply pipe at point B. The disconnection would have to be made at point A.

Diagram
R11.7:
Sealing off redundant pipes.

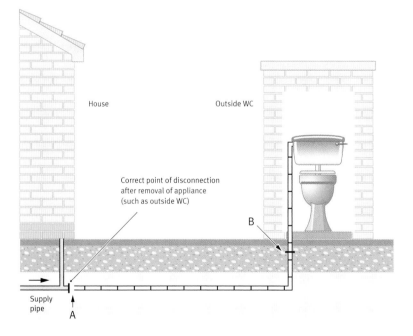

House   Outside WC

Correct point of disconnection after removal of appliance (such as outside WC)

B

Supply pipe

A

Testing

G12.1

The whole installation should be tested hydraulically on completion by subjecting all supply and distributing pipes, fittings and connections to appliances, to an internal test pressure of 1.5 times the maximum operating pressure for the installation or the relevant part.

G12.2

For systems that do not include any plastics pipes (that is, rigid pipe materials such as copper, stainless steel, etc), the requirement shall be deemed to be satisfied if:

a   the whole of the system is subjected internally to the test pressure by pumping, after which the test continues without further pumping;

b   the pressure in the system does not drop below the test pressure over the next one hour period and there is no visible leakage;

in accordance with Clause 3.1.12.3.3 of BS 6700: 1997.

R12.1

Both underground and above ground systems of pipework should be subjected to a final test after completion of the installation and after all builders work has been carried out. The final test is crucial but it is advantageous if buried pipework is tested on an interim basis before being backfilled. In all cases, defects revealed as the result of a test should be rectified and retesting carried out until the result is satisfactory.

R12.2

When testing rigid pipe systems all the outlets in the installation should be sealed and all float-operated valves should be capped off or isolated. The water pressure should then be increased, by pumping, until the internal water pressure at the lowest point in the installation is 50% above the normal operating pressure. This pressure should be maintained for one hour without further pumping.

Water system design and installation

G12.3

For systems that include any plastics pipes, the requirement shall be deemed to be satisfied if, either:

Test A

a. the whole of the system is subjected internally to the test pressure which is maintained by pumping for 30 minutes, after which the test continues without further pumping;

b. the pressure in the system is carefully reduced to one third of the test pressure; and

c. the pressure does not drop over the following 90 minutes and there is no visible leakage;

or in accordance with Clause 3.1.12.3.4 (Test procedure A) of BS 6700: 1997, or

Test B

a. the whole of the system is subjected internally to the test pressure and is maintained by pumping for 30 minutes, after which the pressure is noted and the test is continued without further pumping; and

b. the pressure drop is less than 0.6 bar after a further 30 minutes; and

c. the pressure drop is less than 0.2 bar after the next 120 minutes and there is no visible leakage;

or in accordance with Clause 3.1.12.3.4 (Test procedure B) of BS 6700: 1997.

R12.3

Where systems include plastics pipes, the latter will marginally expand diametrically under the increased pressure due to the elasticity of the plastics material. If pumping ceases the increasing volume will cause the pressure to decrease; thus the pressure cannot be maintained for a period, as occurs with rigid pipes. Two methods have been evolved to overcome this problem and these are described in Clause G12.3 (see Diagrams R12.3a and R12.3b). For further information on these testing methods please refer to BS 6700: 1997.

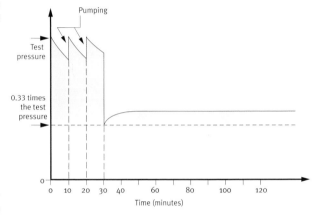

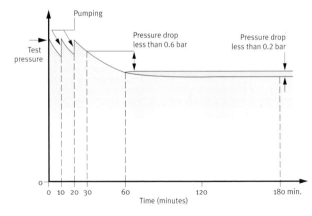

Diagram
R12.3a:
Test A – Testing of pipe systems that include plastics pipes

Diagram
R12.3b:
Test B – Testing of pipe systems that include plastics pipes

Guidance

Recommendations

Flushing

G13.1

Flushing of installations should be in accordance with Clause 3.1.10.1 of BS 6700:1997.

R13.1

It is essential that each length of pipe within the system is flushed to remove any debris, including excess flux, that may have collected in the pipework during installation.

Disinfection

G13.2

After testing and flushing, systems should be disinfected in the following instances:

a. *new installations (except private dwellings occupied by a single family); or*

b. *major extensions or alterations (except private dwellings occupied by a single family); or*

c. *underground pipework (except localised repairs or insertion of junctions); or*

d. *where it is suspected that contamination may have occurred, e.g. fouling by sewage, drainage, animals or physical entry by site personnel for interior inspection, painting or repairs; or*

e. *where a system has not been in regular use and not regularly flushed.*

R13.2

A decision as to whether a system needs to be disinfected should be based on the parameters given in Clause G13.2.

When a comparatively small installation such as a single house is considered it is normally sufficient for the system to be fully inspected and flushed out. Each cistern should be carefully inspected and any deleterious matter removed.

Where new installations, or major extensions or alterations to existing systems have been carried out to other than single houses, for example flats, offices, hotels etc, the whole system should be disinfected before use. This is particularly important where underground services are installed, renovated or modified and where there is any suspicion of contamination of the services by sewage, ground water or the entry into pipes by insects or vermin.

Where required the incoming service pipe between the boundary of the property and the entry to the premises should be disinfected by arrangement with the Water Supplier. This is normally only required for pipes above 50mm I.D but the local requirements of the Water Supplier should be followed.

Where existing systems are not in regular use, such as seasonal occupation of property, the installation should be regularly flushed. Where regular flushing has not been carried out the system should be disinfected before use.

Water system design and installation

Guidance

Recommendations

G13.3

Disinfection of installations should be in accordance with Clause 3.1.10.2 of BS 6700:1997.

R13.3.1 Disinfection procedure

Where required under Clause G13.2 all pipework, both above and below ground level, carrying water for domestic purposes should be disinfected as specified in Clause G13.3 and this Clause.

The general procedure for disinfection of a system, whether chlorine or any other approved disinfectant is used, is as follows:

1. Flush the system.
2. Introduce a disinfecting agent into the system to a specified concentration.
3. Leave the system for a 'contact period' typically of one hour, this period commencing when the system is full of disinfecting fluid at the specified concentration.
4. At the end of the contact period determine the concentration of disinfection within the system.
5. If the concentration is satisfactory, the system should be drained immediately and thoroughly flushed out with drinking water.
6. If the concentration at the end of the contact period is unsatisfactory, the system should be drained of all disinfecting fluid and the procedure, from 2 to 5 inclusive, repeated until a satisfactory result is obtained.
7. Flushing should continue until the free chlorine residual of water in the system is at the level present in the water supplied by the Water Supplier.

After flushing, a sample(s) for bacteriological analysis shall be taken, and analysed, under the supervision of a microbiologist, who shall also determine the number and method of collection of samples. Provided there is no suspicion that the system has been fouled by sewage, drainage or animals prior to disinfection, the installation may be put into service before the result of the bacteriological analysis is known.

Where a bacteriological analysis of the samples indicates that adequate disinfection has not been achieved, after the installation has been flushed and re-disinfected, further samples shall be taken.

Water systems should not be used during any disinfection process and any users normally in attendance during the period should be warned. Outlets from the system to appliances should be suitably marked to this effect.

R13.3.2 Introduction of disinfecting fluid to the water system

Disinfection of supply pipes, including hot water supply pipes, within premises should be carried out through a properly installed injection point fixed immediately on the downstream side of the stopvalve located at the entry point to the premises.

Disinfection of distributing pipes may be carried out by introducing the disinfecting fluid into the system from a storage cistern.

R13.3.3 Disinfection using chlorine

Sodium hypochlorite is often used for disinfection of water systems where chlorine is specified as the disinfectant.

The domestic water system should be filled with disinfection fluid with a chlorine concentration of 50 milligrams per litre (mg/l) or parts per million (ppm). The contact period should be one hour and the concentration of chlorine in the disinfection fluid at the end of the contact period should not be less then 30mg/l (ppm) at all draw-off points.

Recommendations

For disinfection of distributing pipes the system should be filled with water and the servicing valve on the supply to the cistern closed. The capacity of the cistern should be assessed and a calculated quantity of sodium hypochlorite of known strength should be added to the cistern to give a free residual chlorine concentration of 50mg/l (ppm) in the water in the cistern. The chlorinated water should be drawn around the system by successively opening each draw-off fitting, working away from the cistern, and closing it when chlorinated water at 40mg/l to 50mg/l is discharged, as determined by using colorimetric methods.

Where branches or junctions are inserted into existing pipelines or where repairs are carried out, and disinfection is required, fittings should be immersed in a solution of sodium hypochlorite containing 200mg/l (ppm) of available chlorine before installation.

High concentrations of chlorine can adversely affect new coatings in cisterns and release chlorinated or other compounds into water if the coating has not been thoroughly cured before disinfection takes place. When a cistern has been coated it is recommended that the concentration of chlorine residual should not exceed 50mg/l at any time.

Concentrated solutions of chlorine or other disinfectants can be harmful to health and before use all necessary precautions must be taken to protect the health and safety of the users and others. Refer to safety sheets which are required under the Control Of Substances Hazardous to Health (COSHH) Act and ensure a safe operating procedure is devised and followed.

R13.3.4 Disinfection using chemicals other than chlorine

Several different methods and chemicals are available for disinfection of water installations but only those materials listed in the current Drinking Water Inspectorate's List of Substances and Products Approved under Regulation 25 of the Water Supply (Water Quality) Regulations 1989 are acceptable for use with water installations. Many of the methods and materials used for disinfection should only be applied by specialist contractors.

It is essential that the manufacturer's recommendations are followed in respect of concentrations of disinfecting fluids in order to avoid any damage to materials or coatings within the water system.

R13.3.5 Disposal of disinfection fluid

In most cases, water and other fluids which have been used for disinfecting a system may safely be discharged to a public sewer. In some situations, however, particularly in rural areas, the discharge may have an adverse effect upon sewage treatment and the sewerage undertaker should therefore be consulted if in doubt.

On no account should high concentrations of disinfectant solutions be discharged into the natural environment, for example, to water courses via surface water drains. Seek the advice of the Environment Agency before disposing of disinfection fluids.

Schedule 2
Section 5:
Paragraph 14:
**Prevention of
cross connection to
unwholesome water**

Notes

Schedule 2

14.

(1) Any water fitting conveying –

    (a) rain water, recycled water or any fluid other than water supplied by a water undertaker; or

    (b) any fluid that is not wholesome water;

shall be clearly identified so as to be easily distinguished from any supply pipe or distributing pipe.

(2) No supply pipe, distributing pipe or pump delivery pipe drawing water from a supply pipe or distributing pipe shall convey, or be connected so that it can convey, any fluid falling within sub-paragraph (1) unless a device for preventing backflow is installed in accordance with Paragraph 15.

Guidance   **R**ecommendations

Colour coding of pipelines

G14.1

Pipes and cisterns conveying and holding water that is not wholesome should be marked or colour coded in accordance with BS 1710.

R14.1

Schedule 2: Paragraph 14(1) requires that pipes that do not carry wholesome water are readily distinguishable from those that do. The Requirement applies to all pipes that carry water that is not wholesome, for example, water available solely for fire fighting purposes; treated or untreated greywater including rainwater; non-potable water distributed or used for industrial or commercial purposes, or water supplied from a source other than the water supplier's mains.

The purpose of this requirement is to prevent accidental cross-connections that could lead to contamination of wholesome water in supply pipes or distributing pipes. In all premises, where there are pipes conveying unwholesome water, the pipes should be readily identifiable. It is necessary to clearly distinguish those parts of the installation from other pipes carrying wholesome water. This is a matter not only of 'water regulation' concern but also a measure contributing to health and safety.

The Water Supply industry deems that the Regulations will be met if all pipes carrying water for drinking and sanitary purposes are readily distinguishable from all other pipes.

'Readily distinguishable' for pipes means any method of identification or marking. This includes colour pigmentation incorporated in plastics pipes or colour painting of pipes and fittings or permanent marks or labels or, above ground, markings specified in BS 1710: 'Identification of pipelines and services' (see Diagram R14.1).

Plastics pipes laid underground and carrying wholesome water will be acceptable if they are pigmented blue.

Diagram
R14.1:
Examples of BS 1710 colour identification codes

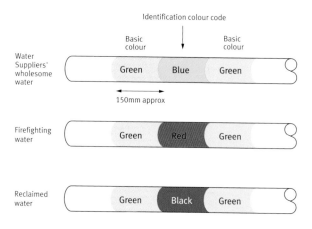

Guidance   **Recommendations**

The colour identification should be placed at junctions; at both inlets and outlets of valves; service appliances and, where pipes pass through walls, at points on the pipe adjacent to both wall surfaces. It is not intended that colour codings for pipes should be prominent in any decorative scheme or should interfere with colour schemes in premises where decorative finishes are provided. A degree of commonsense should prevail in these areas; for instance, the pipe could be marked in an adjacent room or duct.

It should be noted that the identification requirement of Schedule 2: Paragraph 14(1) applies to all water fittings, which includes cisterns and valves. It is important therefore that all fittings, particularly of indeterminate purpose, containing or controlling any fluid, including wholesome water, should be legibly marked in accordance with BS 1710.

G14.2

Any pipe conveying rainwater, recycled water or any other water from a source other than the water undertaker is not to be connected to any pipe carrying wholesome water supplied by the water undertake unless a suitable backflow prevention device or arrangement is installed in accordance with the requirements of Schedule 2: Paragraph 15.

R14.2

Schedule 2: Paragraph 14(2) requires that any pipe carrying fluid that is not wholesome water must not be connected to a pipe carrying wholesome water unless a suitable backflow prevention device is installed. This requirement would be satisfied if wholesome water (Fluid category 1) was delivered into a cistern containing greywater (Fluid category 5) providing that the wholesome water was delivered into the cistern through a backflow prevention device or arrangement suitable for protection against a fluid category 5 risk. For example, Type AA, AB or AD air gap. See Section 6: Paragraph 15 for details of air gaps.

It should be noted that while water derived from a supply pipe is considered 'wholesome water', the water derived from a 'distributing pipe' may not be, depending on what quality of water is contained in the cistern supplying the distributing pipe, and is also dependent on what the distributing pipe is serving. A distributing pipe from a cistern containing wholesome water serving taps over sinks, baths, washbasins and showers could be considered to be serving wholesome water. A distributing pipe serving a hot water supply storage vessel, or a hot water distributing pipe should not be considered as delivering wholesome water and should not have connections made to it for drawing wholesome water.

Schedule 2
Section 6.1:
Fluid categories
Backflow prevention

Backflow prevention

Table G6.1a:	Determination of fluid category 1
Fluid category 1:	Wholesome water supplied by a water undertaker and complying with the requirements of regulations made under section 67 of the Water Industry Act 1991.
Example	Water supplied directly from a water undertaker's main.

Table G6.1b:	Determination of fluid category 2
Fluid category 2:	Water in fluid category 1 whose aesthetic quality is impaired owing to: (a) a change in its temperature; or (b) the presence of substances or organisms causing a change in its taste, odour or appearance, including water in a hot water distribution system.
Examples	Mixing of hot and cold water supplies. Domestic softening plant (common salt regeneration). Drink vending machines in which no ingredients or carbon dioxide are injected into the supply or distributing inlet pipe. Fire sprinkler systems (without anti-freeze). Ice making machines. Water cooled air conditioning units (without additives).

Table G6.1c:	Determination of fluid category 3
Fluid category 3:	Fluid which represents a slight health hazard because of the concentration of substances of low toxicity, including any fluid which contains: (a) ethylene glycol, copper sulphate solution, or similar chemical additives; or (b) sodium hypochlorite (chloros and common disinfectants).
Examples	Water in primary circuits and heating systems (with or without additives) in a house. Domestic washbasins, baths and showers. Domestic clothes and dishwashing machines. Home dialysing machines. Drink vending machines in which ingredients or carbon dioxide are injected. Commercial softening plant (common salt regeneration only). Domestic hand held hoses with flow controlled spray or shut-off control. Hand held fertiliser sprays for use in domestic gardens. Domestic or commercial irrigation systems, without insecticide or fertiliser additives, and with fixed sprinkler heads not less than 150mm above ground level.

Guidance

Table G6.1d:	Determination of fluid category 4
Fluid category 4:	Fluid which represents a significant health hazard due to the concentration of toxic substances, including any fluid which contains: (a) chemical, carcinogenic substances or pesticides (including insecticides and herbicides); or (b) environmental organisms of potential health significance.
Examples	**General** Primary circuits and central heating systems in other than a house. Fire sprinkler systems using anti-freeze solutions. **House gardens** Mini-irrigation systems without fertiliser or insecticide application; such as pop-up sprinklers or permeable hoses. **Food processing** Food preparation. Dairies. Bottle washing apparatus. **Catering** Commercial dishwashing machines. Bottle washing apparatus. Refrigerating equipment. **Industrial and commercial installations** Dyeing equipment. Industrial disinfection equipment. Printing and photographic equipment. Car washing and degreasing plants. Commercial clothes washing plants. Brewery and distillation plant. Water treatment plant or softeners using other than salt. Pressurised fire fighting systems.

G u i d a n c e

Table G6.1e:	Determination of fluid category 5
Fluid category 5:	*Fluid representing a serious health hazard because of the concentration of pathogenic organisms, radioactive or very toxic substances, including any fluid which contains:* *(a) faecal material or other human waste; or* *(b) butchery or other animal waste; or* *(c) pathogens from any other source.*
Examples	**General** *Industrial cisterns.* *Non-domestic hose union taps.* *Sinks, urinals, WC pans and bidets.* *Permeable pipes in other than domestic gardens, laid below or at ground level, with or without chemical additives.* *Grey water recycling systems.* **Medical** *Any medical or dental equipment with submerged inlets.* *Laboratories.* *Bedpan washers.* *Mortuary and embalming equipment.* *Hospital dialysing machines.* *Commercial clothes washing plant in health care premises.* *Non-domestic sinks, baths, washbasins and other appliances.* **Food processing** *Butchery and meat trades.* *Slaughterhouse equipment.* *Vegetable washing.* **Catering** *Dishwashing machines in health care premises.* *Vegetable washing.* **Industrial and commercial installations** *Industrial and chemical plant etc.* *Mobile plant, tankers and gully emptiers.* *Laboratories.* *Sewage treatment and sewer cleansing.* *Drain cleaning plant.* *Water storage for agricultural purposes.* *Water storage for firefighting purposes.* **Commercial agricultural** *Commercial irrigation outlets below or at ground level and/or permeable pipes, with or without chemical additives.* *Insecticide or fertiliser applications.* *Commercial hydroponic systems.*
Note:	*The list of examples of applications shown above for each fluid category is not exhaustive.*

Recommendations

Fluid categories

Fluid category 1

Water undertakers have a duty to supply water which complies with the Water Quality Regulations made under Section 67 of the Water Industry Act 1991, compliance with which ensures a wholesome water suitable for domestic or food production purposes and this quality of water is classified as fluid category 1. Therefore, wherever practicable, water for drinking purposes should be obtained directly from a supply pipe, that is, without any intervening storage before use.

Fluid category 2

Fluid category 2 is water which would be classed as fluid category 1 except that it has undergone a change in taste, odour, appearance or temperature. These changes in water quality are aesthetic changes only and the water is considered to present no human health hazard.

Typical applications of fluid category 2 water in domestic situations are:

a. water heated in a hot water secondary system; and

b. mixtures of fluid categories 1 and 2 water discharged from combination taps or showers; and

c. water that has been softened by a domestic common salt regeneration process.

Note: Where a water softener is installed, water used for mixing with powdered milk for feeding babies should be drawn from an unsoftened water supply. A person on a sodium restricted diet should follow their doctor's instructions regarding the drinking of softened water.

Fluid category 3

Fluids in category 3 represent a slight health hazard and are not suitable for drinking or other domestic purposes.

Typical applications of a category 3 fluid are given below:

a. In houses or other single occupancy dwellings;
  (i) water in primary circuits and heating systems, whether additives to the system have been used or not; and
  (ii) water within washbasins, baths or shower trays; and
  (iii) clothes and dishwashing machines; and
  (iv) home dialysing machines; and
  (v) hand held garden hoses with flow controlled spray or shut-off control; and
  (vi) hand held fertiliser sprays.

b. In premises other than single occupancy dwellings;
  Where domestic fittings, such as washbasins, baths or showers are installed in premises other than single occupancy dwellings, that is, commercial, industrial or other premises, these appliances may still be regarded as fluid category 3, unless there is a potential higher risk. Typical premises in which some, or all, of these appliances may be regarded as justifying a higher fluid risk category include hospitals and other medical establishments.

c. House garden or commercial irrigation systems, without insecticide or fertiliser additives, and with fixed sprinkler heads not less than 150mm above ground level.

Fluid category 4

Fluid category 4 represents a significant health hazard and is not suitable for drinking or other domestic purpose.

'Carcinogenic substances' are those that may, on prolonged exposure, cause cancer.

'Environmental organisms' refer to micro-organisms, bacteria, viruses and parasites of significance for human health, which can occur or survive in the general environment eg. *Legionella* or *Cryptosporidium*.

Some typical general applications of fluid category 4 are:
a. water in primary circuits and heating systems in other than a house, irrespective of whether additives have been used or not; and
b. water treatment or softeners using other than salt; and
c. clothes and dishwashing machines for other than domestic use (see Section 6: Clause R15.16); and
d. mini-irrigation systems in house gardens without fertiliser or insecticide application such as pop-up sprinklers, permeable hoses or fixed or rotating sprinkler heads fixed less than 150mm above ground level.

Fluid category 5

Fluid category 5 represents a serious health hazard and is the most polluting category listed.

'Pathogenic organisms' are micro-organisms such as bacteria, viruses or parasites which are capable of causing illness, especially in humans eg. *Salmonella, Vibrio cholera, Campylobacter*. They generally arise in living creatures and may be released into the environment, for example, in faecal matter, animal wastes or body fluids.

Some typical general applications of a fluid category 5 risk are:
a. sinks, urinals, WC pans and bidets in any location; and
b. permeable pipes or hoses in other than domestic gardens, laid below or at ground level, with or without chemical additives; and
c. grey water recycling systems; and
d. clothes and dishwashing machines in high risk premises (see Section 6: Clause R15.16).

The principle distinction between fluid categories 4 and 5 is that the toxicity or concentrations of substances in category 4 fluids is such that a prolonged period of exposure (days to weeks to months) is generally necessary before serious harm to health occurs. Category 5 fluids are those which contain substances with higher toxicity or at greater concentration than category 4, resulting in them causing harm to health after short exposures (eg. a single or brief (minutes to hours) exposure).

Schedule 2
Section 6.2:
Paragraph 15:
Backflow
prevention

Schedule 2

15.

(1) Subject to the following provisions of this paragraph, every water system shall contain an adequate device or devices for preventing backflow of fluid from any appliance, fitting or process from occurring.

(2) Paragraph (1) does not apply to –

   (a) a water heater where the expanded water is permitted to flow back into a supply pipe, or

   (b) a vented water storage vessel supplied from a storage cistern,

where the temperature of the water in the supply pipe or the cistern does not exceed 25°C.

(3) The device used to prevent backflow shall be appropriate to the highest applicable fluid category to which the fitting is subject downstream before the next such device.

(4) Backflow prevention shall be provided on any supply pipe or distributing pipe –

   (a) where it is necessary to prevent backflow between separately occupied premises, or

   (b) where the water undertaker has given notice for the purposes of this Schedule that such prevention is needed for the whole or part of any premises.

(5) A backflow prevention device is adequate for the purposes of paragraph (1) if it is in accordance with a specification approved by the regulator for the purposes of this Schedule.

Schedule 2
*Section 6.3:
Regulators'
specification for
backflow prevention
arrangements
and devices*

Regulators' specification

S15.1

GENERAL INTERPRETATION OF TERMS RELATING TO BACKFLOW PREVENTION

'**An air gap**' means a visible, unobstructed and complete physical air break between the lowest level of water discharge and the level of potentially contaminated fluid downstream (critical water level) within a cistern, vessel, fitting or appliance, hereinafter called a receptacle, that:

a. is not less than 20mm or twice the internal diameter of the inlet pipe whichever is the greater; and

b. from which water discharges at not more than 15° from the vertical centreline of the water stream.

'**Critical level**' means the physical or piezometric level of the fluid in any part of the receptacle a minimum of two seconds after closing the water inlet, starting from maximum water level.

'**Maximum level**' means the highest physical or piezometric level of the fluid reached in any part of the receptacle when operated continuously under fault conditions,

'**Spillover level**' means the level at which the fluid in a receptacle will first spill over the top edge of a receptacle if the inflow of water exceeds the outflow through any outlet and any overflow pipe.

'**Tap gap**' means the vertical distance between the lowest part of a tap outlet and the spillover level of the appliance or receptacle over which the tap discharges.

An '**upstand**' means either one of two alternative arrangements of water fittings to prevent backflow by backsiphonage:

Type A upstand. An upward flowing supply or distributing pipe surmounted by an anti-vacuum valve (Type DA), or an anti-vacuum valve combined with a single check valve (Type DUK1), any part of the outlet of which is located not less than 300mm above the spillover level of an appliance.

Type B upstand. A branch pipe serving an appliance, where the height of any part of the branch connection to the vented distributing pipe is not less than 300mm above:

a. the spillover level of the appliance; or

b. the highest possible discharge point served by the vented distributing pipe, whichever is the highest.

'**A verifiable backflow prevention device**' means a device, consisting of one or more backflow prevention elements, which can be tested in-situ; usually achieved by the provision of test ports immediately upstream, and between, the mechanical elements comprising the device.

S15.2

INTERPRETATIONS OF BACKFLOW PREVENTION ARRANGEMENTS AS LISTED IN TABLE S15.2

'**Type AA – Air gap with unrestricted discharge**' means a non-mechanical backflow prevention arrangement of water fittings where water is discharged through an air gap into a receptacle which has at all times an unrestricted spillover to the atmosphere.

'**Type AB – Air gap with weir overflow**' means a non-mechanical backflow prevention arrangement of water fittings complying with Type AA, except that the air gap is the vertical distance from the lowest point of the discharge orifice which discharges into the receptacle, to the critical water level of the rectangular weir overflow.

'**Type AC – Air gap with vented submerged inlet and circular overflow**' means a non-mechanical backflow prevention arrangement of water fittings with a vented, but submerged, inlet; the air gap being measured vertically downwards from the lowest point of the air inlet to the critical level.

'**Type AD – Air gap with injector**' means a non-mechanical backflow prevention arrangement of water fittings with a horizontal injector and a physical air gap of 20 millimetres or twice the inlet diameter, whichever is the greater.

'**Type AF – Air gap with circular overflow**' means a non-mechanical backflow prevention arrangement of water fittings with an air gap measured downwards from the lowest point of the discharge orifice, which discharges into the receptacle, to the critical level.

'**Type AG – Air gap arrangement with minimum size circular overflow**' means a non-mechanical backflow prevention arrangement of water fittings with an air gap; together with an overflow, the size of which is determined by measure or a vacuum test.

'**Type AUK1 – Air gap with interposed cistern**' means a non-mechanical backflow prevention arrangement consisting of a cistern with a Type AG overflow and an air gap; the spill-over level of the receiving vessel (WC pan or other receptacle) being located not less than 300 millimetres below the overflow pipe and not less than 15 millimetres below the lowest level of the interposed cistern.

'**Type AUK2 – Domestic tap gap**' means the height of air gap between the lowest part of the outlet of a tap, combination fitting, shower head or other fitting discharging over a domestic sanitary appliance or other receptacle, and the spillover level of that appliance, where a fluid category 2 or 3 risk is present downstream.

Regulators' specification

Type AUK3 – Higher risk tap gap' means the height of an air gap between the lowest part of the outlet of a tap, combination fitting, shower head or other fitting discharging over any appliance or other receptacle, and the spillover level of that appliance, where a fluid category 4 or 5 risk is present downstream.

Type DC – Pipe interrupter with permanent atmospheric vent' means a non-mechanical backflow prevention device with a permanent unrestricted air inlet, the device being installed so that the flow of water is in a vertical downward direction.

Table S15.2: Schedule of non-mechanical backflow prevention arrangements and the maximum permissible fluid category for which they are acceptable

Type	Description of backflow prevention arrangements and devices	Suitable for protection against fluid category	
		Back pressure	Back siphonage
AA	Air gap with unrestricted discharge above spillover level	5	5
AB	Air gap with weir overflow	5	5
AC	Air gap with vented submerged inlet	3	3
AD	Air gap with injector	5	5
AF	Air gap with circular overflow	4	4
AG	Air gap with minimum size circular overflow determined by measure or vacuum test	3	3
AUK1	Air gap with interposed cistern (For example, a WC suite)	3	5
AUK2	Air gaps for taps and combination fittings (tap gaps) discharging over domestic sanitary appliances, such as a washbasin, bidet, bath or shower tray shall not be less than the following:	X	3
	Size of tap or combination fitting / Vertical distance of bottom of tap outlet above spill-over level of receiving appliance		
	Not exceeding G½″ — 20mm		
	Exceeding G½″ but not exceeding G¾″ — 25mm		
	Exceeding G¾″ — 70mm		
AUK3	Air gaps for taps or combination fittings (tap gaps) discharging over any higher risk domestic sanitary appliances where a fluid category 4 or 5 is present, such as: a. any domestic or non-domestic sink or other appliance; or b. any appliances in premises where a higher level of protection is required, such as some appliances in hospitals or other health care premises, shall be not less than 20mm or twice the diameter of the inlet pipe to the fitting, whichever is the greater.	X	5
DC	Pipe interrupter with permanent atmospheric vent	X	5

Notes:

1 X Indicates that the backflow prevention arrangement or device is not applicable or not acceptable for protection against backpressure for any fluid category within water installations in the UK.

2 Arrangements incorporating Type DC devices shall have no control valves on the outlet of the device; they shall be fitted not less than 300 mm above the spillover level of a WC pan, or 150 mm above the sparge pipe outlet of a urinal, and discharge vertically downwards.

3 Overflows and warning pipes shall discharge through, or terminate with, an air gap, the dimension of which should satisfy a Type AA air gap.

Equivalent of Table S6.1 in DETR Guidance document

S15.3

GENERAL INTERPRETATIONS OF BACKFLOW PREVENTION DEVICES AS LISTED IN TABLE S15.3

Type BA – Verifiable backflow preventer with reduced pressure zone' means a verifiable mechanical backflow prevention device consisting of an arrangement of water fittings with three pressure zones with differential obturators and that will operate when potential backflow conditions obtain or there is a malfunction of the valve.

Type CA – Non-verifiable disconnector with different pressure zones' means a non-verifiable mechanical backflow prevention device which provides disconnection by venting the intermediate pressure zone of the device to the atmosphere when the difference of pressure between the intermediate zone and the upstream zone is not greater than 10% of the upstream pressure.

Type DA – Anti-vacuum valve (or vacuum breaker)' means a mechanical backflow prevention device with an air inlet which is closed when water within the device is at or above atmospheric pressure but which opens to admit air if a vacuum occurs at the inlet to the device.

Type DB – Pipe interrupter with atmospheric vent and moving element' means a mechanical backflow prevention device with an air inlet closed by a moving element when the device is in normal use but which opens and admits air if the water pressure upstream of the device falls to atmospheric pressure, the device being installed so that the flow of water is in a vertical, downward direction.

Type DUK1 – Anti-vacuum valve combined with a single check valve' means a mechanical backflow prevention device comprising an anti-vacuum valve with a single check valve located upstream.

Type EA – Verifiable single check valve' means a verifiable mechanical backflow prevention device which will permit water to flow from upstream to downstream but not in the reverse direction.

Type EB – Non-verifiable single check valve' means a non-verifiable mechanical backflow prevention device which will permit water to flow from upstream to downstream but not in the reverse direction.

Type EC – Verifiable double check valve' means a verifiable mechanical backflow prevention device consisting of two verifiable single check valves in series, which will permit water to flow from upstream to downstream but not in the reverse direction.

Regulators' specification

'Type ED – Non-verifiable double check valve' means a non-verifiable mechanical backflow prevention device consisting of two single check valves in series, which will permit water to flow from upstream to downstream but not in the reverse direction.

'Type HA – Hose union backflow preventer' means a mechanical backflow prevention device for fitting to the outlet of a hose union tap and consisting of a single check valve with air inlets that open if the flow of water ceases.

'Type HC – Diverter with automatic return' means a mechanical backflow prevention device used in bath/shower combination tap assemblies which automatically returns the bath outlet open to atmosphere if a vacuum occurs at the inlet to the device.

'Type HUK1 – Hose union tap incorporating a double check valve' means a hose union tap in which a verifiable double check valve has been incorporated into either the inlet or outlet of the tap.

'Type LA – Pressurised air inlet valve' means an anti-vacuum valve or vacuum breaker, similar to Type DA but suitable for conditions where the water pressure at the outlet of the device under normal conditions of use is greater than atmospheric.

'Type LB – Pressurised air inlet valve combined with a check valve downstream' means a mechanical backflow prevention device comprising a Type LA anti-vacuum valve and a single check valve located downstream.

Table S15.3: Schedule of mechanical backflow prevention arrangements and the maximum permissible fluid category for which they are acceptable

Type	Description of backflow prevention arrangements and devices	Suitable for protection against fluid category	
		Back pressure	Back siphonage
BA	Verifiable backflow preventer with reduced pressure zone	4	4
CA	Non-verifiable disconnector with difference between pressure zones not greater than 10%	3	3
DA	Anti-vacuum valve (or vacuum breaker)	X	3
DB	Pipe interrupter with atmospheric vent and moving element	X	4
DUK1	Anti-vacuum valve combined with a single check valve	2	3
EA	Verifiable single check valve	2	2
EB	Non-verifiable single check valve	2	2
EC	Verifiable double check valve	3	3
ED	Non-verifiable double check valve	3	3
HA	Hose union backflow preventer. Only permitted for use on existing hose union taps in house installations	2	3
HC	Diverter with automatic return (normally integral with some domestic appliance applications only)	X	3
HUK1	Hose union tap which incorporates a double check valve. Only permitted for replacement of existing hose union taps in house installations	3	3
LA	Pressurised air inlet valve	X	2
LB	Pressurised air inlet valve combined with a check valve downstream	2	3

Notes:

1 X Indicates that the backflow prevention device is not acceptable for protection against Backpressure for any fluid category within water installations in the UK.

2 Arrangements incorporating a Type DB device shall have no control valves on the outlet of the device. The device shall be fitted not less than 300mm above the spillover level of an appliance and discharge vertically downwards.

3 Types DA and DUK1 shall have no control valves on the outlet of the device and be fitted on a 300mm minimum Type A upstand.

4 Relief outlet ports from Types BA and CA backflow prevention devices shall terminate with an air gap, the dimension of which should satisfy a Type AA air gap.

Equivalent of Table S6.2 in DETR Guidance document

Diagrams of backflow prevention arrangements

All air gaps except AUK2 to be 20mm or twice the inlet bore diameter whichever is the greater. See Table S15.2 on page 6.11 for AUK2 dimensions.

Type AA
Air gap with unrestricted discharge

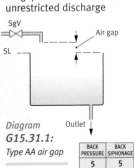

Diagram
G15.31.1:
Type AA air gap

BACK PRESSURE	BACK SIPHONAGE
5	5

Type AB
Air gap with weir overflow

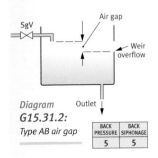

Diagram
G15.31.2:
Type AB air gap

BACK PRESSURE	BACK SIPHONAGE
5	5

Type AC
Air gap with submerged inlet and circular overflow

Diagram
G15.31.3:
Type AC air gap

BACK PRESSURE	BACK SIPHONAGE
3	3

Type AD
Air gap with injector. Often known as a 'jump jet'.

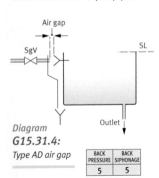

Diagram
G15.31.4:
Type AD air gap

BACK PRESSURE	BACK SIPHONAGE
5	5

Type AF
Air gap with circular overflow

Diagram
G15.31.5:
Type AF air gap

BACK PRESSURE	BACK SIPHONAGE
4	4

Type AG
Air gap device with minimum size circular overflow

An air gap arrangement that satisfies the requirements of BS 6281: Part 2: Specification for Type B air gaps

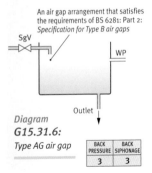

Diagram
G15.31.6:
Type AG air gap

BACK PRESSURE	BACK SIPHONAGE
3	3

Type AUK1
Air gap with interposed cistern. The air gap in the cistern is to conform with Type AG air gap

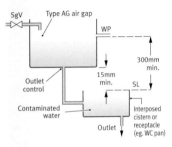

Diagram
G15.31.7:
Type AUK1 air gap

BACK PRESSURE	BACK SIPHONAGE
3	5

Type AUK2
Tap gap for domestic premises eg. basin, bath or bidet

Diagram
R15.31.8:
Type AUK2 tap gap

BACK PRESSURE	BACK SIPHONAGE
-	3

Type AUK3
Tap gap for higher risk premises or appliances eg. medical type premises

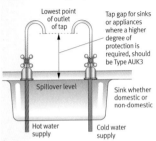

Diagram
R15.31.9:
Type AUK3 tap gap

BACK PRESSURE	BACK SIPHONAGE
-	5

Diagrams of mechanical backflow prevention devices

Type BA

Verifiable backflow preventer with reduced pressure zone

This backflow protection device is commonly known as an 'RPZ Valve Assembly'. A Type AA air gap should be provided between the relief outlet port and the top of the allied tundish.

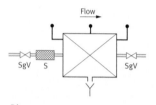

Diagram
G15.31.10:
Type BA device

BACK PRESSURE	BACK SIPHONAGE
4	4

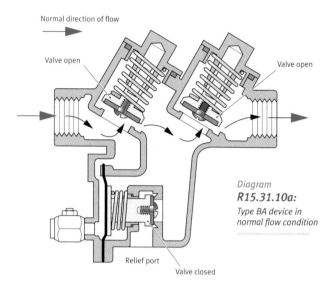

Normal direction of flow

Valve open

Valve open

Diagram
R15.31.10a:
Type BA device in normal flow condition

Relief port

Valve closed

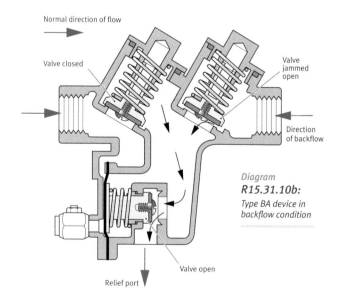

Normal direction of flow

Valve closed

Valve jammed open

Direction of backflow

Diagram
R15.31.10b:
Type BA device in backflow condition

Valve open

Relief port

Type CA

Non-verifiable disconnector with different pressure zones

A Type AA air gap should be provided between the relief outlet port and the top of the allied tundish.

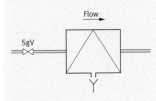

Diagram
G15.31.11:
Type CA device

BACK PRESSURE	BACK SIPHONAGE
3	3

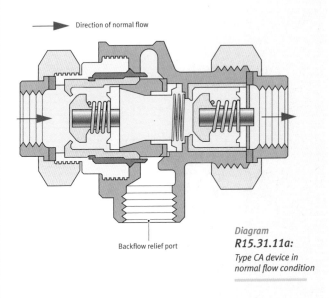

Direction of normal flow

Backflow relief port

Diagram
R15.31.11a:
Type CA device in normal flow condition

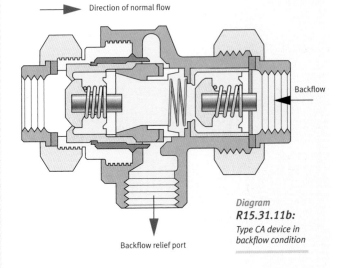

Direction of normal flow

Backflow

Backflow relief port

Diagram
R15.31.11b:
Type CA device in backflow condition

Type DA

**Anti-vacuum valve
(or vacuum breaker)**

*The device must be fitted on
a Type A upstand so that the
outlet is not less than 300mm
above the free discharge point,
or spillover level of the
appliance, and have no valve,
flow restrictor or tap
on its outlet.*

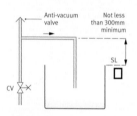

Diagram
G15.31.12:
Type DA device

BACK PRESSURE	BACK SIPHONAGE
–	3

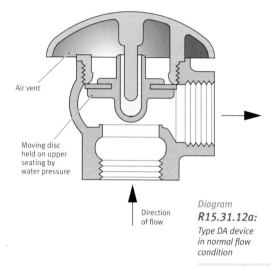

Air vent

Moving disc
held on upper
seating by
water pressure

Direction
of flow

Diagram
R15.31.12a:
*Type DA device
in normal flow
condition*

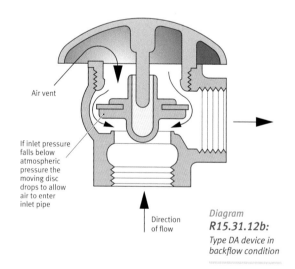

Air vent

If inlet pressure
falls below
atmospheric
pressure the
moving disc
drops to allow
air to enter
inlet pipe

Direction
of flow

Diagram
R15.31.12b:
*Type DA device in
backflow condition*

Type DB

Pipe interrupter with vent and moving element

The device is to be fitted with the lowest point of the air aperture not less than 300mm above the free discharge point, or spillover level of the appliance, and have no valve or restriction on its outlet.

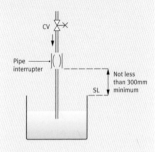

Diagram
G15.31.13:
Type DB pipe interrupter with vent and moving element air gap

BACK PRESSURE	BACK SIPHONAGE
–	4

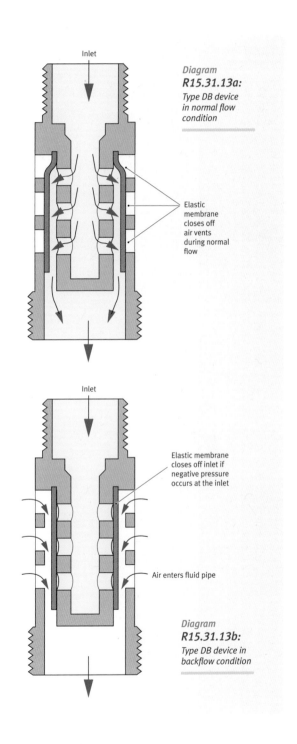

Diagram
R15.31.13a:
Type DB device in normal flow condition

Elastic membrane closes off air vents during normal flow

Elastic membrane closes off inlet if negative pressure occurs at the inlet

Air enters fluid pipe

Diagram
R15.31.13b:
Type DB device in backflow condition

Type DC

Pipe interrupter with permanent atmospheric vent

Except for urinals, this device must be fitted with the lowest point of the air aperture not less than 300mm above the free discharge point, or spillover level of an appliance, and have no valve, flow restrictor or tap on its outlet. In the case of urinals the device is to be fixed not less than 150mm above the sparge outlet.

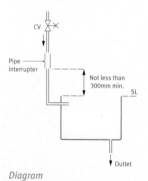

Diagram
G15.31.14:

Type DC pipe interrupter with permanent vent

BACK PRESSURE	BACK SIPHONAGE
–	5

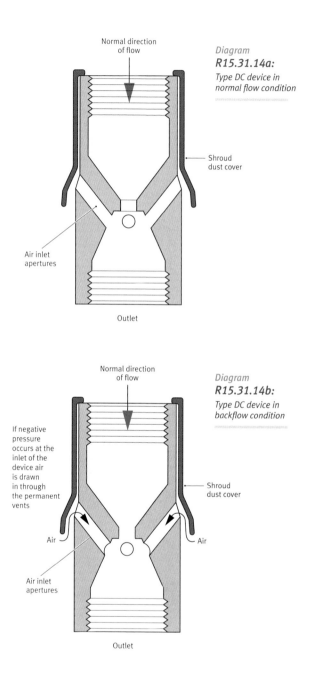

Diagram
R15.31.14a:
Type DC device in normal flow condition

Diagram
R15.31.14b:
Type DC device in backflow condition

Type DUK1

Anti-vacuum valve combined with verifiable check valve

The device must be fitted on a Type B upstand so that the outlet of the device is not less than 300mm above the free discharge point, or spillover level of the appliance, and have no valve, flow restrictor or tap on its outlet.

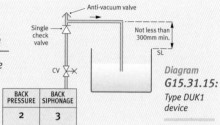

BACK PRESSURE	BACK SIPHONAGE
2	3

Diagram G15.31.15:

Type DUK1 device

Type EA

Verifiable single check valve

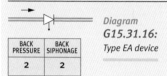

Diagram G15.31.16:

Type EA device

BACK PRESSURE	BACK SIPHONAGE
2	2

Type EB

Non-verifiable single check valve

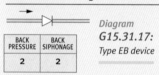

Diagram G15.31.17:

Type EB device

BACK PRESSURE	BACK SIPHONAGE
2	2

Type EC

Verifiable double check valve

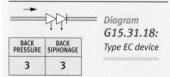

Diagram G15.31.18:

Type EC device

BACK PRESSURE	BACK SIPHONAGE
3	3

Type ED

Non-verifiable double check valve

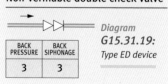

Diagram G15.31.19:

Type ED device

BACK PRESSURE	BACK SIPHONAGE
3	3

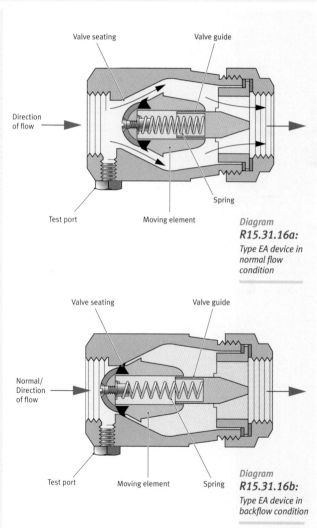

Diagram R15.31.16a:

Type EA device in normal flow condition

Diagram R15.31.16b:

Type EA device in backflow condition

Type HA

Hose union backflow preventer

Not to be used in new installations. Only permitted outside houses for fitting to existing hose union taps that do not incorporate any backflow prevention device.

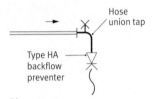

Diagram
G15.31.20:
Type HA device

BACK PRESSURE	BACK SIPHONAGE
2	3

Type HC

Diverter with automatic return
(Integral with some domestic appliance applications only)

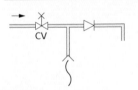

Diagram
G15.31.21:
Type HC device

BACK PRESSURE	BACK SIPHONAGE
–	3

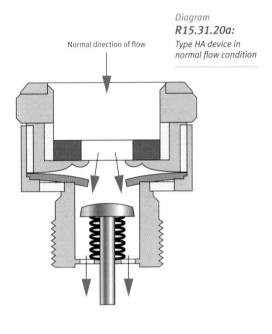

Normal direction of flow

Diagram
R15.31.20a:
Type HA device in normal flow condition

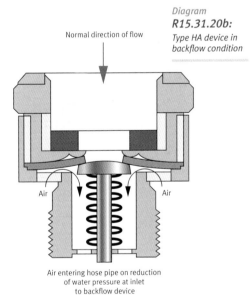

Normal direction of flow

Diagram
R15.31.20b:
Type HA device in backflow condition

Air entering hose pipe on reduction of water pressure at inlet to backflow device

Type HUK1

Hose union tap incorporating verifiable double check valve

Not to be used in new installations. Only permitted outside houses for replacement of existing hose union taps that do not incorporate any backflow prevention device.

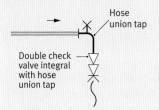

Hose union tap

Double check valve integral with hose union tap

Diagram
G15.31.22:
Type HUK1 device

BACK PRESSURE	BACK SIPHONAGE
3	3

Type LB

Pressurised air inlet valve combined with a check valve downstream

Use is limited to locations where operational waste is acceptable, eg. in gardens or similar.

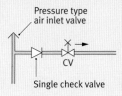

Pressure type air inlet valve

CV

Single check valve

Diagram
G15.31.24:
Type LB device

BACK PRESSURE	BACK SIPHONAGE
2	3

Type LA

Pressurised air inlet valve

Use is limited to locations where operational waste is acceptable, eg. in gardens or similar.

Pressure type air inlet valve

CV

Diagram
G15.31.23:
Type LA device

BACK PRESSURE	BACK SIPHONAGE
–	2

Notes

6

Schedule 2
Section 6.4: Guidance Clauses relating to backflow prevention

Backflow prevention

General

G15.1

Except where expanded water from hot water systems or instantaneous water heaters is permitted to flow back into a supply or distributing pipe, every water fitting through which water is supplied for domestic purposes should be installed in such a manner that no backflow of fluid from any appliance, fitting or process can take place.

R15.1

Schedule 2: Paragraph 15(1), generally, prohibits any backflow of fluid from appliances into the water system. However, Paragraph 15(2) permits expanded water from hot water heaters or storage vessels to flow back into a supply pipe or cistern providing that the temperature of the water in the supply pipe or cistern does not exceed 25°C.

This temperature limitation is of particular importance in any cistern or local pipe that serves a tap where water for drinking may be obtained, as under the Water Quality Regulations a water temperature of 25°C must not be exceeded. While a temperature of 25°C is quoted in Schedule 2: Paragraph 15(2) it is preferable that this temperature be limited to 20°C for the reasons given in Section 4: Clause R9.1.

Three cases need to be considered:

a. An instantaneous heater or combination boiler without thermal storage less than 15 litres capacity.

   In this case the volume of water in the heater is generally small and any backflow due to expansion can be ignored.

b. An unvented hot water storage system supplied from a supply pipe or combination boiler with storage and having the thermal storage supplied with water from a supply pipe.

   In theory, the expansion of water when heating up the entire contents of the storage vessel from cold could be considerable. In practice, much of the initial expansion of water takes place in the upper part of the storage vessel, the cooler water at the lower part of the vessel passing into the supply pipe and contributing only marginally to the temperature of water in the supply pipe. Practical tests have been undertaken and in many cases no perceptible increase in water temperature has been detected at a point in the supply pipe three metres upstream of the storage vessel; this finding may only be taken as a guideline and it is the responsibility of the installer to ensure that the temperature of water at any water taps upstream of the storage vessel does not exceed 25°C when the hot water system is operating normally.

c. A vented or unvented hot water storage system supplied from a distributing pipe. This is similar to 'b' except that it is essential that the temperature of the water in the storage cistern supplying the system is not raised to a temperature in excess of 25°C, wherever practicable.

Guidance

Recommendations

G15.2

Avoidance of backflow should be achieved by good system design and the provision of suitable backflow prevention arrangements and devices, the type of which depends on the fluid category to which the wholesome water is discharged. A description of fluid risk categories is shown in Schedule 1 of the Regulations and some suggested examples relating to the fluid categories are shown in Schedule 1: Tables G6.1a to G6.1e.

R15.2

Examples of fluid categories for domestic and some non-domestic fluids are given in Section 6.1, Schedule 1: Tables G6.1a to G6.1e and fluid categories 1 to 5 in the Recommendations. These are only typical and in some situations, particularly non-domestic situations, advice of the Water Supplier should be sought to determine the category of fluid against which protection is required.

G15.3

The type of backflow protection for a given situation is related to the fluid risk categories downstream of the backflow prevention device.

R15.3

The terms 'upstream' and 'downstream' are illustrated in Diagram R15.3.

Diagram R15.3: Orientation of flow

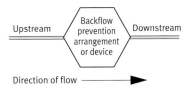

G15.4

Schedules of backflow prevention arrangements and backflow prevention devices, and the maximum permissible fluid risk category for which they are acceptable, are shown in Tables S15.2 and S15.3. Details of the arrangements and devices are shown in Diagrams G15.31.1 to G15.31.24.

R15.4

Tables S15.2 and S15.3 in the Regulators' specification (see Section 6.3) show the types of non-mechanical backflow prevention arrangements and mechanical backflow prevention devices available and list the types, description and their suitability for protection against a particular fluid category. Backflow prevention arrangements and devices are illustrated in Diagrams G15.31.1 to G15.31.24 and Diagrams R15.31.8 to R15.31.20 (see Section 6.3).

TYPE OF DEVICE

The nomenclature for devices is as follows;

The first letter denotes the 'family'; for example, air gap (A), pipe interrupter (D) or check valve (E). This together with the second letter denotes the 'type'; for example, air gap with injector (AD) or, pipe interrupter with permanent atmospheric vent (DC) or verifiable single check valve (EA).

Backflow prevention

Guidance

Recommendations

SUITABILITY FOR PROTECTION AGAINST FLUID CATEGORY

This column in Tables S15.2 and S15.3 lists the fluid category for which the device or arrangement is acceptable for backflow protection of the wholesome water upstream of the device. Both arrangements and devices are listed, for their suitability, under two categories:

a. **Backpressure** – This is the situation where the pressure within a system is greater than atmospheric pressure and the upstream pressure is less than the downstream pressure at any point and at the same elevation, thus causing backflow to occur.

Typical backflow prevention devices or arrangements for use against backpressure are those where the outlet control valve, or tap, are located downstream of the backflow device, such as devices of the B, C, E and L families. For example RPZ valves, check valves, non-verifiable disconnectors and pressurised air inlet valves.

b. **Backsiphonage** – This is the situation where the downstream end of a pipe or device is subjected to atmospheric pressure only and the pressure upstream is less than atmospheric at the same elevation.

Typical backflow prevention devices or arrangements for use against backsiphonage are those where the control valve is located prior to the device, such as devices of the A, D or H families. For example, an air gap or tap gap, a pipe interrupter or anti-vacuum valve.

Depending on the type of device, some are suitable for both backpressure and backsiphonage, but may not be suitable for the same fluid category.

G15.5
Wherever practicable, systems should be protected against backflow without the necessity to rely on mechanical backflow protection devices; this can often be achieved by point of use protection such as a 'tap gap' above the spillover level of an appliance. Minimum tap gaps for different sizes of taps and applications are shown in Table S15.2.

R15.5
Non-mechanical backflow prevention arrangements principally involve the use of an air gap either with or without a cistern. Descriptions of these devices are given in Sections S15.2 and Table S15.2 and are illustrated in Diagrams G15.31.1 to G15.31.7 and Diagrams R15.31.8 and R15.31.9.

Section S15.1 of the Regulators' Specification shows the requirements for the dimension of an air gap to be 'not less than 20mm or twice the internal diameter of the inlet pipe whichever is the greater'. It should be noted that for this purpose, the 'diameter of the inlet pipe' is to be taken as the largest internal diameter of:

a. the branch inlet pipe within one metre of the air gap; or

b. the internal diameter of the inlet to the tap or air gap, whichever is the greater.

Guidance

Recommendations

G15.6

In cistern fed systems secondary backflow prevention can often be achieved for appliances by the use of permanently vented distributing pipes (see Diagram G15.24b).

R15.6

This method of secondary backflow protection may be suitable in separate, two storey premises (see Clause R15.24).

G15.7

Mechanical backflow protection devices which, depending on the type of device, may be suitable for protection against backpressure or backsiphonage, or both, should be installed so that:

a. they are readily accessible for inspection, operational maintenance and renewal; and

b. except for Types HA and HUK1, backflow prevention devices for protection against fluid categories 2 and 3, they should not be located outside premises; and

c. they are not buried in the ground; and

d. vented or verifiable devices, or devices with relief outlets, are not installed in chambers below ground level or where liable to flooding; and

e. line strainers are provided immediately upstream of all backflow prevention devices required for fluid category 4. Where strainers are provided, servicing valves are to be fitted upstream of the line strainer and immediately downstream of the backflow prevention device; and

f. the lowest point of the relief outlet from any reduced pressure zone valve assembly or similar device should terminate with a Type AA air gap located not less than 300mm above the ground or floor level.

Note: For information on the installation and maintenance of reduced pressure zone devices (RPZ valve assemblies) see Installation and Guidance Note No. 9-03-02 published by the Water Regulations Advisory Scheme.

R15.7

Backflow protection devices and arrangements should be readily accessible at all times for operation, maintenance and renewal, see Section 4: Clauses G10.1 and G10.2.

Some backflow devices, such as double check valves, are very susceptible to damage by freezing and should not normally be located outside buildings. An exception is made in the case of existing hose union taps where a hose pipe is to be used in the circumstances described in Clause G15.21.

For both the above reasons it is not acceptable for backflow protection devices to be buried in the ground.

It is not acceptable for backflow prevention devices or arrangements that are verifiable, vented, or those with operational relief ports, to be located in chambers below ground level or where there is any chance of flooding occurring. In all cases these devices should be located so that any vent, port or operational outlet from the device should be at least 300mm above any flood level. Where line strainers are provided there should be adequate space around them so that cleaning can be carried out effectively.

It should be noted that while Clause G15.7e requires the provision of servicing valves downstream of backflow prevention devices for fluid category 4 risks, control valves or servicing valves should not be provided downstream of pipe interrupters as this could cause a malfunction and discharge of water from the air inlet ports of the interrupter (see also Clause R11.1).

Backflow prevention

Appliances incorporating, or supplied with water through, pumps

G15.8
Where pumped showers or other appliances supplied through or incorporating pumps, are installed, care should be taken in positioning branches from distributing pipes.

R15.8
Pipework installations should be designed to provide the calculated simultaneous demands of the system; however, due allowance should also be made for those devices where a full demand is required at all times. This is particularly relevant in distributing pipe systems where branches serve pumped showers or other appliances. No pumped showers, or other appliances incorporating a pump, should draw water from any supply or distributing pipe which serves an appliance categorised as fluid risk 4 or 5, for example, a pipe serving a bidet with an ascending spray and/or a flexible hose and spray/jet.

Bidets (including WCs adapted as bidets) with flexible hose and spray handset fittings or with submerged water inlets

G15.9
Bidets with flexible hose and spray handset fittings and/or water inlets below the spillover level of the appliance, are a fluid Category 5 risk and should not be supplied with water directly from a supply pipe.

R15.9
Appliances, taps, combination tap assemblies and mixing valves to which hoses serving sprays or jets are attached, are a serious backflow risk and the degree of backflow protection required is determined on the basis of the fluid category in an appliance or receptacle in which the end of the spray or jet could be immersed. The 'zone of backflow risk' for any appliance which is served by a spray or jet attached to a flexible hose is the area covered in a vertical and horizontal plane by the spray or jet with a radius subtended by the length of the hose. This applies to all types of appliances to which a spray is attached. See Diagram R15.9a which illustrates the principle involved.

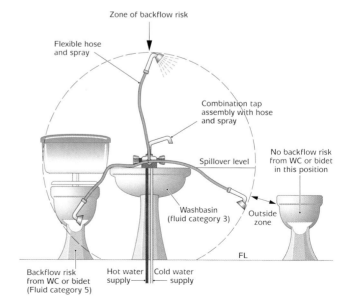

Diagram
R15.9a:
Illustration of the principle of a zone of backflow risk

Guidance

Recommendations

Bidets, including WCs adapted as bidets, incorporating an ascending spray inlet or utilising a flexible hose or an arrangement with a spray or jet, are a fluid category 5 risk in that the ascending spray inlet could be contaminated with urine or other matter and the spray or jet handset could be deposited in the bidet or WC. Bidets of this type must not be supplied with water from a cold or hot water supply pipe or common distributing pipe. The zone of backflow risk is shown and the highest part of this zone must be not less than 15mm below any cistern serving the bidet (see Diagram R15.9b).

Diagram
R15.9b:

Illustration of zone of backflow risk for a bidet with hose and spray

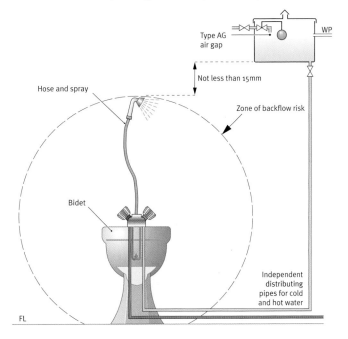

G15.10

Bidets of this type may:

a. *be supplied with cold and/or hot water through Type AA, AB or AD backflow prevention arrangements serving the bidet only; or*

b. *be supplied with cold water from an independent distributing pipe serving the bidet only, (see Diagram G15.10); or a common distributing pipe serving the bidet and which may also serve a WC or urinal flushing cistern only; or*

c. *be supplied with hot water from a water heater, which is supplied from an independent distributing pipe that serves the bidet only, (see Diagram G15.10); or*

d. where the bidet is at a lower elevation than any other outlets or appliances, be supplied with water from a common cold and/or hot water vented distributing pipe providing that:

(i) the elevation of the spillover level of the bidet, if there is no flexible hose; or

(ii) the elevation of the spray outlet, with the hose extended vertically above the spillover level of the bidet;

whichever is the highest, is not less than 300mm below the point of connection of the branch distributing pipe serving the bidet, to the point of connection of other outlets or appliances served by the main distributing pipe.

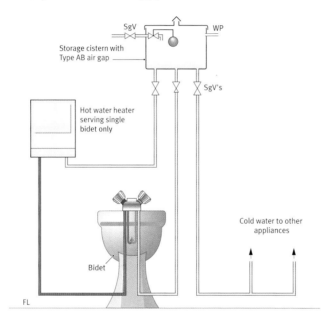

Diagram G15.10:

A method of supplying cold and hot water to a bidet with ascending spray inlet

R15.10.1

One method of supplying water to an ascending spray and/or hose and spray bidet is described in Clause G15.10a and the principle is illustrated in Diagram R15.10.1 but the method described in the formal guidance is difficult to operate effectively. The backflow prevention device or air gap should be located at least 300mm above the fully extended hose and spray, or zone of backflow risk, and this height may need to be increased to provide sufficient water pressure, to overcome friction loss in the pipes and fittings, in order to operate the ascending spray and hose spray effectively. This method of supplying blended water to a

Recommendations

bidet involves complicated control methods as the control of water to the bidet itself has to be linked with the control of water flow, and temperature, to the air gap, blended water cistern or backflow prevention device.

Diagram
R15.10.1:

A method of supplying cold and hot water to a bidet with hose and spray (see Clause R15.10.1 for practicability)

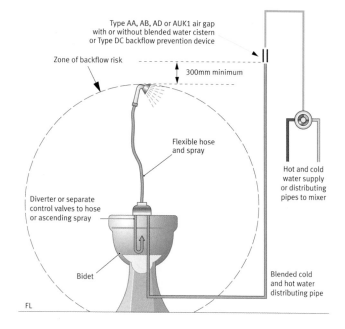

Type AA, AB, AD or AUK1 air gap with or without blended water cistern or Type DC backflow prevention device

Zone of backflow risk

300mm minimum

Flexible hose and spray

Hot and cold water supply or distributing pipes to mixer

Diverter or separate control valves to hose or ascending spray

Bidet

Blended cold and hot water distributing pipe

FL

R15.10.2

A method of supplying cold and hot water to this type of bidet is also described in Clauses G15.10b and c, and is illustrated in Diagram G15.10. In the latter case the cold water supply to the bidet is taken from an independent distributing pipe, which may also supply a WC or urinal flushing cistern. The hot water supply is derived from an instantaneous type water heater which is also supplied from an independent distributing pipe. The top of the zone of backflow risk (in Diagram G15.10 this will be the spillover level of the bidet) should be at least 15mm below the base of the cistern in accordance with the requirements for a Type AUK1 air gap.

Backflow prevention

Guidance   *Recommendations*

R15.10.3

The method of supplying water to this type of bidet, where the bidet is located at a lower elevation than any other outlets or appliances, is described in G15.10d and is illustrated for a bidet with an ascending spray only in Diagram R15.10.3.

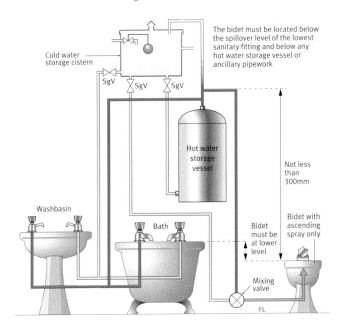

Diagram
R15.10.3:
A method of supplying cold and hot water to a bidet where the bidet is at the lowest level

Within diagram:
Cold water storage cistern

The bidet must be located below the spillover level of the lowest sanitary fitting and below any hot water storage vessel or ancillary pipework

SgV   SgV   SgV

Hot water storage vessel

Not less than 300mm

Washbasin

Bath

Bidet must be at lower level

Bidet with ascending spray only

Mixing valve

FL

Bidets with water inlets above spillover level only

G15.11

Bidets in domestic locations with taps or mixers located above the spillover level of the appliance, and not incorporating an ascending spray inlet below spillover level or spray and flexible hose, may be served from either a supply pipe or a distributing pipe provided that the water outlets discharge with a Type AUK2 air gap above the spillover level of the appliance (see Table S15.2).

R15.11

Bidets in domestic locations of the over-rim type, that have no ascending spray or spray and/or flexible hose may be supplied with cold and hot water through single or combination tap assemblies from either a supply pipe or a distributing pipe providing that a Type AUK2 air gap is maintained between the outlet of the water fitting and the spillover level of the bidet (see Diagrams G15.12 and R15.13.1a).

G u i d a n c e   R e c o m m e n d a t i o n s

WCs and urinals

G15.12

The water supply to a manually operated WC or urinal pressure flushing valve may be derived from either a supply pipe or a distributing pipe. The pressure flushing valve should be located above the WC pan or urinal and must incorporate, or discharge through, a pipe interrupter with a permanent atmospheric vent, that is Type DC in Table S15.2.

The lowest part of the vent opening of the pipe interrupter should be located not less than 300mm above the spillover level of the WC pan or not less than 150mm above the sparge outlet of a urinal. See Diagram G15.12 for typical installation details.

Diagram
G15.12:

Typical installation of sanitary appliances served from a supply pipe in other than dwellings

Diagram labels: Bidets to have water inlets above spillover level and no hoses; WC cistern; SL; WC; FL; WC flushing valve and pipe interrupter; To other appliances on same floor only; Bidet; WC; FL; Not less than 300mm; SL; Bidet; WC; FL; Bidet; WC; FL; Supply pipe

R15.12.1

Manually operated pressure flushing valves for WCs and urinals that incorporate a permanent vent may be supplied with water from either a supply or distributing pipe. Where pressure flushing valves are used that do not incorporate a permanent vent, a pipe interrupter with permanent atmospheric vent should be provided on the outlet side of, and immediately adjacent to, each flushing valve, the vents being located at the minimum height shown in Diagrams R15.12.1a and R15.12.1b.

Backflow prevention

Pressure flushing valves that do not incorporate a permanent vent, or do not have a pipe interrupter installed on the outlet side of the valve, are acceptable providing the valves are located at the minimum heights shown in Diagrams R15.12.1a and R15.12.1b, and are supplied with water from a dedicated cistern, the inlet of which is provided with a Type AG air gap.

For further details of pressure flushing valves for WCs, see Section 9: Clause R25.2 and for further details of pressure flushing valves for urinals (see Section 9: Clause R25.9).

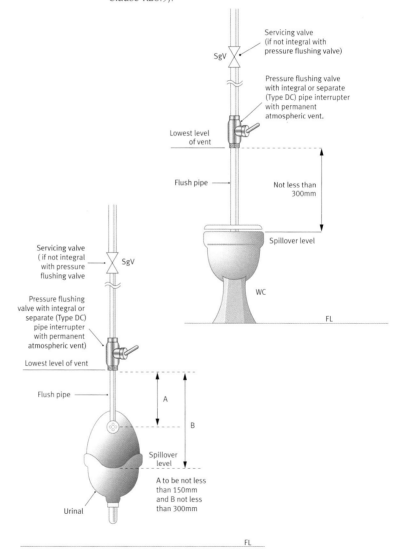

Diagram
R15.12.1a:

Location of pressure flushing valve for WC

Servicing valve (if not integral with pressure flushing valve)

SgV

Pressure flushing valve with integral or separate (Type DC) pipe interrupter with permanent atmospheric vent.

Lowest level of vent

Flush pipe

Not less than 300mm

Spillover level

WC

FL

Diagram
R15.12.1b:

Location of pressure flushing valve for urinal

Servicing valve (if not integral with pressure flushing valve

SgV

Pressure flushing valve with integral or separate (Type DC) pipe interrupter with permanent atmospheric vent)

Lowest level of vent

Flush pipe

A

B

Spillover level

A to be not less than 150mm and B not less than 300mm

Urinal

FL

R15.12.2

A hose union or other tap to which a hose with a spray or jet may be attached at the outlet, and which may be located adjacent to ordinary WCs or squatting toilets, is a fluid category 5 risk, in that the tap outlet could be contaminated directly with urine or other matter and, if a hose is provided, the spray or jet could be deposited in the WC. Taps for this purpose must not be supplied with water from a supply pipe, but can be supplied from an independent distributing pipe providing that the highest part of the zone of the backflow risk is not less than 300mm below any cistern serving the tap (see Diagrams R15.12.2a and R15.12.2b).

Diagram
R15.12.2a:

Illustration of backflow risk for a tap with hose and spray or jet located adjacent to an ordinary WC

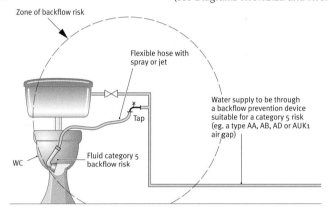

Diagram
R15.12.2b:

Illustration of backflow risk for a tap with hose and spray or jet located adjacent to a squatting type WC

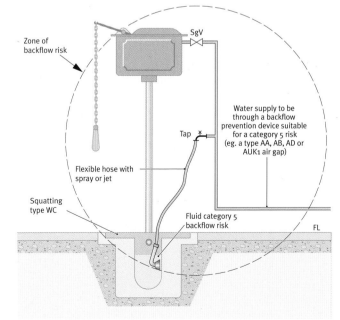

Backflow prevention

Shower heads or tap inlets to baths, washbasins, sinks and bidets

G15.13

Except where suitable additional backflow protection is provided, all single tap outlets, combination tap assembly outlets, or fixed shower heads terminating over washbasins, baths or bidets in domestic situations should discharge above the spillover level of the appliance with a tap gap (Type AUK2) as scheduled in Table S15.2. For a sink in a domestic or non-domestic location, and for any appliances in premises where a higher level of protection is required, such as some appliances in hospitals or other health care premises, a tap gap (Type AUK3) is required, (see Table S15.2).

R15.13.1

Wherever practical, backflow protection at tap or combination tap assembly units or mixers should be achieved by the provision of a tap gap. Where an acceptable tap gap is not achievable, mechanical backflow protection should be provided in accordance with Clause R15.14. Diagram R15.13.1a shows the tap gap for a wash basin, bath or bidet in domestic situations and Diagram R15.13.1b shows the tap gap for a sink, or other appliance where a higher degree of protection is required.

It should be noted that the tap gap is measured from the spillover level of the appliance to the lowest part of the tap outlet. If the tap shelf of the washbasin or other appliance is lower than the spillover level, the tap should be raised so that the required height of tap gap above the spillover level is achieved, or additional protection measures should be provided as described in paragraph G15.14.

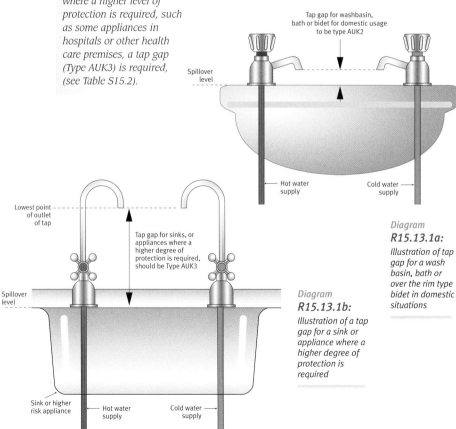

Diagram
R15.13.1a:
Illustration of tap gap for a wash basin, bath or over the rim type bidet in domestic situations

Diagram
R15.13.1b:
Illustration of a tap gap for a sink or appliance where a higher degree of protection is required

R15.13.2

Where combination tap assemblies, either with or without a hose and shower head, or shower mixer taps are installed, and both cold and hot water (that is, fluid category 1 and 2) are mixed in the body of the tap, it may be considered reasonable, where pressures are unbalanced, for there to be single check valves on both the cold and hot inlets to the combination tap or mixer as shown in Diagram R15.13.2a. Under the previous Byelaws single check valves were required to prevent the possibility, under fault conditions, of the 'cold side' pressurising the 'hot side' and, under vacuum conditions, of hot water returning to the mains 'cold side'. The Water Supply Industry supports the provision of single check valves where there are unbalanced pressures.

Where a combination tap or mixer with water mixing in the body is used with balanced pressures (that is, both inlets are fed from supply pipes or both are from storage), the 'cold side' is now rated as Fluid Category 1, and the 'hot side' is now rated Fluid Category 2, and single check valves should

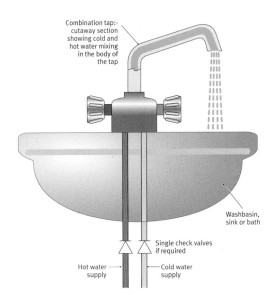

Combination tap:-
cutaway section
showing cold and
hot water mixing
in the body of
the tap

Diagram
R15.13.2a:

Provision of check valves to cold and hot pipes serving combination taps or mixer fittings under unbalanced pressures where water mixes in the body of the tap

Washbasin, sink or bath

Single check valves if required

Hot water supply — — Cold water supply

therefore – according to the Regulations – be installed on both 'sides' (see Diagram R15.13.2a). Alternatively, a combination tap with separate waterways as illustrated in Diagram R15.13.2b may be used.

The Water Supply Industry deems that the particular requirement of the Regulation will be met if there are no check valves on either 'side' of the supplies to 'mixer' taps where water mixes within the body and the supplies are on balanced pressures.

Diagram
R15.13.2b:
Illustration of combination tap with separate waterways

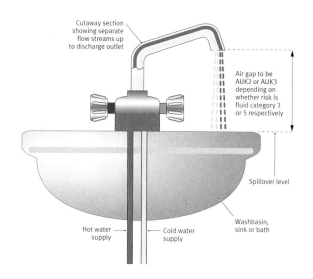

Cutaway section showing separate flow streams up to discharge outlet

Air gap to be AUK2 or AUK3 depending on whether risk is fluid category 3 or 5 respectively

Spillover level

Washbasin, sink or bath

Hot water supply — Cold water supply

Submerged inlets to baths and washbasins

G15.14
Submerged inlets to baths or washbasins in any house or domestic situation are considered to be a fluid category 3 risk; they should be supplied with water from a supply or distributing pipe through a double check valve. Submerged inlets to baths or washbasins in other than a house or domestic situation, and sinks in any location, are considered to be a fluid category 5 risk and appropriate backflow protection is required for this level of risk.

R15.14
Where the outlets of taps, combination taps or mixer fittings to washbasins or baths are submerged, the branch pipes serving cold and hot water to the taps should each be protected against a fluid category 3 risk, that is, with a double check valve (see Diagram R15.14a).

Recommendations

Diagram
R15.14a:

Illustration of wash basin with submerged tap outlets in domestic situation

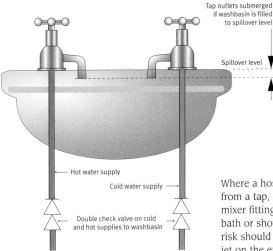

Where a hose with a spray or jet is served from a tap, combination tap assembly or mixer fitting located over a wash basin, bath or shower tray the zone of backflow risk should be ascertained. If the spray or jet on the end of the hose is capable of entering any washbasin, bath or shower tray located within the zone of backflow risk, a fluid category 3 backflow prevention device, such as a double check valve, should be provided on each inlet pipe to the appliance (see Diagram R15.14b and R15.14c).

Where the inlet fitting incorporates an integral self-cancelling diverter, a single check valve must be provided on both the cold and hot water inlets.

If any appliance such as a sink, WC or bidet is located within the zone of backflow risk of a flexible hose, the cold and hot water supplies to the hose should be protected against a fluid category 5 risk. Alternatively, a fixed shower only should be installed, that is, an arrangement without any flexible hose (see Diagram R15.14d).

Diagram
R15.14b:

Illustration of a fluid category 3 risk from a wash basin, bath or shower tray where no integral self-cancelling diverter (HC device) is provided

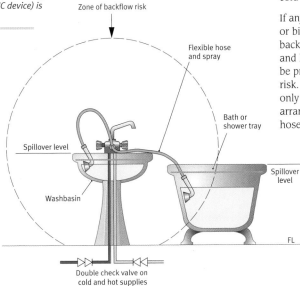

Backflow prevention

Diagram
R15.14c:

Illustration of a backflow risk for a shower mixer fitting from a fluid category 3 risk

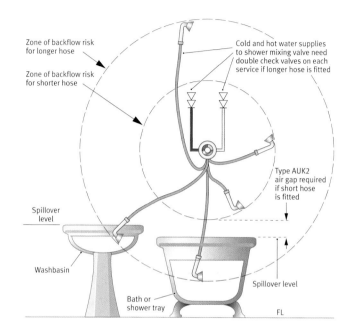

Zone of backflow risk for longer hose

Zone of backflow risk for shorter hose

Cold and hot water supplies to shower mixing valve need double check valves on each service if longer hose is fitted

Type AUK2 air gap required if short hose is fitted

Spillover level

Washbasin

Bath or shower tray

Spillover level

FL

Diagram
R15.14d:

Illustration of a backflow risk for a bath mixer fitting from a fluid category 5 risk

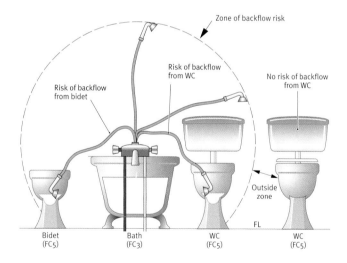

Zone of backflow risk

Risk of backflow from WC

No risk of backflow from WC

Risk of backflow from bidet

Outside zone

FL

| Bidet (FC5) | Bath (FC3) | WC (FC5) | WC (FC5) |

Drinking water fountains

G15.15
Drinking water fountains should be designed so that the outlet of the water delivery jet nozzle is at least 25mm above the spillover level of the bowl. The nozzle should be provided with a screen or hood to protect it from contamination.

Washing machines, washer-dryers and dishwashers

G15.16
Household washing machines, washer-dryers and dishwashers are manufactured to satisfy a fluid category 3 risk. Where they are likely to be used in a non-domestic situation, appropriate backflow protection for a higher fluid risk category should be provided.

R15.16
Washing machines, washer-dryers and dishwashers, including coin-operated types, for use in single family houses and flats, and where the use is classed as domestic in other buildings, are considered a fluid category 3 risk and backflow protection against this level of risk is normally built into domestic type machines. Washing machines, washer-dryers and dishwashers for use in other than the above applications must be provided with backflow protection suitable to the level of risk according to the following applications. If the inbuilt protection is inadequate additional external protection must be provided.
For further information see WRAS Guidance 9–04–01.

Fluid category 4 –
Applications
For example: Restaurants, hotels, launderettes and laundries where no medical or other high risk laundry is likely to be processed.

Fluid category 5 –
Applications
For example: Hospitals and other premises where health care is provided. Also laundries where medical or other high risk items are processed.

Hose pipes for house garden and other applications

G15.17
Hand held hoses should be fitted with a self-closing mechanism at the outlet of the hose.

R15.17
Hoses should only be used where the outlet nozzle is designed to be held in the hand and water can only discharge when under user control. This will reduce the risk of backflow into the supply pipe if the hose end is dropped on the ground and also promotes water conservation.

Commercial and other installations excluding house gardens

G15.18
Any taps and fittings used for supplying water for non-domestic applications, such as commercial, horticultural, agricultural or industrial purposes should be provided with:

a. backflow protection devices appropriate to the downstream fluid category; and,

b. where appropriate, a zone protection system.

Backflow prevention

Guidance

Recommendations

G15.19

Soil watering systems installed in close proximity to the soil surface (that is, where the watered surface is less than 150mm below the water outlet discharge point) for example, irrigation systems, permeable hoses etc., are considered to be a fluid category 5 risk and should only be supplied with water through a Type AA, AB, AD or AUK1 air gap arrangement.

R15.19

Porous hose irrigation systems, either laid on the ground or buried below the surface, are a serious potential backflow risk and the pipe supplying these devices should be protected against a fluid category 5. Soil watering systems where the installation consists of fixed sprinkler heads located not less than 150mm above ground level, and without the use of insecticide or fertiliser additives, are considered a fluid category 3 risk.

House garden installations

G15.20

Taps to which hoses are, or may be, connected and located in house garden locations are to be protected against backflow by means of a double check valve. The double check valve should be located inside a building and protected from freezing (see Diagram G15.20).

R15.20

This paragraph is also taken to refer to recreational areas excluding agricultural and horticultural use. A double check valve is considered a suitable type of backflow prevention device for this fluid category 3 risk. Double check valves have been shown to be susceptible to frost damage and should therefore be protected against freezing by being installed inside a building, or by other means.

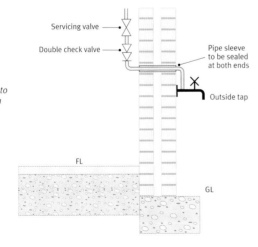

Diagram
G15.20:

Backflow protection to external hose taps in house gardens only (thermal insulation omitted)

Servicing valve

Double check valve

Pipe sleeve to be sealed at both ends

Outside tap

FL

GL

Backflow prevention

Guidance

Recommendations

G15.21
Where, in existing house installations, a hose pipe is to be used from an existing hose union tap located outside a house and which is not provided with backflow protection, either:

a. the existing hose union tap should be provided with a double check valve located inside the building; or

b. the tap should be replaced with a hose union tap that incorporates a double check valve (Type HUK1); or

c. a hose union backflow preventer (Type HA) or a double check valve should be permanently secured to the outlet of the tap.

R15.21
While the Regulations are not retrospective appropriate measures must be taken against any known situation where there is a potential backflow risk from hoses. The offence will be deemed to have been committed when the hose was attached and not when the tap was first installed.

Where an outside tap is being installed in a new location, a double check valve (Type EC or ED) should be provided and fixed inside the envelope of the thermal insulation of a building.

Where an existing outside tap is being replaced:

a. If practicable: a double check valve should be provided on the supply to the tap and should be located inside the thermal envelope of the building; or

b. where it is not practicable to locate the double check valve within a building the tap could be replaced with;

　(i) a hose union tap that incorporates a double check valve (Type HUK1); or

　(ii) a tap which has a hose union backflow preventer (Type HA) or a double check valve (Type EC or ED) should be fitted and permanently secured to the outlet of the tap.

In the case of 'b' in weather when the air temperature is likely to drop below freezing, the supply to the tap should be turned off at the servicing valve and the hose tap left open to drain water from within the double check valve.

G15.22
Where fixed or hand-held devices are used with hose pipes for the application of fertilisers or domestic detergents the minimum backflow protection provided should be suitable for protection against a fluid category 3 risk. Backflow protection against a fluid category 5 risk should be provided where these devices are used for the application of insecticides.

R15.22
While these fixed or hand-held devices, supplied from a protected hose tap, are considered satisfactory for the application of fertilisers they should not be used for the application of insecticides without additional backflow protection measures being included to give protection against a fluid category 4 risk.

Backflow prevention

G15.23

Where mini-irrigation systems, such as porous hoses, are installed in house garden situations only, a hose union tap with backflow protection in accordance with Clauses G15.20 or G15.21 combined with a pipe interruptor with atmospheric vent and moving element device (Type DB) at the connection of the hose to the hose union tap, or not less than 300mm above the highest point of the delivery point of the spray outlet or the perforated surface of the porous hose, whichever is the highest, is acceptable (see Diagrams G15.23a and G15.23b).

R15.23

Porous hose irrigation systems laid on the ground surface, in house gardens only, may be installed in accordance with clause G15.23 and Diagrams G15.23a and G15.23b. A Type DB backflow prevention device may be unsuitable where the hose can generate backpressure (eg. if buried in soil).

Irrigation systems in house garden situations consisting of fixed sprinkler heads located not less than 150 mm above ground level, and without the use of insecticide or fertiliser additives, are considered a fluid category 3 risk and may be served from a hose union tap protected against this category of fluid risk, by a Type DB or no less effective device.

Irrigation systems in house garden situations or recreational areas, excluding agricultural and horticultural use, consisting of pop-up sprinklers without the use of insecticide or fertiliser additives are considered a fluid category 4 risk and should be protected by a verifiable backflow preventer with a reduced pressure zone (BA device) or no less effective device.

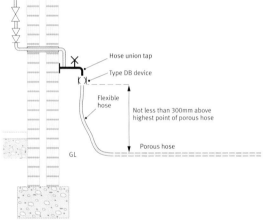

Diagram
G15.23a:

Mini-irrigation or porous hose in house situation where ground surface is level or sloping away from house

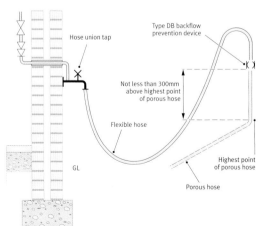

Diagram
G15.23b:

Mini-irrigation or porous hose in house situation where ground level is rising away from the house

Guidance

Whole site and zone protection

Diagram
G15.24a:

Secondary backflow protection of supply pipes using double check valves

G15.24

A whole-site or zone backflow prevention device should be provided on the supply or distributing pipe, such as a single check valve or double check valve, or other no less effective backflow prevention device, according to the level of risk as judged by the Water Undertaker where:

a. *a supply or distributing pipe conveys water to two or more separately occupied premises (whether or not they are separately chargeable by the water supplier for a supply of water); or,*

b. *a supply pipe conveys water to premises which under any enactment are required to provide a storage cistern capable of holding sufficient water for not less than 24 hours ordinary use (see Diagrams G15.24b and G15.24c).*

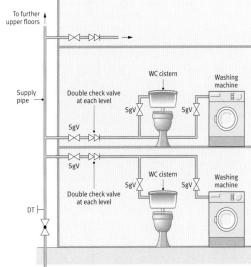

Diagram
G15.24c:

Secondary backflow protection of distributing pipes using double check valves

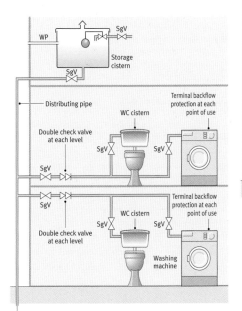

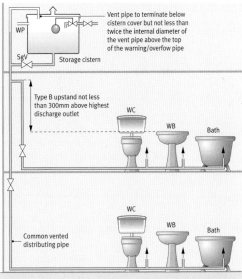

Diagram
G15.24b:

Example of secondary backflow protection to two storey premises using a vented distributing pipe

R15.24.1

Clause R15.13 deals with protection of the supply and with protection at points of use. In certain installations however the risks are increased because of the possibility of internal backflow within installations in buildings in multiple occupation. In these cases Schedule 2: Section 6.2: Paragraph 15(4) requires that certain additional precautions should be taken in the event of low pressure to prevent or limit backflow in certain supply and distributing pipes. These include the main supply pipes or distributing pipes serving several dwelling units such as in blocks of flats where contaminated water might pass from one flat to another. The requirement also applies to industrial premises, schools, offices, hospitals, etc. but does not apply to, and within, any separately occupied premises with its own supply pipe. The requirements for backflow protection should be applied in the following cases:

a. on the common supply pipe system serving two or more premises and on any common distributing pipe system serving two or more such premises; and

b. on the supply pipes of individual premises arranged to receive an intermittent supply of water.

R15.24.2

Clause R15.24.3 deals with secondary backflow protection associated with supply pipes and Clause R15.24.4 deals with secondary backflow protection that is associated with distributing pipes. In each case the requirement of the Regulations would be accepted as being satisfied if the measures indicated are taken. For re-circulatory hot water systems it is not practicable to provide secondary backflow protection except in cases where the hot water feed pipe to individual premises is not itself a re-circulatory flow and return system. Except in this latter event, secondary backflow protection would not therefore be required but special care should be taken to ensure full conformity with other backflow requirements. In all cases appliances should be down-fed from ceiling level and high risk appliances (e.g. bedpan washers) should only be fed from dedicated distributing pipes.

R15.24.3   SECONDARY BACKFLOW PROTECTION ON SUPPLY PIPES

It is recommended that secondary backflow protection be installed at every floor level as indicated in Diagram G15.24a. Where the backflow risk does not exceed fluid category 3 the acceptable protection devices would consist of double check valve assemblies installed immediately downstream of the stop valve on each branch supply pipe to the level or floor under consideration.

R15.24.4   SECONDARY BACKFLOW PROTECTION ON DISTRIBUTING PIPES

It is recommended that secondary backflow protection be installed at every floor level as indicated in Diagram G15.24c. Where the backflow risk does not exceed fluid category 3 the acceptable protection devices would consist of double check valve assemblies installed immediately downstream of the stop valve on each branch supply pipe to the level or floor under consideration.

An alternative method is shown in Diagram G15.24b. This method, which has been accepted and used in the past as secondary backflow protection against fluid category 3, depends on a vented distributing pipe which serves two floor levels only. With this system great care is required in the sizing and connections of pipework to ensure adequate backflow protection of the lower floor appliances. All appliances served should have point of use backflow protection. To be effective it is recommended that:

a. A vent pipe is connected and arranged on each distributing pipe at its junction with the associated storage cistern. Every vent pipe should be the same size as the distributing pipe at the point of connection to the cistern; and

b. No part of any branch pipe is at a higher elevation than the point of its junction with the distributing pipe; and

c. Every branch pipe is arranged in such a way that the overflowing level of associated fixed appliances served by a draw-off fitting connected to the branch pipe is at a level not less than 300mm below the point of the junction of the branch pipe with the falling length of distributing pipe.

G15.25

The provision of zone or whole-site backflow protection should be in addition to individual requirements at points of use and within the system.

G15.26

Zone protection may be required in other than domestic premises where particular industrial, chemical or medical processes are undertaken.

R15.26

Zone protection is often used in industrial, chemical or medical premises to group particular areas of activity and risk. A typical outline of such a system is illustrated in Diagram R15.26.

Diagram
R15.26:

Schematic layout of zoned water system

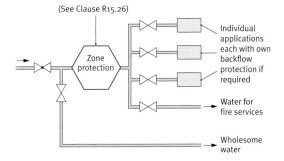

(See Clause R15.26)

Zone protection

Individual applications each with own backflow protection if required

Water for fire services

Wholesome water

Backflow prevention

Fire protection systems

G15.27

Wet sprinkler systems (without additives), first-aid fire hose reels and hydrant landing valves are considered a fluid category 2 backflow risk. Wet sprinkler systems with additives to prevent freezing are considered a fluid category 4 risk.

R15.27

Water services to buildings for fire sprinkler systems without additives, which are independent of the domestic water supply are considered a fluid category 2 risk. This is only necessary due to the likelihood of the water remaining stagnant and as such a single check valve, or equivalent, is acceptable for backflow protection (see Diagram R15.27a). Check valves to the appropriate BS are at present only available up to DN 54; if the pipe is larger than DN 54 it may be necessary to use non-return valves, preferably with soft faced seals and spring loaded, if available.

Additives are often added to the water in sprinkler systems in exposed situations to prevent freezing at low ambient temperatures and in these conditions the contents of the system are considered to be a fluid category 4 risk. This would therefore necessitate a Type BA backflow prevention device such as an RPZ valve (see Diagram R15.27a).

Diagrams R15.27b, R15.27c and R15.27d show cases where sprinklers are supplied with water from storage or where the storage is supplemented by a supply from another source.

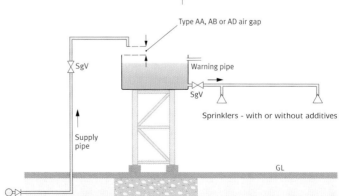

Diagram
R15.27a:
Backflow protection to sprinkler systems

Diagram
R15.27b:
Elevated storage serving water for sprinklers only

Guidance   *Recommendations*

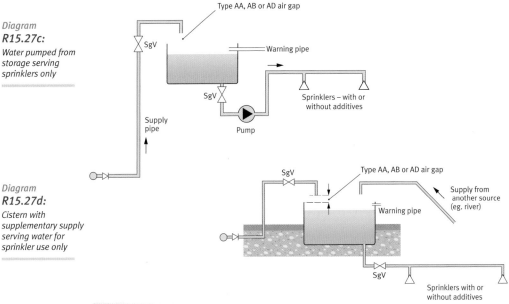

Diagram
R15.27c:
Water pumped from storage serving sprinklers only

Diagram
R15.27d:
Cistern with supplementary supply serving water for sprinkler use only

G15.28
Fluids contained within large cylindrical hydro-pneumatic pressurised vessels are considered to be fluid category 4 risk.

G15.29
Where fire protection systems and drinking water systems are served from a common domestic supply pipe, the connection to the fire systems should be taken from the supply pipe immediately on entry to the building and appropriate backflow protection devices should be installed.

R15.29
While some Water Suppliers may insist on separate service pipes for domestic water supplies and fire water supplies, others will permit the installation of a single service pipe to serve both purposes. Generally, first aid fire hosereels and fire landing valves are considered a fluid category 2 risk for which a single check valve would be sufficient. Details of a combined domestic and fire service pipe arrangement is shown in Diagram R15.29a.

Diagram
R15.29a:
Arrangement of common service to domestic and fire supply pipe

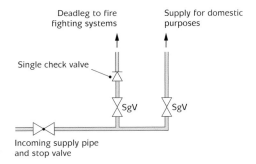

Backflow prevention

Miscellaneous commercial and industrial applications

R15.30

All wholesome water derived from supply or distribution pipes and used in commercial, industrial, marine, scientific and medical establishments, situations and processes should be adequately protected against backflow. Water supplies to laboratories and similar scientific establishments for non-domestic purposes are generally considered to be a fluid category 5 risk unless a risk assessment clearly shows that a lower category of risk exists. Where a fluid category 5 exists supplies should always be taken from distributing pipes supplied with water from an independent storage cistern. Each water outlet should be individually protected to prevent backflow between individual points of draw-off. Where water is required at a higher pressure than is attainable from a storage cistern, the supply should be pumped from a cistern (see Diagram R15.30a).

Diagram
R15.30a:

Pumped water supply to laboratory fittings

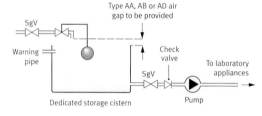

Safety/drench showers and eyewash fountains should be supplied with water directly off the supply pipe.

Water supplies to chemical dosing tanks, water tankers and other fluid category 5 risk applications, or where the water supply is supplemented from an alternative source, should only be supplied with water through a Type AA, AB, AD or AUK1 backflow prevention arrangement (see Diagrams R15.30b, R15.30c and R15.30d).

Diagram
R15.30b:

Separation of wholesome water from supplementary sources

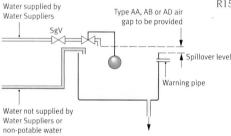

Diagram
R15.30c:

Separation of wholesome water from water that has been used

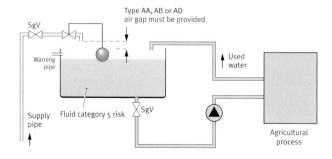

Recommendations

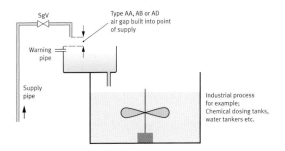

Diagram
R15.30d:

Water supply to a fixed or mobile appliance in industrial or commercial premises.

Backflow protection should be provided at all points of connection of a wholesome water supply to boats, ships, trains etc. Diagrams R15.30e to R15.30j show several different applications.

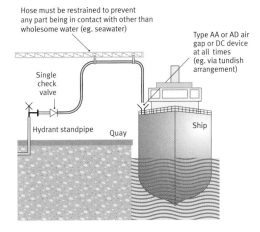

Diagram
R15.30e:

Water supply taken directly from supply pipe to ship

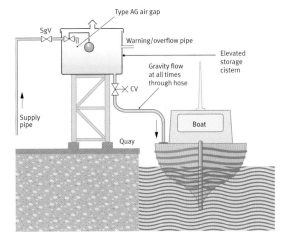

Diagram
R15.30f:

Water supply taken by gravity from storage on quayside

Backflow prevention

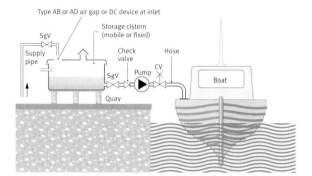

Diagram R15.30g:

Water supply pumped from storage on quayside

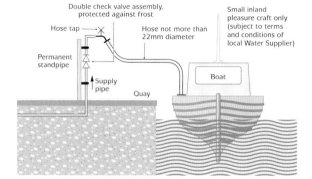

Diagram R15.30h:

Water supply taken from hose union tap on quayside

Diagram R15.30i:

Water supply taken by gravity from storage

Diagram R15.30j:

Water supply pumped from storage

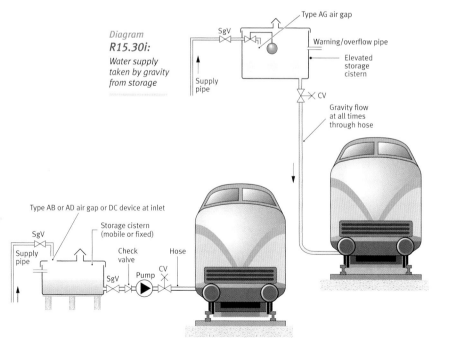

Schedule 2
Section 7:
Paragraph 16:
Cold water services

Notes

Schedule 2

16.

(1) Every pipe supplying water connected to a storage cistern shall be fitted with an effective adjustable valve capable of shutting off the inflow of water at a suitable level below the overflowing level of the cistern.

(2) Every inlet to a storage cistern, combined feed and expansion cistern, WC flushing cistern or urinal flushing cistern shall be fitted with a servicing valve on the inlet pipe adjacent to the cistern.

(3) Every storage cistern, except one supplying water to the primary circuit of a heating system, shall be fitted with a servicing valve on the outlet pipe.

(4) Every storage cistern shall be fitted with –

    (a) an overflow pipe, with a suitable means of warning of an impending overflow, which excludes insects;

    (b) a cover positioned so as to exclude light and insects; and

    (c) thermal insulation to minimise freezing or undue warming.

(5) Every storage cistern shall be so installed as to minimise the risk of contamination of stored water. The cistern shall be of an appropriate size, and the pipe connections to the cistern shall be so positioned, as to allow free circulation and to prevent areas of stagnant water from developing.

Cold water services

Float operated valves

G16.1

Float operated valves and other fittings for controlling flow to cisterns, including flushing cisterns, should:

a. *be capable of controlling the flow of water into any cistern or apparatus and, when closed, be watertight and remain watertight; and*

b. *incorporate, as applicable, a renewable seat and a washer which are resistant to both corrosion and erosion by water, or have some other no less effective valve closure assembly; and*

c. *as applicable, have a float which is constructed of a material capable of withstanding without leaking any water temperature in which it operates or is likely to operate, and has a lifting effort such that when not more than half immersed, the valve is capable of drop-tight closure against the maximum operating pressure at that elevation in the building; and*

d. *when acting via an operating lever, and when the valve is closed, will withstand without bending or distorting a force twice that to which it is ordinarily subject and, in the case of a G^1/$_2$ size valve, is constructed so that the water shut-off level may be altered or adjusted without bending the float lever; and*

e. *where used in cisterns storing water other than for drinking purposes, the installation of the fitting should be such that it is capable of satisfying backflow prevention requirements when the water level in the cistern is level with the centreline of the float operated valve.*

G16.2

The requirements for float-operated valves may be satisfied as follows:

a. *for use in WC cisterns – should comply with BS 1212. Parts 2, 3 or 4; and*

b. *for use elsewhere – should comply with BS 1212: Part 1, 2, 3 or 4.*

R16.2

Float operated valves that satisfy Clause G16.1 are:

BS 1212: Part1: 1990: Specification for piston type float operated valves (copper body alloy) (excluding floats)

Note: Unless there is a suitable backflow prevention device (for example, a double check valve) immediately upstream of the float operated valve, BS1212: Part 1 float valves are not acceptable in a WC cistern or in any other location where any part of the valve may be submerged when the overflow pipe is in operation. See Clause G16.1e.

BS 1212: Part 2: 1990: Specification for diaphragm type float operated valves (copper alloy body) (excluding floats)

BS 1212: Part 3:1990: Specification for diaphragm type float operated valves (plastics bodied) for cold water services only (excluding floats)

BS 1212: Part 4:1991: Specification for compact type float operated valves for WC flushing cisterns (including floats)

The Part 2, Part 3 and Part 4 valves are capable of withstanding a backflow test when the water level is as high as the centre line of the valve whereas a Part 1 valve will not withstand such a test.

Recommendations

Schedule 2: Section 7: Paragraph 16(1) would be accepted as being satisfied if any float is of the appropriate size having regard to the working pressure and it complies with either:

a. BS 1968: Floats (copper) for float operated valves; or

b. BS 2456: Floats (plastics) for float operated valves for hot and cold water.

There are many float operated valves available which do not comply with BS 1212 and therefore reference should be made to the WRAS Water Fittings & Materials Directory for other acceptable types. Care should be taken to ensure that they are installed so as to satisfy the backflow prevention requirements of Schedule 2: Section 6: Paragraph 15.

Clause G16.1d requires not only that the lever of a float operated valve should be strong enough but that in the case of every G$1/2$ sized valve the float should be fitted with some easily adjustable device for setting the water level. Bending of the float arm will not be accepted as a means of meeting the latter provision and BS 1212: Part 2 illustrates an acceptable method (see Diagram R16.2).

Methods of water level inlet control other than float operated valves may be used, such as control by water level sensors controlling remote electrically or pneumatically operated valves. In all cases the methods and installation should be suitable for the purpose and comply with all aspects of the Regulations.

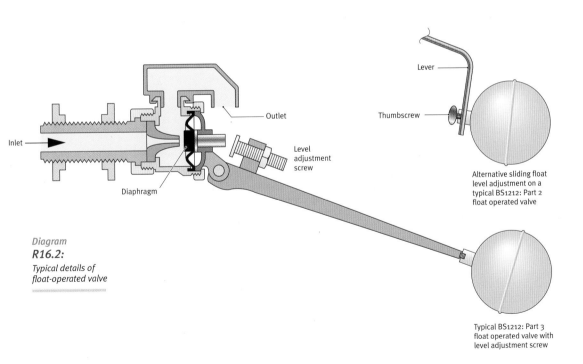

Diagram
R16.2:
Typical details of float-operated valve

Outlet

Inlet

Diaphragm

Level adjustment screw

Lever

Thumbscrew

Alternative sliding float level adjustment on a typical BS1212: Part 2 float operated valve

Typical BS1212: Part 3 float operated valve with level adjustment screw

G16.3

Float operated valves which are subject to hot water at the inlet should conform to Clause G16.1 and be constructed of materials capable of withstanding without leaking any ordinary operating water temperature to which they are likely to be subjected. So far as is reasonably practicable, their operation should not be prevented or impaired by scale. Having regard to any scale which is likely to be deposited on the valve or float, the valve should be capable of being adjusted to prevent any flow through the valve above the required water level.

R16.3

Except in the case of the cistern element of a hot water storage combination unit where in BS 3198 the temperature is permitted to rise to not more than 39°C (see Clause R16.13.4) this guidance is not intended to apply to float operated valves conveying cold water to feed cisterns supplying hot water apparatus, except that the float must be capable of withstanding an occasional rise in temperature due to any expansion water being received in the cistern. Floats conforming to BS 2456 and BS 1968 will be accepted as satisfying this requirement.

Floats conforming to BS 2456 are not designed for continuous contact with hot water and copper floats for such a purpose should have brazed or equivalent seams. Float operated valves conveying hot water must not incorporate materials unsuitable for continuous or frequent contact with hot water; BS 1212 does not include relevant requirements.

Inlets to cisterns

G16.4

Inlets to all cisterns should be provided with a servicing valve to facilitate maintenance, and a float operated valve or some other no less effective device which is capable of controlling the flow of water into the cistern. The servicing valve should be fitted as close as reasonably practical to the float operated valve or other device. This does not apply to a pipe connecting two or more cisterns each of which has the same overflowing level.

R16.4

A solenoid valve responding to a level switch will be acceptable as a no less effective device to a float operated valve

G16.5

Float-controlled valves or equivalent inlet devices should be securely and rigidly attached to the cistern and installed so that the valve closes when the level of the water is not less than 25mm below the overflowing level of the cistern. Where the cistern is fitted with an approved alternative to a warning pipe, such as an indicator instrument or a visual or audible alarm, the inlet valve is to close when the water level is not less than 50mm below the overflowing level of the cistern.

R16.5

Inlet valves installed to provide an air gap, either within or above a cistern must be firmly and rigidly fixed and arrangements made to avoid splashing.

Guidance   *Recommendations*

Outlets from cisterns

G16.6

Where practicable all outlets from a cistern should be taken from the bottom of the cistern.

R16.6

The recommendation for bottom outlets in Clause G16.6 does not preclude the use of outlets taken from the side of a cistern but the guidance recommends that where practicable outlets are located in the bottom of the cistern (see Diagram R16.6).

This recommendation is to reduce the retention of sediment in the bottom of a cistern below the level of the lowest outlet as this deposited matter may harbour or provide nutrient for bacteria and other organisms. To ensure that a system operates safely it is essential that any sediment in the bottom of the cistern is routinely removed and the temperature of the water is maintained below 20°C whenever possible.

The need for different levels of draw-off from a cistern is particularly relevant where mechanical shower mixing valves or combination taps are supplied with both cold and hot water from a common storage cistern. In these cases it is recommended that the outlet serving a hot water system is taken from the cistern at a slightly higher level than the outlet serving cold water to appliances. This will ensure that in the event of the cistern being drawn down the hot water will cease to flow at the shower or combination tap before the cold water, thus preventing any possible scalding of a person using the appliance (see Diagram R16.6).

'A' or 'B' to be not less than internal diameter of outlet of cold water distributing pipe

Diagram
R16.6:

Illustration showing position of cistern outlets

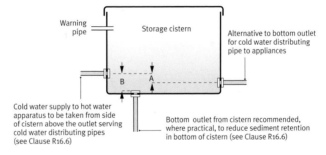

G16.7

Except for cisterns supplying water to primary circuits or heating circuits, all outlets other than vent pipes, overflow pipes, and warning pipes relating to storage cisterns supplying water to cold water taps and secondary hot water systems, should be fitted with a servicing valve as close to the cistern as is reasonably practicable.

R16.7

It is not normal to provide servicing valves on the outlets of cisterns serving primary circuits because of the danger of boiling and shortage of feed water if the outlet servicing valve is inadvertently closed and a fault in the temperature control system occurs. As cisterns used for this purpose are usually of relatively small capacity, little wastage of water occurs if the inlet servicing valve to the cistern is used for maintenance purposes and the cistern, and system, is drained.

Warning and overflow pipes

G16.8

All cisterns, except automatically operated urinal flushing cisterns, should be provided with a warning pipe, or some other no less effective device, installed in such a manner that it discharges immediately the water in a cistern reaches the defined overflowing level. Where an alternative no less effective device is installed instead of a warning pipe, an overflow pipe should also be installed. The outlet end of a warning or overflow pipe is not to be at a higher level than the inlet end; it should be installed on a downward inclined plane, and not comprise, include, or have connected to it, any flexible hose.

R16.8

In many cases an adequately sized warning pipe will also act as an overflow pipe, but there is nothing to prevent both a warning pipe and an overflow pipe being provided. However, it is suggested that a single warning/overflow pipe should be sufficient for a cistern of 1,000 litres or less actual capacity (see Diagram R16.8a).

It should be noted that the 'actual capacity' of a cistern means the volume of water which the cistern is capable of holding measured to its overflowing level.

With cisterns that have an actual capacity greater than 1,000 litres it is recommended that a warning pipe and an overflow pipe should be provided, the warning pipe discharging in a conspicuous position and the overflow pipe discharging in a suitable position elsewhere. This method is often used with large cisterns (see Diagram R16.8b).

Diagram
R16.8a:

Cistern 1,000 litres
capacity or less

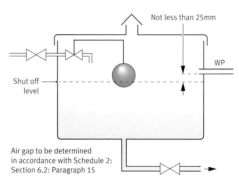

Diagram
R16.8b:

Cistern more than
1,000 litres capacity

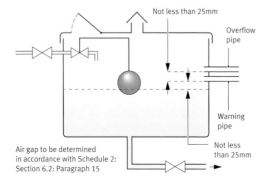

Cisterns with an actual capacity in excess of 5,000 litres should be provided with an overflow that operates when the water level is 50mm above the normal shut off level. A warning pipe may be omitted but a level indicator should be provided with an audible or visible alarm which operates when the water reaches 25mm below the invert of the overflow. This latter provision would not be required if, in addition to the float operated valve or other device controlling the inflow, there is an independent control to shut off the inflow when the water level reaches the overflowing level of the warning pipe or lowest overflow pipe as the case may be (see Diagram R16.8c).

In all cases the level of the outlet of the float operated valve or other inlet device and the location and position of termination of any warning or overflow pipe must comply with the backflow requirements of Schedule 2: Section 6: Paragraph 15.

Every warning pipe shall be installed so as to discharge water immediately the water in the cistern reaches overflowing level. Any warning/overflow pipe must be securely fixed and have a falling gradient towards its outlet and should not comprise, include or have connected to it, any flexible hose.

Air gap to be determined in accordance with Schedule 2: Section 6.2: Paragraph 15

Diagram
R16.8c:
Cistern 5,000 litres capacity or more

Overflow pipe

25mm

Shut off level

Level at which audible or visible alarm is actuated

Not less than 50mm between invert of overflow pipe and shut off level

G16.9
Warning or overflow pipes from any cistern should not be installed to discharge into any other cistern.

R16.9
Wherever possible warning pipes should discharge outside a building, however, where this is not practicable owing to the design of the building, they may be discharged internally provided the discharge is conspicuous. The following are examples of acceptable arrangements for the discharge of warning/overflow pipe.

a. In dwellings. The pipe discharges outside an external wall or it discharges internally with a type AA air gap over a tundish, or not less than 150mm above the rim of a WC pan or shower tray, etc. Alternatively, the pipe may terminate into a combined bath overflow manifold as illustrated in Diagram R16.9.

b. Common pipe. Each pipe discharges into a tundish in a normally visible position (that is, not in a duct or similar) such that there is a type AA air gap between the point of discharge and the rim of the tundish. The tundish itself may drain into a common pipe discharging outside an external wall.

Cold water services

Diagram
R16.9:
Principle of operation
of combined bath
overflow manifold

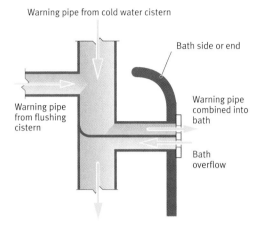

Warning pipe from cold water cistern

Bath side or end

Warning pipe
from flushing
cistern

Warning pipe
combined into
bath

Bath
overflow

G16.10
A warning/overflow pipe
should be not less than
19mm internal diameter,
but the actual internal
diameter of the pipe(s)
installed should be capable
of taking the possible flow
in the pipe arising from any
failure of the inlet valve.

R16.10
While a 19mm diameter warning/overflow pipe may be
adequate to take the flow from a cistern if the reason for
failure is a worn washer in a float operated valve, it may
not be adequate for a major breakdown of the valve.
The size of warning/overflow pipe provided should therefore
be determined taking into consideration the nominal size
of float operated valve, or no less effective device, or the
diameter of the orifice in the valve and the pressure
available at the inlet to the valve.

G16.11
When determining the size
of an overflow pipe,
account should be taken of
any insect or vermin screen
installed, which may reduce
the nominal flow capacity
of the overflow pipe.

R16.11
The restriction on the flow of water through any insect
or vermin screen located at the point of connection of a
warning/overflow pipe to a cistern or, at the terminal end of
the warning/overflow pipe, should be taken into account
when determining the size of the mesh of the screen.

Guidance

Recommendations

G16.12

When two or more cisterns have a common warning pipe the pipework should be arranged so that the overflow from any cistern cannot enter another. The location of the cistern overflowing must be readily identifiable and the discharge should be in a conspicuous position.

R16.12

Where two or more cisterns have a common warning or overflow pipe it should be installed so that the source of any warning or overflow may be readily identified and shall be so arranged that any overflow from any one cistern cannot discharge into another.

The joining together of two or more warning/overflow pipes from similar type cisterns to form a common warning pipe is acceptable providing the discharge is readily seen and the combined overflow pipe is designed so that the overflow from one cistern cannot discharge into another.

Cold water storage cisterns

G16.13

Cisterns storing water for domestic purposes should be watertight and, where required, be lined or coated with a suitable impermeable material; they shall be provided with warning and overflow connections, as appropriate, which are so constructed and arranged as to exclude insects. They should have a rigid, close fitting and securely fixed cover which is not airtight but which excludes light and insects from the cistern; be made of a material or materials which do not shatter or fragment when broken and which will not contaminate any water which condenses on its underside; and, in the case of a cistern storing more than 1,000 litres of water, be constructed so that the cistern may be inspected and cleansed without it having to be wholly uncovered (see Diagrams G16.13a and G16.13b).

Diagram
G16.13a:
Principal details of cistern for storing water for domestic purposes

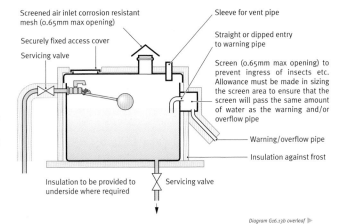

Screened air inlet corrosion resistant mesh (0.65mm max opening)

Securely fixed access cover

Servicing valve

Insulation to be provided to underside where required

Sleeve for vent pipe

Straight or dipped entry to warning pipe

Screen (0.65mm max opening) to prevent ingress of insects etc. Allowance must be made in sizing the screen area to ensure that the screen will pass the same amount of water as the warning and/or overflow pipe

Warning/overflow pipe

Insulation against frost

Servicing valve

Diagram G16.13b overleaf ▶

Guidance

Recommendations

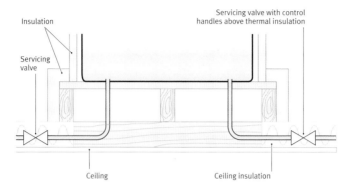

Insulation

Servicing valve with control
handles above thermal insulation

Servicing valve

Ceiling

Ceiling insulation

Diagram
G16.13b:

Details of lower part of cistern for storing water for domestic purposes where the cistern is located in a roof void of a house (Typical for a house where the ceiling thermal insulation is omitted below cistern)

R16.13.1

All cisterns storing water for domestic purposes should be made from or lined with a material which is approved for contact with drinking water (see WRAS Water Fittings & Materials Directory). The requirements of Clause G16.1 for cisterns storing cold water for domestic use can normally be satisfied for housing by the use of single piece storage cisterns and covers conforming to BS 7181. Cisterns manufactured of polyolefin or olefin copolymer conforming to BS 4213 are available up to 500 litres capacity. One piece cisterns manufactured of glass fibre reinforced plastics up to 500 litres are available conforming to BS 7491: Part 1 and larger cisterns in the same material up to 25,000 litres nominal capacity to BS 7491: Part 2. Cisterns and covers from 18 litres up to 3,364 litres capacity are manufactured of galvanised low carbon steel conforming to BS 417: Part 2. For larger capacity cisterns, or where access is limited, sectional steel or glass fibre reinforced plastics cisterns are available.

Reinforced concrete cisterns or reservoirs, buried or partly sunk in the ground, are acceptable when they conform with Clause G16.1 and have been designed, constructed and tested in accordance with BS 8007: Code of practice for the design of concrete structures for retaining aqueous liquids.

R16.13.2

All cisterns for storing cold water for domestic purposes should be constructed to conform with the requirements of Clause G16.13 (see also Section 4: Clause G8.6).

They will generally be accepted when they:

a. are placed wholly above ground level, preferably on a well drained site, not liable to flooding, such that the cistern base is not less than 600mm above the highest known flood level (see Section 4: Clause G8.6): or

b. They are located in a watertight basement below ground level with facilities for the disposal of water if the cistern is emptied for maintenance.

R16.13.3
To restrict microbiological growth it is important that stored wholesome water should be kept at as low a temperature as practicable, ideally less than 20°C. Insulation should be provided against heat gain and/or from frost depending on the ambient conditions and the following procedures are recommended.

a. Where cisterns are sited in locations where a high ambient temperature could occur the cisterns should be adequately insulated and the capacity of the cistern restricted to a minimum essential capacity so that the throughput of water is maximised. In hotels, hospitals, medical centres, etc. and in large commercial and industrial type buildings consideration should be given to providing cooling facilities to ensure that stored drinking water remains wholesome. Specialist advice and contractors should be sought when cooling equipment is to be installed.

b. Immersion heaters may exceptionally be provided in cold water storage cisterns that are located in frost vulnerable locations, where the heat is provided solely to prevent freezing of water in the cistern. The heaters should be automatically controlled and it is suggested that they cut-in when the temperature of the water in the cistern is reduced to 1°C and cut-out at 5°C. It is also preferable that the system be fitted with a visual indicator to operate when the heaters are in operation.

R16.13.4
In the case of the cistern element of a hot water storage combination unit the temperature is permitted in BS 3198 to rise to not more than 39°C. Such a cistern would be accepted as meeting the requirements providing that:

a. the unit only supplies hot water for domestic purposes; and
b. the cistern is incorporated as an integral part of the unit; and
c. no water is drawn from it except to the hot water storage vessel; and
d. it is effectively insulated against frost; and
e. in all other respects it meets with the requirements of Clause G16.13.

R16.13.5
Feed and expansion cisterns serving primary circuits should conform generally with Clause G16.13 but do not need to fulfil all the requirements for the cover or for the warning/overflow pipe to have a screen.

Cold water services

G16.14

Every cistern should be adequately supported to avoid distortion or damage and only installed in a place or position where the inside may be readily inspected and cleansed, and any float operated valve or other controls may be readily installed, repaired, renewed or adjusted. The cistern should have a minimum unobstructed space above of not less than 350mm (see Diagrams G16.14a, G16.14b and G16.14c).

Diagram
G16.14a:

Minimum unobstructed space for conventionally shaped cistern of 1,000 litres actual capacity or less

Diagram
G16.14b:

Minimum unobstructed space for a cistern with a bolted-on lid for cisterns greater than 1,000 litres actual capacity

Diagram
G16.14c:

Minimum unobstructed space for hot water combination units

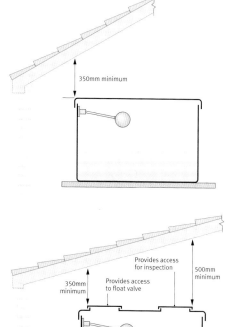

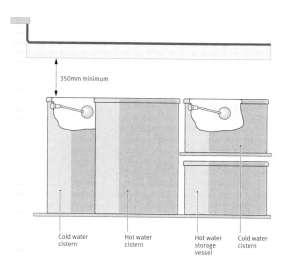

Guidance

Recommendations

R16.14

Where a cistern is made of rigid materials, for example, galvanised steel, it can be placed directly on support beams spaced at not more than 350mm centres.

The requirements would be deemed to be satisfied if a storage cistern made of plastics, fibreglass, etc. is supported on close boarded timber laid on support beams (see Diagram R16.14).

Diagram
R16.14:

Example of close boarded support to plastics cistern

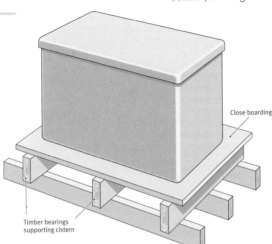

Close boarding

Timber bearings
supporting cistern

G16.15

Where the required capacity of water is provided by the use of two or more cisterns, the inlets and the outlets of the cisterns should be located so that water passes through the whole of the cisterns and short-circuiting does not occur.

R16.15

Where two or more cisterns are used to provide the storage capacity required the cisterns should be connected in parallel and, to avoid stagnation, the float operated valves adjusted so that they all operate to the same maximum water level. The cisterns should be connected in such a manner that there is an equal flow of water through each cistern and also so that any of the cisterns may be drained for maintenance while still maintaining water supplies from the remainder of the cisterns.

Schedule 2
Section 8:
Paragraphs 17, 18, 19, 20, 21, 22, 23 & 24:
Hot water services

Notes

Schedule 2

17.

(1) Every unvented water heater, not being an instantaneous water heater with a capacity not greater than 15 litres, and every secondary coil contained in a primary system shall –

  (a) be fitted with a temperature control device and either a temperature relief valve or a combined temperature and pressure relief valve; or

  (b) be capable of accommodating expansion within the secondary hot water system.

(2) An expansion valve shall be fitted with provision to ensure that water is discharged in a correct manner in the event of a malfunction of the expansion vessel or system.

18.

Appropriate vent pipes, temperature control devices and combined temperature pressure and relief valves shall be provided to prevent the temperature of the water within a secondary hot water system from exceeding 100°C.

19.

Discharges from temperature relief valves, combined temperature pressure and relief valves and expansion valves shall be made in a safe and conspicuous manner.

20.

(1) No vent pipe from a primary circuit shall terminate over a storage cistern containing wholesome water for domestic supply or for supplying water to a secondary system.

(2) No vent pipe from a secondary circuit shall terminate over any combined feed and expansion cistern connection to a primary circuit.

21.

Every expansion cistern or expansion vessel, and every cold water combined feed and expansion cistern connected to a primary circuit, shall be such as to accommodate any expansion water from that circuit during normal operation.

22.

(1) Every expansion valve, temperature relief valve or combined temperature and pressure relief valve connected to any fitting or appliance shall close automatically after a discharge of water.

(2) Every expansion valve shall –

  (a) be fitted on the supply pipe close to the hot water vessel and without any intervening valves; and

  (b) only discharge water when subjected to a water pressure of not less than 0.5 bar (50 kPa) above the pressure to which the hot water vessel is, or is likely to be, subjected in normal operation.

23.

(1) A temperature relief valve or combined temperature and pressure relief valve shall be provided on every unvented hot water storage vessel with a capacity greater than 15 litres.

(2) The valve shall –

  (a) be located directly on the vessel in an appropriate location, and have a sufficient discharge capacity, to ensure that the temperature of the stored water does not exceed 100°C; and

  (b) only discharge water at below its operating temperature when subjected to a pressure of not less than 0.5 bar (50 kPa) in excess of the greater of the following –

    (i) the maximum working pressure in the vessel in which it is fitted, or

    (ii) the operating pressure of the expansion valve.

(3) In this paragraph 'unvented hot water storage vessel' means a hot water storage vessel that does not have a vent pipe to the atmosphere.

24.

No supply pipe or secondary circuit shall be permanently connected to a closed circuit for filling a heating system unless it incorporates a backflow prevention device in accordance with a specification approved by the regulator for the purposes of this Schedule.

Unvented hot water systems

G17.1

Every unvented water heater or storage vessel, and every secondary coil contained in a heater and not being an instantaneous water heater or a thermal storage unit of 15 litres or less capacity, should be fitted with:

a. a temperature control device; and

b. either a temperature relief valve or combined temperature and pressure relief valve; and

c. an expansion valve; and

d. unless the expanded water is returned to the supply pipe in accordance with Schedule 2: Paragraph 15(2)(a), either;

   (i) an expansion vessel; or

   (ii) contain an integral expansion system,

such that the expansion water is contained within the secondary system to prevent waste of water.

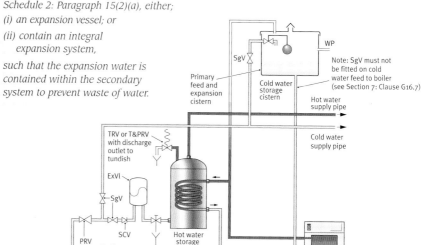

Diagram
G17.1a:

Unvented hot water storage system of capacity greater than 15 litres with vented primary circuit

Diagram
G17.1b:

Unvented hot water storage system of capacity greater than 15 litres with sealed primary circuit

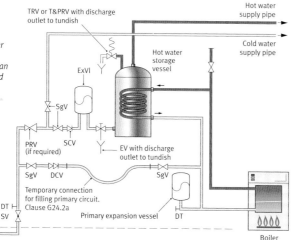

Recommendations

R17.1.1
In addition to the items listed in Clauses G17.1a to G17.1d, the Building Regulations require an unvented hot water storage system to have a non-self re-setting thermal cut-out.

a. DIRECTLY HEATED SYSTEMS
A directly heated unit should have a minimum of two temperature activated safety devices operating in sequence, namely:

A non self re-setting thermal cut-out; and

(i) one or more temperature relief valves; or

(ii) other safety devices providing at least an equivalent degree of safety in preventing the temperature of stored water exceeding 100°C at any time.

These are additional to any thermostatic control that is fitted to maintain the temperature of the stored water.

b. INDIRECTLY HEATED SYSTEMS
Indirectly heated units require safety devices as for directly heated units but the non self re-setting thermal cut-out should be wired to a motorised valve or some other suitable device to shut off the flow to the primary heater.

Where an indirectly heated unit has any alternative direct method of water heating fitted, a non self re-setting thermal cut-out will also be needed on the direct source(s). An illustration of an unvented hot water system with the appropriate primary controls is shown in Diagram R17.1.1a.

Further information is contained in 'The Building Regulations 1991 Approved Document G – Hygiene', published by HMSO.

Diagram
R17.1.1a:

Illustration of unvented hot water storage and heating system, showing arrangement of controls on primary circulation

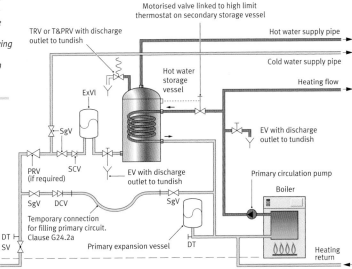

c. INDEPENDENT WATER HEATERS

It should be noted that Clauses G17.1a to G17.1d do not apply to independent water heaters, combination boilers or thermal storage units, unless the capacity exceeds 15 litres.

Where these units incorporate a primary thermal store exceeding 15 litres storage capacity, the system shall be provided with the safety devices required for directly heated systems in Clause R17.1.1a above. A typical arrangement for an electrically heated primary thermal store is illustrated in Diagram R17.1.1b.

Diagram
R17.1.1b:

Illustration of typical arrangement of thermal store exceeding 15 litres storage capacity

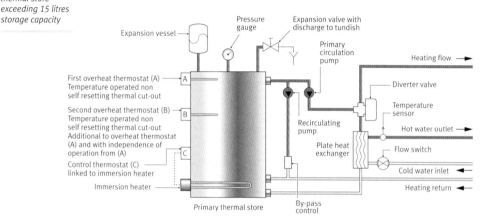

R17.1.2

Diagram G17.1a shows a typical unvented hot water system where the primary circuit is vented; the primary circuit being automatically maintained with water from a feed cistern. Diagram G17.1b illustrates an unvented system where the primary circuit is sealed and requires regular maintenance to ensure that the primary circuit is always filled with water at the recommended pressure. In both these cases the hot water in the secondary part of the system expands on heating, into the expansion vessel.

R17.1.3

Alternative methods of accommodating expansion water in unvented hot water secondary systems are:

Diagram
R17.1.3a:

Unvented hot water storage system with integral expansion system (bubble top)

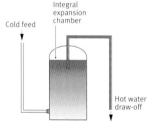

a. BY MEANS OF INTEGRAL STORAGE OF EXPANSION WATER

In this case an airspace is maintained in the top of the hot water storage system where expanded water can be accommodated; this is often known as the 'bubble top' method. With this system there should be minimal operational waste of water. An illustration of the system is shown in Diagram R17.1.3a.

b. BY MEANS OF EXPANDED WATER BEING ACCOMMODATED IN THE SUPPLY PIPE

This system is permitted under Section 6: Paragraph 15 whereby the expanded water is allowed to expand back into the supply pipe; in this case the single check valve on the cold water inlet to the hot water storage vessel and the expansion vessel is omitted. See Diagram R17.1.3b for details. With this system it is essential that none of the expanded water can enter the supply pipe and be drawn off as drinking water; therefore the final length of the branch supply pipe should be of sufficient length and diameter such that it can accommodate all the expansion water and prevent the temperature of the water in the supply pipe from rising above the statutory limit of 25°C or preferably, the recommended limit of 20°C.

Diagram
R17.1.3b:

Unvented hot water storage system where water is allowed to expand into the supply pipe

Servicing valve with fixed washer plate

Pipe sized so capacity can accommodate expansion water

Supply pipe

Hot water draw-off

Cold water draw-off

G17.2

An expansion valve should be fitted to all unvented hot water storage systems, with a capacity in excess of 15 litres, to ensure that expansion water is discharged in a correct manner in the event of a malfunction of the expansion vessel or system (see Diagrams G17.1a and G17.1b).

R17.2

Where, due to unsatisfactory maintenance or other unusual occurrences, a malfunction of the expansion vessel occurs or the bubble is lost, expansion water is allowed to escape to waste through an expansion valve (see Clause R22.2). Any such discharge should be visible at a tundish and is an indication that the containment means is not functioning correctly.

G17.3

Where expansion water is accommodated separately the expansion vessel should preferably be of an approved 'flow through type' and should comply with the requirements of BS 6144 and BS 6920.

R17.3

When water is heated from 4°C to 100°C it expands in volume by approximately 4% of its initial volume; it is therefore usual to provide an expansion capacity of 4% of the volume of the hot water storage system.

Where expansion vessels are used to accommodate expansion water on unvented hot water storage systems the expansion vessels consist of a pressure vessel in which there is a bag type membrane; expanded water entering the membrane bag expands the bag against an air or inert gas cushion. This principle is shown in Diagram R17.3.

The vessel must be sized correctly to ensure that it is capable of accepting at least 4% of the total system's water content in order to prevent unacceptably high pressures arising within the system. In all cases careful note should be taken of the manufacturer's installation instructions when installing these vessels.

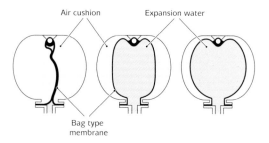

Diagram
R17.3:

Principle of operation of single entry air or gas loaded expansion vessels

Some doubts have been expressed about the desirability of using single entry expansion vessels on hot water systems. The use of single entry expansion vessels effectively forms a vertical dead-leg through which there is no flow of water and concern has been expressed about the possibility of bacterial growth within the vessel. It is considered preferable therefore, that an expansion vessel with both inlet and outlet connections should be installed, wherever practicable, so that the water content of the vessel is constantly changed.

Temperature of hot water within a storage system

G18.1

Irrespective of the type of fuel used for heating, the temperature of the water at any point within a hot water storage system should not exceed 100°C and appropriate vent pipes, temperature control devices and other safety devices should be provided to prevent this occurring.

R18.1

The limitation that the temperature of water within a hot water system should not exceed 100°C at any point in the system applies to all instantaneous, vented or unvented hot water systems. Methods of achieving the limitation in water temperature are described in other parts of this Section.

Hot water distribution temperatures

G18.2
Hot water should be stored at a temperature of not less than 60°C and distributed at a temperature of not less than 55°C. This water distribution temperature may not be achievable where hot water is provided by instantaneous or combination boilers.

R18.2
While a distribution temperature in excess of 50°C may be desirable to prevent microbial growth, it could be physically dangerous, as above 50°C there is a danger of scalding; the degree of risk depending on temperature and the time of contact. At 50°C the risk to most people is likely to be negligible. However, the risk, particularly to young children, the very old, and to those with sensory loss, will be greater, in which case slightly lower temperatures would be advisable.

G18.3
The maintenance of acceptable water temperatures may be achieved by efficient routing of pipes, reducing the lengths of pipes serving individual appliances and the application of good insulation practices to minimise freezing of cold water pipes and to promote energy conservation for hot water pipes. For references, see Comments and Recommendations of Clause 2.6.4 of BS 6700: 1997.

Temperature of hot water supplies at terminal fittings and on surfaces of hot water pipes

G18.4
Where practicable the hot water distribution system should be designed and installed to provide the required flow of water at terminal fittings to sanitary and other appliances at a water temperature of not less than 50°C and within 30 seconds after fully opening the tap. This criteria may not be achievable where hot water is provided by instantaneous or combination boilers.

R18.4
In hot water storage systems, the requirement of a minimum temperature of water after a stated time after opening a tap, can often be achieved by careful design and, in larger installations, the use of a secondary circulation. However, where hot water is supplied from instantaneous heaters or combination boilers, and the temperature of the water discharged is inversely proportional to the flow rate, difficulty may be experienced in achieving the suggested criteria (see Table G18.7).

G18.5
Terminal fittings or communal showers in schools or public buildings, and in other facilities used by the public, should be supplied with water through thermostatic mixing valves so that the temperature of the water discharged at the outlets does not exceed 43°C.

R18.5
Non-thermostatically operated/manually set cold and hot water mixers continue to be available, but for reasons of safety, thermostatically controlled cold and hot water mixers should be used in all installations, whether domestic or public. This is particularly relevant where children in schools or aged or disabled people are using showers in public buildings and are unsupervised.

G18.6

The temperature of water discharged from terminal fittings and the surface temperature of any fittings in health care premises should not exceed the temperatures recommended in HS(G)104 – Safe hot water and surface temperatures.

Energy conservation

G18.7

All water fittings forming part of a primary or secondary hot water circulation system and all pipes carrying hot water to a tap that are longer than the maximum length given in Table G18.7 should be thermally insulated in accordance with BS 5422.

R18.7

Where the location of hot water outlets within a building require long lengths of pipe (dead-legs) to serve them, heat energy is lost in running water to waste until the water discharged at the outlet is at a suitable temperature. It is recommended that the length of dead-legs should be as short as possible, not more than those shown in Table G18.7, and all hot water pipes including those forming part of any secondary circulation system, should be thermally insulated.

Table G18.7: *Maximum recommended lengths of uninsulated hot water pipes*

OUTSIDE DIAMETER OF PIPE IN MILLIMETRES	MAXIMUM LENGTH IN METRES
12	**20**
Over 12 and up to and including 22	**12**
Over 22 and up to and including 28	**8**
Over 28	**3**

Equivalent of Table 8.1 in DETR guidance document

Discharge pipes from safety devices

G19.1

Discharge pipes from expansion valves, temperature relief valves and combined temperature and pressure relief valves should be installed in accordance with the guidance given in this document and should also comply with the requirements of Building Regulation G3.

R19.1

Apart from the requirements of the Regulations for any hot water installation, other legislation concerning the installation of unvented hot water storage systems with a capacity in excess of 15 litres is referred to in the Building Regulations. These are administered by the local Building Control Officer to whom application to install these systems should be made.

Discharge pipes from expansion valves, temperature relief valves and combined temperature and pressure relief valves should not be connected directly to a drain. In all cases the discharge should pass through a visible tundish, with a AUK3 air gap, and be located adjacent to the device.

The diameter of the discharge pipe from safety devices must be at least the diameter of the outlet of the device. The diameter of the discharge pipe from the tundish should be at least one size larger than the outlet of the safety device and may need to be increased in diameter depending on its total length (see Clause G19.3).

Guidance

Recommendations

G19.2

Where discharge pipes pass through environments outside the thermal envelope of the building they should be thermally insulated against the effects of frost.

R19.2

It is important that discharge pipes have no restriction in their cross-sectional area.

G19.3

The discharge pipe from a temperature relief valve or combined temperature and pressure relief valve should:

a. *be through a readily visible air gap discharging over a tundish located in the same room or internal space and vertically as near as possible and in any case within 500mm of the point of outlet of the valve; and*

b. *be of non-ferrous material, such as copper or stainless steel, capable of withstanding any temperatures arising from a malfunction of the system; and*

c. *have a vertical drop of 300mm below the tundish outlet, and thereafter be laid to a self draining gradient; and*

d. *be at least one size larger than the nominal outlet size of the valve, unless its total equivalent hydraulic resistance exceeds that of a straight pipe 9 metres long. Where the total length of the pipe exceeds 9 metres equivalent resistance,*

R19.3

Depending on the water pressure within a hot water storage vessel the temperature of water or steam discharged from safety devices such as temperature relief valves and combined temperature and pressure relief valves on default will generally be approaching, or at least 100°C. It is therefore imperative that the terminal point of the discharge pipe is located where a sudden discharge cannot cause injury. It should also be noted that as the discharge will consist of scalding water and steam, materials such as asphalt, roofing felt and non-metallic rainwater gutters and rainwater pipes may be damaged by such discharges.

Examples of acceptable discharge arrangements are:

a. Ideally below a fixed grating and above the water seal in a trapped gully.

b. Downward discharges at low level; that is, not more than 100mm above external surfaces such as car parks, hard standings, grassed areas etc are acceptable providing that where children may play or otherwise come into contact with discharges a wire cage or similar guard is positioned to prevent contact. The point of discharge must be visible.

c. Discharges at high level: for example, into a metal hopper and metal down pipe with the end of the discharge pipe clearly visible or onto a roof capable of withstanding high temperature discharges of water at least 3m from any plastics guttering system that would collect such discharges (tundish visible).

d. Where a single pipe serves a number of discharge pipes, such as in blocks of flats, the number served should be limited to not more than six systems so that any installation discharging can be traced. The single common discharge pipe from the tundishes should be at least one pipe size larger than the largest individual discharge pipe to be connected.

G u i d a n c e

R e c o m m e n d a t i o n s

the pipe shall be increased in size by one nominal diameter for each additional, or part of, equivalent 9 metres resistance length. The flow resistance of bends in the pipe should be taken into consideration when determining the equivalent length of pipe; and

(Note: Alternatively, the size of the discharge pipe may be determined in accordance with Annex D of BS 6700: 1997.)

e. *terminate in a safe place where there is no risk to persons in the vicinity of the point of discharge (see Building Regulation G3).*

e. If unvented hot water storage systems are installed where discharges from safety devices may not be apparent, that is, in dwellings occupied by blind, infirm or disabled people, consideration should be given to the installation of an electronically operated device to warn occupants when discharge takes place.

A typical discharge pipe arrangement is shown in Diagram R19.3.

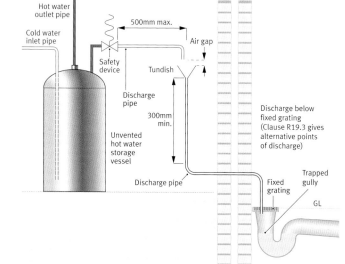

Diagram
R19.3:

Typical discharge pipe arrangement

Guidance   **R**ecommendations

Discharge pipes from expansion valves

G19.4

The discharge pipe from an expansion valve may discharge into the tundish used for the discharge from a temperature relief valve or from a combined temperature and pressure relief valve as described in G19.3, or:

a. *discharge through a readily visible air gap over a tundish located in the same room or internal space and vertically as near as possible and in any case within 500mm of the point of outlet of the valve; and*

b. *be of non-ferrous material, such as copper or stainless steel; and*

c. *discharge from the tundish through a vertical drop outlet and thereafter be laid to a self draining gradient; and*

d. *not be less than the nominal outlet size of the expansion valve and discharge external to the building at a safe and visible location.*

R19 .4

The discharge from expansion valves will normally be at a much lower temperature and a much lower rate of flow than that from discharge pipes serving safety devices considered in G19.3 and therefore the safety risk is less than the higher temperature discharges from safety devices.

Vent pipes

G20.1

Vent pipes from primary hot water circuits and vent pipes from secondary hot water storage systems should be of adequate size, but not less than 19mm internal diameter. They may terminate over their respective cold water feed and expansion cisterns or storage cisterns (or elsewhere) providing there is a physical air gap, at least equivalent to the size of the vent pipe, above the top of the warning pipe, or overflow if there is one (or above any point of obstruction if elsewhere), at the point of termination.

R20.1

Diagram R20.1 shows the recommended dimension for an air gap at the termination point of a vent pipe, from a primary or secondary hot water system, above the level of the top of the float operated valve, in a storage or feed and expansion cistern. This is greater than the minimum dimension suggested in the Guidance, to provide additional protection of the air gap between the discharge point of the vent pipe and the maximum water level.

Diagram
R20.1:
Air gap at vent pipe termination over a cistern

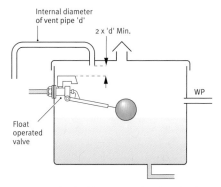

Vent pipe should terminate not less than twice the internal diameter of the vent pipe above the level of the top of the float operated valve

Hot water services

G u i d a n c e R e c o m m e n d a t i o n s

G20.2
Vent pipes from hot water secondary storage systems should be of adequate size but not less than 19mm internal diameter and should be insulated against freezing.

G20.3
Where vent pipes, from either a primary or secondary system, terminate over their respective cold water feed cisterns, they should rise to a height above the top water level in the cistern sufficient to prevent any discharge occurring under normal operating conditions. See Diagram G20.3 for determination of minimum height required to prevent discharge.

R20.3
Although vent pipes from both primary and secondary systems may terminate over their respective cisterns there should be no discharge from the vent pipes at any time under normal circumstances, as the water in the system is not permitted to exceed 100°C. Diagram G20.3 shows a method of determining the minimum height of the top of a primary or secondary vent pipe above the top of a warning pipe, or overflow pipe if one is provided, in a cistern.

This method of determining the height of a vent pipe is only applicable where gravity systems of supply and circulation are used. Where circulation pumps are used in primary or secondary systems, due allowance should be made for pressure variations within the system. The pressure variations will depend on the location of the pump within the system, the pressure and capacity of the pump used, together with frictional head losses in the circulation pipes.

Diagram
G20.3:
Determination of minimum height of top of vent pipe

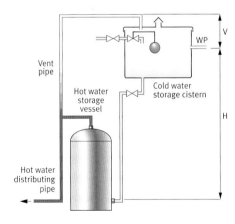

1. Minimum height of top of vent pipe above top of overflow pipe to be determined by V = 0.04H + 0.15 where V and H are in metres.

2. The above minimum height relates to gravity circulation systems. If a circulation pump is installed due allowance should be made for any induced head.

3. The above method can also be used for determination of the height of a vent pipe in a vented primary circuit.

Hot water systems supplied with water from storage cisterns

G20.4

In any cistern-fed vented or unvented hot water storage system the storage vessel should:

a. be capable of accommodating any expansion water; or

b. be connected to a separate expansion cistern or vessel; or

c. be so arranged that expansion water can pass back through a feed pipe to the cold water storage cistern from which the apparatus or cylinder is supplied with water (see Diagrams G20.4a below, and G20.4b overleaf).

Diagram
R20.4.1a:

Illustration of unvented system, with integral secondary expansion capacity, supplied from a cistern

R20.4.1

Diagram R20.4.1a illustrates an unvented hot water system with integral expansion capacity (or 'bubble top') supplied with water from a cold water storage cistern. In this case any expanded secondary water is accommodated in the space below the air/vapour cushion at the top of the storage vessel.

A single check valve is installed in the cold feed pipe to prevent expanded water from passing back into the storage cistern.

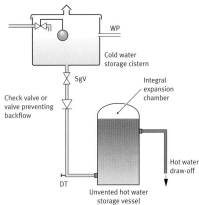

Diagram
G20.4a:

Directly heated and vented hot water storage system

See Clauses G20.6 and G20.7 to determine whether a dedicated storage cistern is required

Cold water storage cistern

Directly heated hot water storage vessel

To drinking water supply over sink

Hot water distributing pipe to sanitary appliances

Stopvalve

Boiler

Hot water services

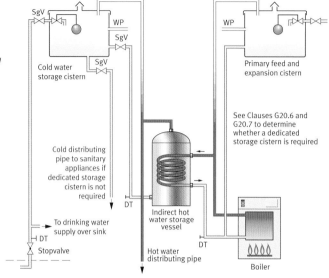

Diagram
G20.4b:

Double feed indirectly heated and vented hot water storage system

SgV
WP
SgV
SgV
Cold water storage cistern

WP

Primary feed and expansion cistern

See Clauses G20.6 and G20.7 to determine whether a dedicated storage cistern is required

Cold distributing pipe to sanitary appliances if dedicated storage cistern is not required

DT
Indirect hot water storage vessel

DT

To drinking water supply over sink

DT
Stopvalve

Hot water distributing pipe

Boiler

Diagram R20.4.1b: illustrates a conventional unvented system with secondary system expansion capacity supplied with water from a cistern.

Although not shown in detail the controls and safety devices required for all these applications would be the same as for any unvented system with a capacity in excess of 15 litres and supplied with water from a supply pipe.

Diagram
R20.4.1b:

Illustration of conventional unvented system with secondary supplied with water from a cistern

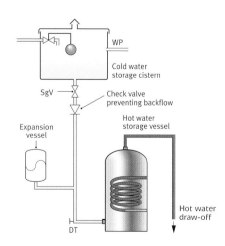

WP

Cold water storage cistern

SgV

Check valve preventing backflow

Expansion vessel

Hot water storage vessel

Hot water draw-off

DT

Recommendations

R20.4.2
Diagrams G20.4a and G20.4b illustrate two alternative vented hot water storage systems, the former being a directly heated system and the latter being an indirectly heated system. In both of these systems expanded water can pass back into the feed pipe as described in Clause G20.4c.

R20.4.3
The directly heated hot water storage system shown in Diagram G20.4a should preferably only be used in soft water areas, that is, where the water supplied by the water undertaker is not subject to the precipitation of hardness scale on heating. If used with hard water the cistern shown in Diagram G20.4a may cause an accumulation of scale in the cylinder resulting in thermal inefficiency and blockage. In hard water areas it is preferable to use a double feed indirectly heated system as shown in Diagram G20.4b.

Another type of hot water storage system referred to as the single feed indirectly heated system is illustrated in Diagram R20.4.3a.

With this system the primary system is fed with water from the secondary system by using a hot water storage vessel incorporating a special primary heat exchanger in which an air pocket separates the secondary hot water from the primary heating water. No corrosion inhibitors or additives are to be used with this system. The operation of a single feed indirect storage vessel is illustrated in Diagram R20.4.3b overleaf.

Diagram
R20.4.3a:

Single feed indirectly heated and vented hot water storage system

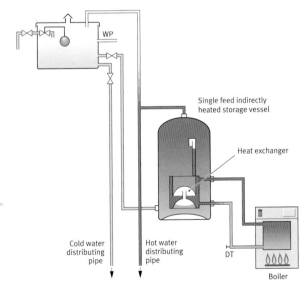

WP

Single feed indirectly heated storage vessel

Heat exchanger

Cold water distributing pipe

Hot water distributing pipe

DT

Boiler

Hot water services

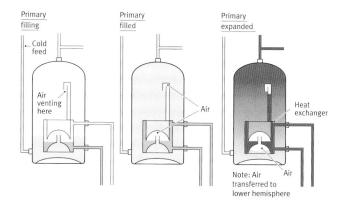

Diagram
R20.4.3b:
Filling sequence of a single feed indirect storage vessel

Primary filling — Cold feed — Air venting here

Primary filled — Air

Primary expanded — Heat exchanger — Note: Air transferred to lower hemisphere — Air

G20.5

Where the cold water storage cistern supplying water to a vented hot water storage vessel is also used to supply wholesome water to sanitary or other appliances, any expansion water entering the cistern through the feed pipe should preferably not raise the temperature of the wholesome water in the cistern to more than 20°C.

R20.5

The need for strict control of water temperatures in storage cisterns is described in detail in Section 4: Clause R9.1 and in Section 10: Clause R27.2, where the reasons for maintaining wholesome water at a temperature of 20°C or less are described.

Vented systems requiring dedicated storage cisterns or mechanical safety devices

G20.6

Every vented and directly heated hot water storage vessel, single feed indirectly heated hot water storage vessel, or any directly or indirectly heated storage vessel where an electrical immersion heater is installed, should be supplied with water from a dedicated storage cistern unless:

a. where the energy source is gas, oil or electricity, a non-self-setting thermal energy cut-out device is provided in addition to the normal temperature-operated automatic-reset cut-out; or

R20.6

In most circumstances the hot water supply system should be fed with water from a dedicated cistern that supplies no other services or appliances. In this case, if boiling does occur and there is a hot water discharge from the vent pipe into the dedicated cistern, it will not affect the temperature or quality of any wholesome water (see Diagram R20.6a).

Schedule 2: Section 8: Paragraph 18 limits the temperature of the water at any point in the system to 100°C; if this temperature is not exceeded in any part of a system there should be no discharge of water from a vent pipe into a cistern. Where a directly heated system is installed the temperature of the system is normally controlled by a thermostat which limits the maximum temperature to a predetermined limit, say 60°C. Two instances need to be considered:

a. Where the energy source is gas, oil or electricity, and there is a failure of the thermostatic control, there is a possibility of the temperature rising to 100°C or above, depending on the pressure within the system. The consequences of this possibility can be overcome by the provision of a non-self-setting thermal energy cut-out device (see Diagram R20.6b option a).

Guidance	Recommendations
b. where the energy source is solid fuel, a temperature relief valve complying with BS 6283: Part 2, or a combined temperature and pressure relief valve complying with BS 6283: Part 3, is provided complete with a readily visible air-break to drain device and discharge pipe as described in G19.3.	b. Where the energy source is solid fuel it is not practicable to provide a sufficiently rapid reaction for shutting down fuel in the event of a sudden rise in water temperature and a temperature relief valve or preferably, a combined temperature and pressure relief valve should be installed to operate in the event of high water temperatures occurring. The relief valve should be self-setting (see Diagram R20.6b option b).

Diagram
R20.6a:

Vented direct or indirect hot water storage system supplied with water from a dedicated storage cistern

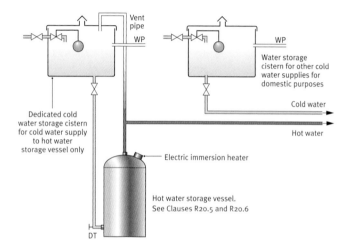

Diagram
R20.6b:

Vented direct or indirect hot water storage system with non-self-setting thermal cut out device

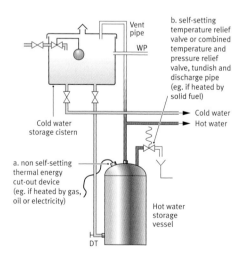

G20.7

Every double feed indirectly heated hot water storage system which is heated by a sealed (unvented) primary circuit, or the primary circuit heating medium is steam or high temperature hot water, or where an electric immersion heater is installed, should:

a. be supplied with water for the secondary circuit from a dedicated cold water storage cistern; or

b. be provided with a non-self-setting thermal energy cut-out device to control the primary circuit, and any electric immersion heaters, in addition to any temperature-operated automatic-reset cut-out.

R20.7

Where the temperature of the medium in the sealed primary (unvented) side of an indirect system is derived from steam or high temperature hot water where the temperature is in excess of 100°C, or where a fault occurs with the thermostat of an immersion heater, there is a danger of the water in the secondary side of the installation being raised above the maximum permitted temperature of 100°C. Therefore, a dedicated cistern supplying water to the secondary system should be provided which should not supply any other services or appliances (see Diagram R20.6a).

Alternatively, the system should be provided with a non-self-setting thermal cut-out device to control the primary circuit energy source and any immersion heaters, in addition to any temperature-operated automatic reset cut-outs (see Diagram R20.6b).

G20.8

No water in the primary circuit of a double feed indirect hot water storage vessel should connect hydraulically to any part of a hot water secondary storage system.

G20.9

Vent pipes from primary circuits should not terminate over cold water storage cisterns containing wholesome water for supply to sanitary appliances or secondary hot water systems.

G20.10

Vent pipes from secondary hot water systems should not terminate over feed and expansion cisterns supplying water to primary circuits.

G20.11

No water in the primary circuit of a single feed indirect hot water storage vessel, under normal operating conditions, should mix with water in the secondary circuit. Single feed indirect hot water storage vessels should be installed with a permanent vent to the atmosphere.

G u i d a n c e   **R e c o m m e n d a t i o n s**

Primary feed and expansion cisterns

G21.1

Every expansion cistern, and every cold water combined feed and expansion cistern connected to a primary or heating circuit should be capable of accommodating any expansion water from the circuit and installed so that the water level is not less than 25mm below the overflowing level of the warning pipe when the primary or heating circuit is in use (see Diagram G21.1).

R21.1

In a cistern fed system, expansion water in the primary circuit returns through the feed pipe into the feed and expansion cistern. The volume is approximately 4% of the total volume of water in the primary circuit. To avoid overflow the cistern capacity and the setting of the float valve must be designed to accommodate this volume. This is done by setting the level of water in the cistern when the system is cold, and the water level sufficiently low so that when the system heats up the water rises to a point not higher than 25mm below the warning pipe (see Diagram G21.1). Note, the volume of water in the cistern when the system is cold is not prescribed but it must be sufficient to permit the satisfactory operation of the float operated valve.

Vent pipe shall terminate not less than twice the internal diameter of the vent pipe above the top of the float operated valve 'a' or top of the overflow pipe 'b' whichever is the higher. (See G21.1)

Diagram
G21.1:

Details of relative water levels in feed and expansion cisterns to primary circuits

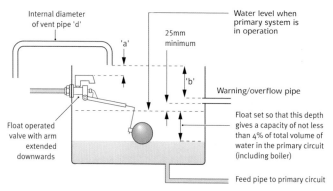

Internal diameter of vent pipe 'd'

25mm minimum

'a'

Water level when primary system is in operation

'b'

Warning/overflow pipe

Float operated valve with arm extended downwards

Float set so that this depth gives a capacity of not less than 4% of total volume of water in the primary circuit (including boiler)

Feed pipe to primary circuit

Expansion and safety devices

G22.1

Expansion valves, temperature relief valves or combined temperature and pressure relief valves connected to any fitting or appliance should close automatically after an operational discharge of water and be watertight when closed.

R22.1

Because pressures in the water undertaker's mains can vary considerably and are usually higher at night, care should be taken in selecting expansion and safety devices, ensuring that they are appropriate at all conditions of mains pressure. If in doubt, the Water Undertaker should be consulted as it may be necessary to install a pressure reducing valve. Expansion valves and safety devices should be marked clearly with their maximum pressure ratings and should be capable of withstanding 1.5 times the maximum pressures to which they are likely to be subjected.

Guidance   **R**ecommendations

G22.2
Expansion valves should comply with BS 6283: Part 1. They should be fitted on the supply pipe close to the hot water vessel and without any intervening valves, and only discharge water when subjected to a water pressure of not less than 0.5 bar (50 kPa) above the pressure to which the hot water vessel is, or is likely to be, subjected to in normal operation.

R22.2
Under normal conditions of operation, expansion of water on heating up is referred to in Guidance Clause G17.1 and under those circumstances no discharge should take place from expansion valves. Only under malfunction conditions of the means of accommodating expansion water should an expansion valve operate and discharge water. An illustration of an expansion valve is shown in Diagram R22.2 and details of discharge pipes from expansion valves are described in Clause G19.4.

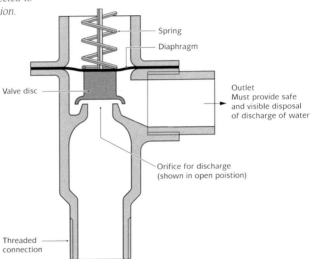

Spring

Diaphragm

Valve disc

Outlet
Must provide safe and visible disposal of discharge of water

Diagram
R22.2:
Illustration of typical expansion valve

Orifice for discharge (shown in open poistion)

Threaded connection

Temperature and combined temperature and pressure relief valves

G23.1
Except for unvented hot water storage vessels of a capacity of 15 litres or less, a temperature relief valve complying with BS 6283: Part 2, or a combined temperature and pressure relief valve complying with BS 6283: Part 3, should be provided on every unvented hot

R23.1
Temperature relief valves or combined temperature and pressure relief valves should only discharge water at the temperature, and pressure where applicable, determined in accordance with Guidance Clause G23.1. For details of discharge pipes and their termination see Clauses G19.1, G19.2 and G19.3.

The recommendation in Clause G23.1 is that the temperature of the water does not exceed 100°C. To provide a reasonable margin below this

*water storage vessel.
The valve should:*

a. be located directly on the storage vessel, such that the temperature of the stored water does not exceed 100°C; and

b. only discharge water at below its operating temperature when subjected to a pressure not less than 0.5 bar (50 kPa) greater than the maximum working pressure in the vessel to which it is fitted, or 0.5 bar (50 kPa) greater than the operating pressure of the expansion valve, whichever is the greater.

temperature, and except where the valve is provided in accordance with Clause G23.2, it is suggested that any temperature relief valve or combined temperature and pressure relief valve, whether self-setting or non-self-setting, should operate at a temperature not exceeding 95°C.

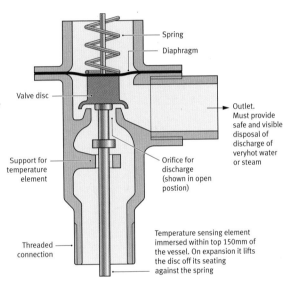

Diagram
R23.1:
Illustration of typical temperature relief valve

Labels for diagram:
- Spring
- Diaphragm
- Valve disc
- Outlet. Must provide safe and visible disposal of discharge of veryhot water or steam
- Support for temperature element
- Orifice for discharge (shown in open postion)
- Threaded connection
- Temperature sensing element immersed within top 150mm of the vessel. On expansion it lifts the disc off its seating against the spring

Non-mechanical safety devices

G23.2
If a non-mechanical safety device such as a fusible plug is fitted to any hot water storage vessel, that vessel requires a temperature relief valve or combined temperature and pressure relief valve designed to operate at a temperature not less than 5°C below that at which the non-mechanical device operates or is designed to operate.

R23.2
Non-mechanical safety devices such as fusible plugs have sometimes been installed in the past in directly heated hot water systems to prevent the system being subjected to boiling caused by a malfunction of the energy control. The problem is that when the fusible plug operates it discharges water and/or steam, depending on the temperature and pressure of the water at the moment of operation. To avoid a dangerous health and safety situation, Guidance Clause G23.2 requires a temperature relief valve or a combined temperature and pressure relief valve to be fitted which will operate at a temperature of not less than 5°C below that at which the non-mechanical safety device is designed to operate. In this situation the non-mechanical safety device would never operate unless the relief valve failed and the overall effectiveness and benefits derived from installing the non-mechanical device need to be considered.

Hot water services

Guidance   **R**ecommendations

Filling of closed circuits

G24.1

No primary or other closed circuit should be directly and permanently connected to a supply pipe unless it incorporates an approved backflow prevention arrangement.

G24.2

A connection may be made to a supply pipe for filling or replenishing a closed circuit by providing a servicing valve and an appropriate backflow prevention device, the type of which will depend on the degree of risk arising from the category of fluid contained within the closed circuit, providing that the connection between the backflow prevention device and the closed circuit is made by:

a. a temporary connecting pipe which must be completely disconnected from the outlet of the backflow prevention device and the connection to the primary circuit after completion of the filling or replenishing procedure (Diagram G17.1b shows an acceptable method, of filling a closed circuit, providing that the fluid in the closed circuit is not a greater hazard than fluid category 3); or

b. a device which in addition to the backflow prevention device incorporates an air gap or break in the pipeline which cannot be physically closed while the primary circuit is functioning; or

c. an approved backflow prevention arrangement.

R24.1

Primary and other closed circuits have to be initially filled with water and may require additional 'topping-up' at intervals during use. Primary circuits may contain additives and the water can be heavily contaminated, therefore they are not to be permanently connected to any supply pipe without an adequate backflow prevention device.

R24.2

Where a connection is made to a supply pipe, or a distributing pipe in some instances, for supplying water for filling or replenishing water in a closed circuit, such as a hot water primary circuit and/or a space heating system, it is essential that:

a. there is no backflow of water, at any time, from the primary circuit into the water supply; and

b. the water supply is disconnected, or vented to atmosphere during the periods between filling and subsequent replenishing of the water in the primary circuit.

Under normal operating conditions, the pressure in a primary heating circuit is less than in the pipe supplying water to the circuit. However, in the event of a malfunction of an expansion valve or pressure relief valve in the primary circuit, pressure may rise above the pressure in the supply pipe. In such an instance, a mechanical backflow prevention device could be damaged and cease to function. If there is no discontinuity or venting to atmosphere and, as frequently happens, the valve controlling the water supply has been left in the open position, fluid from the primary circuit may return to the supply pipe.

It is therefore essential that when the filling or the replenishing of a primary circuit is completed, there shall be a discontinuity at the point of connection, or the type of backflow prevention device installed shall be of a type that allows any fluid resulting from excess pressure in the primary circuit to discharge to waste.

The type of backflow prevention device required should be suitable for a fluid Category 3 risk in the case of a house or for fluid category 4 risk for installations in premises other than a house (see examples in Section 6.1: Tables G6.1c and G6.1d). It is however essential that there is a discontinuity in the connecting pipework or a backflow prevention arrangement is used in which any fluid resulting from backflow from the primary circuit is discharged to waste.

To avoid control valves being tampered with and left in an open position it is recommended that all control valves used in connection with filling loops should be lockshield type valves with a loose key.

A satisfactory method of filling or replenishing a primary circuit in a house is described in Clause G24.2a and Diagram R24.2a, where the temporary connecting pipe is completely disconnected after filling or replenishment.

Recommendations

Another method that is considered acceptable for a fluid category 3 risk in a house and satisfies Clause G24.2b is the installation of a Type CA: 'Non-verifiable disconnector with different pressure zones' backflow prevention device (see Diagram R24.2b).

In other than a house, where backflow protection against a fluid category 4 risk is required, a Type BA: 'Verifiable backflow preventer with reduced pressure zone' backflow preventer (RPZ valve), with a strainer on the inlet, could be used (see Diagram R24.2c).

Unless using an approved backflow prevention device which is permitted to operate continuously, methods of supplying feed water to a closed circuit are to be manually operated and are only to be used when make up water is required.

Diagram
R24.2a:
Approved method for temporary connection for filling a closed circuit in a house

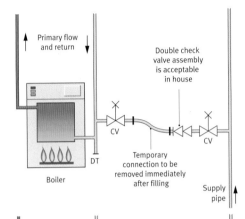

Diagram
R24.2b:
Alternative method of filling and replenishing a closed circuit in a house, using a Type CA backflow prevention device

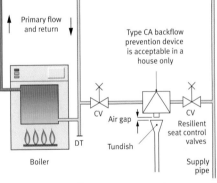

Diagram
R24.2c:
Method of filling a closed circuit in a system installed in other than a house, using a Type BA backflow prevention device

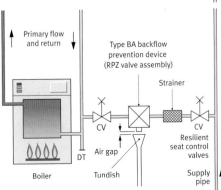

Schedule 2
Section 9:
Paragraph 25:
WCs, flushing devices and urinals

WRAS

Water Regulations Advisory Scheme®

Notes

25.

(1) Subject to the following provisions of this paragraph –

(a) every water closet pan shall be supplied with water from a flushing cistern, pressure flushing cistern or pressure flushing valve, and shall be so made and installed that after normal use its contents can be cleared effectively by a single flush of water, or, where the installation is designed to receive flushes of different volumes, by the largest of those flushes;

(b) no pressure flushing valve shall be installed –

　(i) in a house, or

　(ii) in any building not being a house where a minimum flow rate of 1.2 litres per second cannot be achieved at the appliance;

(c) where a pressure flushing valve is connected to a supply pipe or distributing pipe, the flushing arrangement shall incorporate a backflow prevention device consisting of a permanently vented pipe interrupter located not less than 300mm above the spillover level of the WC pan or urinal;

(d) no flushing device installed for use with a WC pan shall give a single flush exceeding 6 litres;

(e) no flushing device designed to give flushes of different volumes shall have a lesser flush exceeding two-thirds of the largest flush volume;

(f) every flushing cistern, other than a pressure flushing cistern, shall be clearly marked internally with an indelible line to show the intended volume of flush, together with an indication of that volume;

(g) a flushing device designed to give flushes of different volumes –

　(i) shall have a readily discernible method of actuating the flush at different volumes; and

(ii) shall have instructions, clearly and permanently marked on the cistern or displayed nearby, for operating it to obtain the different volumes of flush;

(h) every flushing cistern, not being a pressure flushing cistern or a urinal cistern, shall be fitted with a warning pipe or with a no less effective device;

(i) every urinal that is cleared by water after use shall be supplied with water from a flushing device which –

   (i) in the case of a flushing cistern, is filled at a rate suitable for the installation;

   (ii) in all cases, is designed or adapted to supply no more water than is necessary for effective flow over the internal surface of the urinal and for replacement of the fluid in the trap; and

(j) except in the case of a urinal which is flushed manually, or which is flushed automatically by electronic means after use, every pipe which supplies water to a flushing cistern or trough used for flushing a urinal shall be fitted with an isolating valve controlled by a time switch and a lockable isolating valve, or with some other equally effective automatic device for regulating the periods during which the cistern may fill.

(2) Every water closet, and every flushing device designed for use with a water closet, shall comply with a specification approved by the regulator for the purposes of this Schedule.

(3) The requirements of sub-paragraphs (1) and (2) do not apply where faeces or urine are disposed of through an appliance that does not solely use fluid to remove the contents.

(4) The requirement in sub-paragraph (1)(i) shall be deemed to be satisfied –

(a) in the case of an automatically operated flushing cistern servicing urinals which is filled with water at a rate not exceeding –

   (i) 10 litres per hour for a cistern serving a single urinal;

   (ii) 7.5 litres per hour per urinal bowl or stall, or, as the case may be, for each 700mm width of urinal slab, for a cistern serving two or more urinals;

(b) in the case of a manually or automatically operated pressure flushing valve used for flushing urinals which delivers not more than 1.5 litres per bowl or position each time the device is operated.

(5) Until 1 January 2001 paragraphs (1)(a) and (d) shall have effect as if they provided as follows –

(a) 'every water closet pan shall be supplied with water from a flushing cistern or trough of the valveless type which incorporates siphonic apparatus;'

(d) 'no flushing device installed for use with a WC pan shall give a single flush exceeding 7.5 litres'.

(6) Notwithstanding sub-paragraph (1)(d) a flushing cistern installed before 1 July 1999 may be replaced by a cistern which delivers a similar volume and which may be either single flush or dual flush; but a single flush cistern may not be so replaced by a dual flush cistern.

(7) In this paragraph –

'PRESSURE FLUSHING CISTERN' means a WC flushing device that utilises the pressure of water within the cistern supply pipe to compress air and increase the pressure of water available for flushing a WC pan;

'PRESSURE FLUSHING VALVE' means a self-closing valve supplied with water directly from a supply pipe or a distributing pipe which when activated will discharge a pre-determined flush volume;

'TRAP' means a pipe fitting, or part of a sanitary appliance, that retains liquid to prevent the passage of foul air; and

'WARNING PIPE' means an overflow pipe whose outlet is located in a position where the discharge of water can be readily seen.

WCs, flushing devices and urinals

General

G25.1

Every WC pan should be flushed and its contents cleared effectively by a single flush of water or, where alternative volumes of flush water are available, by the largest of the available flushes.

R25.1

The contents of WC pans must be cleared by a single flush of water. Where two different volumes of flush capacity are installed, either may be used if effective. Irrespective of the type of flushing mechanism the contents of the pan should be effectively cleared.

Where dual flush devices are installed, a single lower flush volume should be adequate to clear urine and paper, a single larger flush volume should clear all faeces and paper.

Methods of flushing WC pans

G25.2

Except in a house, or any other building where a minimum flow rate of 1.2 litres per second cannot be achieved at the appliance, a WC pan may be flushed by a manually operated pressure flushing valve directly connected to a supply or distributing pipe, provided that the flushing arrangement incorporates a backflow prevention arrangement or device appropriate to fluid category 5. See Section 6: Schedule 2: Paragraph 15.

R25.2

Pressure flushing valves are not permitted in houses. These valves require a minimum rate of flow of 1.2 litres per second to be available at the WC pan and may be installed in premises, other than houses, where this amount of water for flushing is available at the WC. Many smaller premises have a total flow demand of less than 1.2 litres per second, therefore pressure flushing valves are not permitted for these applications.

Pressure flushing valves may be served with water from either a supply pipe or, in suitable circumstances, a distributing pipe. The outlet of the pressure flushing valve should incorporate, or be provided with, a pipe interrupter with a permanent atmospheric vent; the flushing valve being installed so that the level of the lowest vent aperture is not less than 300mm above the spillover level of the WC pan. Unless a servicing valve is integral with the pressure flushing valve it is recommended that a separate servicing valve be provided on the branch pipe to each pressure flushing valve. A suitable arrangement is shown in Diagram R25.2 opposite.

If manually operated solenoid or equivalent pressure flushing valves are installed the valve must be of the normally closed type or non-latching.

Pressure flushing valves that do not incorporate a permanent vent, or where a pipe interrupter is not installed on the outlet of the valve, are acceptable providing that the pressure flushing valves are supplied with water from a dedicated cistern supplied through a Type AG air gap.

Guidance   **Recommendations**

Diagram
R25.2:
WC with pressure flushing valve

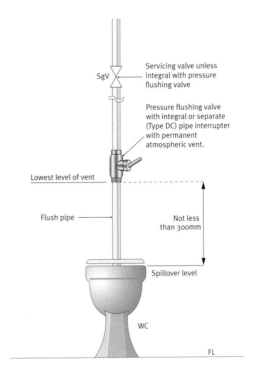

SgV — Servicing valve unless integral with pressure flushing valve

Pressure flushing valve with integral or separate (Type DC) pipe interrupter with permanent atmospheric vent.

Lowest level of vent

Flush pipe

Not less than 300mm

Spillover level

WC

FL

G25.3

Flushing apparatus for use with a WC pan should be designed to deliver a maximum flush volume not exceeding 6 litres and the lesser volume of water for a dual flush apparatus should not exceed two-thirds of the large flush volume.

R25.3

Schedule 2: Section 9: Paragraph 25 (1)(d) requires that any type of flushing device installed from 1 January 2001 must deliver a flush volume of not more that 6 litres to a WC pan. Where a dual flush flushing arrangement is provided, the maximum flush volume for the larger flush must be 6 litres and the lesser flush volume must not exceed two thirds of the larger flush volume. Interruptable flushing devices, which permit the flush to be stopped after a variable volume up to the maximum are not permitted as the lesser flush volume may exceed two thirds of the maximum flush volume.

G25.4

Except in the case of a pressure flushing cistern, a clearly marked line should indicate the water level and the volume of flush.

R25.4

Except for pressure flushing cisterns, WC flushing cisterns must be marked within the cistern with an indelible line to indicate the maximum water level at which the cistern may be flushed and must also show the volume of water that will be flushed at that level.

WCs, flushing devices and urinals

Guidance   *Recommendations*

G25.5

*Every flushing mechanism
designed or adapted to give
flushes of different volumes
should have instructions for
operating and obtaining the
different volumes of flush
clearly and permanently
marked on the cistern, or
displayed near the
flushing mechanism.*

R25.5

Problems have arisen in the past where the operation
of dual flush cisterns has not been fully understood and
repeated flushing at the lower flush volume has not
cleared all the faeces from the WC pan. To avoid
problems in use it is recommended that where any dual
flush devices are used in a building, the dual flush
devices should be installed in all WCs.

Schedule 2: Section 9: Paragraph 25 (g)(i) requires that
a readily discernable method of operating dual flush
cisterns must be provided. Suitable methods may consist
of separate buttons or handles, segmented (one third/two third) buttons, wall
plates with different sized pressure pads, handles which operate one way or
the other, and many other variations.

Schedule 2: Section 9: Paragraph 25 (g)(ii) requires that instructions for
operation are clearly and permanently displayed for all users. It is important
therefore that flushing devices that incorporate dual flushing arrangements
should have instructions for operating the two methods of flush either on the
cistern or displayed nearby. Instructions should be clear, unambiguous and
permanently marked, particularly in public buildings. It is recommended that
dual flush devices be arranged so that they operate the larger flush volume if
the flushing device defaults in operation.

Warning pipes

G25.6

*Except for pressure flushing
cisterns, all WC flushing
cisterns should be provided
with a connection for a
warning pipe, the outlet of
which is to discharge in a
prominent position, or
other equally effective
device.*

R25.6

WC flushing cisterns must be provided with a warning
pipe connection or other no less effective device.

A 'no less effective device' is an alternative to a warning
pipe but which still provides a warning of a failure of the
water inlet valve to a WC cistern.

The Water Supply Industry considers that WCs that have an
internal overflow discharging into the WC pan shall be
deemed to meet the requirement of the Regulations in that
the internal overflow will be regarded as a no less effective
device (in place of a warning pipe). A warning pipe may also discharge directly
into the flush pipe (without a tundish) as this may be considered equivalent to
an internal overflow. These two interpretations are conditional upon measures
to reduce the likelihood of the internal overflow being used. For compact inlet
valves (eg. those manufactured to BS1212: Part 4) the provision of a gauze
strainer incorporated in, or fitted upstream of, the float-operated inlet valve to
trap debris (swarf, etc) which might cause premature failure of the valve, is
required. Manufacturers are to be encouraged to supply, as a unit, the
cistern with a valve and a strainer.

The following are also considered no less effective devices:
a. a visible warning, for example, a tundish, sight glass,
   mechanical signal or an electrically operated device
   such as an indicator lamp; or
b. an audible signal; or

Recommendations

c. a mechanical device which disables the flush, thereby indicating to the user that there is a fault condition in the WC flushing system; or

d. a device that detects when the water level rises above the maximum operating level and closes the water supply to the float operated valve.

In order to provide a Type AG air gap between the lowest level of the outlet of the float-operated valve and any water discharging from the warning pipe, it is preferable that a float-operated valve is installed with an ' up and over' discharge which conforms with BS 1212: Part 2 or 3, or is of a type that provides the necessary air gap. A float operated valve conforming to Part 1 of BS 1212 should not be installed in a WC flushing cistern unless it is protected against backflow with an acceptable backflow prevention device upstream. The valve must also be adjustable without bending the float arm.

See Section 7: Clauses G16.8 to G16.12 and the corresponding 'R' Clauses for further information on warning pipes and combined warning pipes.

Diagram
R25.6:

Relationship between float operated valve outlet, elevated overflow level and alternative warning pipes in a WC flushing cistern

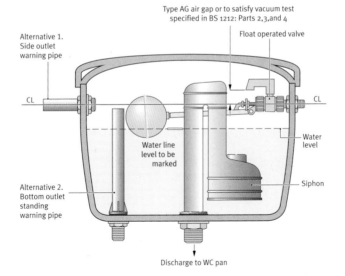

WCs, flushing devices and urinals

G25.7

Where warning pipe(s) discharge over a tundish, the tundish must be visible.

R25.7

Any tundish receiving water from a warning pipe must incorporate a type AA air gap and must be located in a prominent position so that any discharge into it can readily be seen. Unless a viewing window aperture or sight glass is provided in a WC compartment or toilet area, a tundish located in a duct, cupboard or room only infrequently visited would not be acceptable.

A warning pipe may discharge into the flush pipe of a WC either directly or if required, through a visible tundish.

For reasons of health, the outlet from a tundish must not discharge to a soil or waste discharge pipe, or a drain, downstream of any trap or gully. It is not sufficient to provide the tundish with its own trap as the water in the trap will evaporate.

G25.8

A warning pipe may be installed to discharge water into a WC pan providing it discharges into the air not less than 150mm above the top edge of the WC pan.

R25.8

The water supply industry considers that an internal overflow, discharging into the flush pipe of the WC pan is acceptable as an equally effective alternative to a warning pipe (see Clause R25.6). The termination point of any warning pipe discharging over a urinal channel or above a drainage gully grating must be at least 150mm above the top edge of the urinal channel or floor level of the surrounding area.

Urinal flushing devices

G25.9

Urinals may be flushed with either:

a. *a manual or automatically operated cistern; or,*

b. *a pressure flushing valve directly connected to a supply or distributing pipe which is designed to flush the urinal, either manually or automatically, provided that the flushing arrangement incorporates a backflow prevention arrangement or device appropriate to fluid category 5 (see Schedule 2: Paragraph 15).*

R25.9

Urinals are usually provided with automatically operated flushing cisterns; however, a manually operated flushing cistern may be provided for a single urinal (see Diagram R25.9a opposite).

Where pressure flushing valves or solenoid valves, either manually operated or automatically operated after use by electronic means, are installed, the valves may be served with water from either a supply pipe or a distributing pipe which is capable of delivering 1.5 litres per urinal bowl, or position, each time the device is operated.

Pressure flushing valves may be served with water from either a supply pipe or, in suitable circumstances, a distributing pipe. The outlet of the pressure flushing valve should incorporate, or be provided with, a pipe interrupter with a permanent atmospheric vent; the flushing valve being installed so that the level of the lowest vent aperture is not less than 150mm above the sparge outlet and not less than 300mm above the spillover level of the urinal. Unless a

Recommendations

servicing valve is integral with the pressure flushing valve it is recommended that a separate servicing valve be provided on the branch pipe to each pressure flushing valve. A suitable arrangement is shown in Diagram R25.9b below.

If manually operated solenoid or equivalent pressure flushing valves are installed the valve must be of the normally closed type or non-latching.

Pressure flushing valves that do not incorporate a permanent vent, or where a pipe interrupter is not installed on the outlet of the valve, are acceptable providing that the pressure flushing valves are supplied with water from a dedicated cistern supplied through a Type AG air gap.

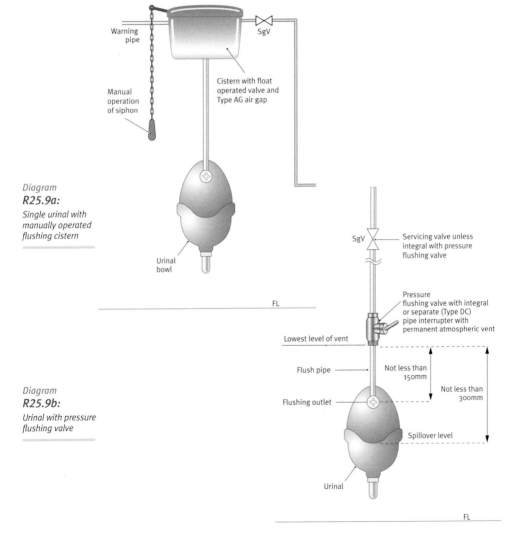

Diagram
R25.9a:

Single urinal with manually operated flushing cistern

Diagram
R25.9b:

Urinal with pressure flushing valve

WCs, flushing devices and urinals

G25.10

Unless a urinal cistern is manually operated, or fills and flushes by a device operated by an electronic sensor, pressure pad or no less suitable device which ensures that the urinal is only flushed after it is used, the inlet to the flushing cistern is to be controlled by a time switch opening an inlet valve or some other equally effective automatic device which regulates the periods during which the cistern may fill.

R25.10

This requirement prevents the flow of water to urinal cisterns during the periods when the building is unoccupied thus conserving water supplies. This is normally achieved by:

a. incorporating a time operated switch controlling a solenoid valve which cuts off the water supply to the urinal flushing cistern(s) (see Diagram R25.10a); or

b. an 'impulse' initiated automatic system which only permits water to pass to a urinal cistern when other appliances are used (see Diagram R25.10b); or

c. proximity, or sensor control devices.

Diagram
R25.10a:

Automatically operated urinal flushing cistern with period time switch control

Diagram
R25.10b:

Automatically operated urinal flushing cistern controlled by hydraulically operated valve

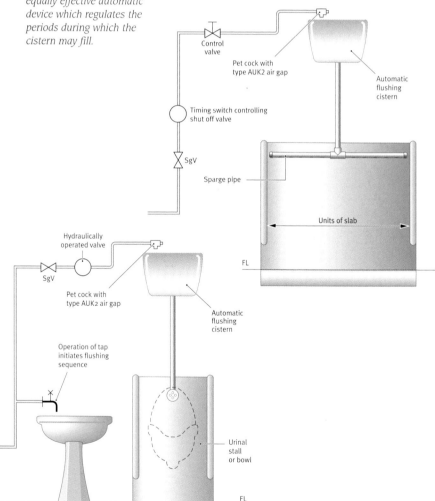

Guidance   *Recommendations*

WC pans and WC flushing devices

G25.11

All WC pans and all flushing devices for WC pans should conform to a specification approved by the Regulator.

R25.11

WC pans and WC flushing cisterns have to conform to the requirements of a specification approved by the Regulator and the types of flushing devices for use with WC pans are described below.

WC flushing cisterns may incorporate flushing devices as follows;

a. FLUSHING CISTERN WITH SIPHONIC OUTLET

This is the traditional WC 'valveless' flushing cistern where the water from the cistern can only be used to flush a WC when the siphon is primed by the user. When the flushing arrangement is not being operated it cannot pass any water to the WC pan.

When the operating handle in Diagram R25.11a is depressed the plunger rises displacing water which pushes air out of the siphon into the flush pipe and initiating the flush. When the water level reaches 'A', air enters the siphon and stops the flush.

Diagram
R25.11a:

WC flushing cistern with siphonic discharge to WC pan

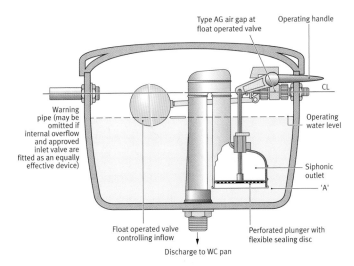

Type AG air gap at float operated valve

Operating handle

CL

Warning pipe (may be omitted if internal overflow and approved inlet valve are fitted as an equally effective device)

Operating water level

Siphonic outlet

'A'

Float operated valve controlling inflow

Perforated plunger with flexible sealing disc

Discharge to WC pan

Recommendations

b. DUAL FLUSH FLUSHING CISTERN WITH SIPHONIC OUTLET

This is similar to 'a' but incorporates an arrangement whereby air can be admitted through an aperture in the siphon, thus breaking the flow. If the lower flush volume has been selected, the aperture admits air when the falling water level reaches it, thus only part of the water in the cistern is discharged. If the larger flush volume is selected the entry of air into the siphon is prevented and the full amount of water in the cistern is discharged.

c. FLUSHING CISTERN WITH 'DROP' OR 'FLAP' VALVE OUTLET

These 'valve outlet' type cisterns have a valve on the outlet which is normally closed. With the cistern full of water the operating lever is activated and the drop valve (see Diagram R25.11b) or flap valve (see Diagram R25.11c) is opened and water passes to the flush pipe. With the 'drop' type valve the valve lifts around the full circumference of the outlet, whereas with the 'flap' valve one side of the lifting valve is hinged. There is an arrangement whereby the valve is held open automatically until the whole of the flush has passed, after which the valve closes. The 'drop' type of flushing cistern outlet valve is also available with dual flush mechanisms.

Diagram
R25.11b:
WC flushing cistern with drop valve outlet

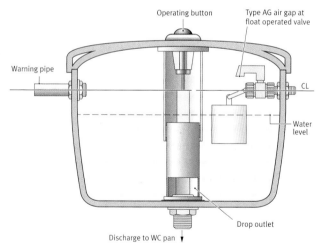

Operating button

Type AG air gap at float operated valve

Warning pipe

CL

Water level

Drop outlet

Discharge to WC pan

Guidance   Recommendations

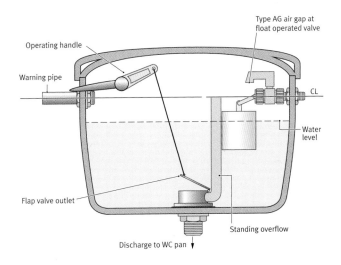

Diagram
R25.11c:
WC flushing cistern with flap valve outlet

Automatic urinal cistern filling rates

G25.12

An automatically operated flushing cistern serving urinals should be filled with water at a rate not exceeding:

a. *10 litres per hour per urinal bowl for a cistern serving a single urinal; or*

b. *7.5 litres per hour per urinal bowl or position or, as the case may be, for each 700mm width of urinal slab for a cistern serving two or more urinals.*

R25.12

This requirement will be accepted as being satisfied if any flushing cistern delivering water to a urinal installation complies with BS 1876: Specification for automatic flushing cisterns for urinals.

An automatic flushing cistern for use with a urinal, (see Diagram R25.12), contains a syphon arrangement which prevents water flowing down the flush pipe until the cistern is full. At this point water flows down the flush pipe, thus creating a negative pressure upstream of the discharge in the flush pipe, and the remaining water is siphoned out of the cistern by atmospheric pressure. Flow continues until the cistern is nearly empty and air can enter the syphon at the inlet. The cistern commences refilling and the cycle is automatically repeated.

Diagram R25.12 overleaf ▷

Guidance   Recommendations

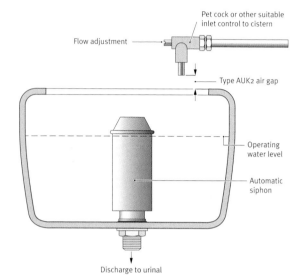

Pet cock or other suitable
inlet control to cistern

Flow adjustment

Type AUK2 air gap

Diagram
R25.12:
Details of an
automatic urinal
flushing cistern

Operating
water level

Automatic
siphon

Discharge to urinal

The frequency of operation of an automatic flushing
cistern depends on the control of the rate of filling.
Under Clause G25.12 the rate of filling must be
controlled to not more than 7.5 litres per hour for each
urinal unit where the cistern delivers to two or more
units. Where only one unit is being supplied accurate
control of inflow becomes difficult and an increased
filling rate of up to 10 litres per hour is permitted.

G25.13
Where manually or
automatically operated
pressure flushing valves are
used for flushing urinals,
the flushing valve should
deliver a flush volume not
exceeding 1.5 litres per
bowl or position each time
the device is operated.

R25.13
Schedule 2: Paragraph 25(4)(b) requires that
where individual manual or automatically operated
pressure flushing valves are installed that are
operated after use, the volume of flush must not
exceed 1.5 litres per position.

Limitation of capacity of WC flushing cisterns and method of flushing

G25.14
Until January 2001:

a. every WC pan should be flushed with water from a flushing cistern of the valveless type, that is, one that incorporates siphonic apparatus for providing the means of flushing; and

b. no flushing apparatus for use with a WC pan should give a single flush volume greater than 7.5 litres.

R25.14
Prior to 1 January 2001 the following apply:

a. flushing cisterns of the valveless type, that is, with siphonically operated outlet devices, will be the only type permitted to be installed; and

b. the maximum volume of flush for a WC will be 7.5 litres.

Therefore, prior to the end of the year 2000, while a 6 litre or lower flush volume was permitted for flushing a WC pan, the only method of flushing the pan was by the use of a flushing cistern containing a siphonically operated outlet. From 1 January 2001, flushing by the use of 'drop' or 'flap' valves in cisterns, or pressure flushing valves in other than houses, is permitted.

The above only applies to the flushing of WC pans. The use of a manually operated cistern with a drop valve or flap valve outlet, or a pressure flushing valve, for flushing a urinal was permitted from 1 July 1999.

Renewal of existing WC cisterns

G25.15
Notwithstanding G25.14, where any existing flushing cistern installed before 1 July 1999 needs to be replaced without changing the WC pan, the new cistern should be of the same flush volume as the one being replaced, which may be a single or dual flush. A single flush cistern may not be replaced with a dual flush cistern. Where dual-flush cisterns are renewed the lesser flush volume is not to be greater than 2/3 of the total flush volume.

R25.15
From the 1 January 2001 the maximum flush permitted for a WC is 6 litres except that cisterns replacing those giving the larger or a dual flush should be of a similar capacity to the original, unless the complete suit replaced.

Where a complete installation of a WC suite comprising a flushing cistern and WC pan is being replaced, the installation will be treated as new and not as a replacement, therefore the WC suite will need to comply with the current Regulations.

Schedule 2
Section 10:
Paragraphs 26, 27 & 28: Baths, sinks, showers and taps

Notes

Schedule 2

26.

All premises supplied with water for domestic purposes shall have at least one tap conveniently situated for the drawing of drinking water.

27.

A drinking water tap shall be supplied with water from –

(a) a supply pipe;

(b) a pump delivery pipe drawing water from a supply pipe; or

(c) a distributing pipe drawing water exclusively from a storage cistern supplying wholesome water.

28.

(1) Subject to paragraph (2), every bath, wash basin, sink or similar appliance shall be provided with a watertight and readily accessible plug or other device capable of closing the waste outlet.

(2) This requirement does not apply to –

(a) an appliance where the only taps provided are spray taps;

(b) a washing trough or wash basin whose waste outlet is incapable of accepting a plug and to which water is delivered at a rate not exceeding 0.06 litres per second exclusively from a fitting designed or adapted for that purpose;

(c) a wash basin or washing trough fitted with self-closing taps;

(d) a shower bath or shower tray;

(e) a drinking water fountain or similar facility; or

(f) an appliance which is used in medical, dental or veterinary premises and is designed or adapted for use with an unplugged outlet.

Baths, sinks, showers and taps

Drinking water points

G26.1

*All premises supplied
with water for domestic
purposes should have at
least one conveniently
situated tap for supplying
drinking water directly
from the supply pipe.*

R26.1

Wherever practicable in any new or altered water supply
installation where water is required for drinking, a
drinking water tap, supplied directly from the supply
pipe, should be provided. Where the drinking water tap
cannot be provided with water from a supply pipe, the
tap should be supplied from a cistern containing water
of drinking water quality (see Clauses G27.2 and R27.2).

G26.2

*In houses, a drinking
water draw-off tap should
normally be sited over the
kitchen sink.*

R26.2

In houses a drinking water tap should be located over
the kitchen sink and be connected to the supply pipe.
Where drinking water is required in premises which use
a water softener, an unsoftened drinking water tap
should be provided.

Drinking water supplies

G27.1

*All taps supplying drinking
water should be fed from a
source of wholesome water
and preferably be supplied
with water directly off a
supply pipe. Where
insufficient water pressure
is available in the supply
pipe and:*

*a. the demand is less than
0.2 litres per second; or*

*b. if a larger demand is
required and the water
undertaker agrees,*

*drinking water may be
pumped directly off the
supply pipe.*

R27.1

Where it is impracticable to supply water directly off
the supply pipe due to insufficient water pressure being
available, it may be necessary to install pumps or a
booster system. If the amount of water required is less
than 0.2 litres per second it is permissible to pump
directly off the supply pipe. However, if a greater flow
capacity is required to serve the premises the written
consent of the Water Supplier will be required either for
pumping directly or indirectly (via a cistern or closed
vessel) from the supply pipe. If an indirect system of
pumping is installed it is required that the system is of
a type that minimises the possibility of deterioration
of the quality of the water.

G27.2

*Where it is impracticable to
supply drinking water from
the supply pipe, the water
should be taken from a
distributing pipe drawing
wholesome water from a
storage cistern.*

R27.2

An alternative to supplying drinking water from the
supply pipe is to supply it from a storage cistern
containing potable water installed in accordance with
Clause G16.13. However, it is preferable that, wherever
practicable, water for drinking purposes is derived
directly from a supply pipe.

While drinking water derived from a storage cistern
may be wholesome, it is recommended that:

a. the interior of the cistern is kept clean; and

b. the quantity of water stored is restricted to a
minimum essential capacity so that the throughput
of water is maximised; and

R e c o m m e n d a t i o n s

c. the water is below a temperature of 20°C (bearing in mind that cisterns are often placed in roof spaces or voids and subjected to wide temperature variations); and

d. the cistern is insulated, ventilated and fitted with a screened warning and/or overflow pipe in accordance with Diagram G16.13a; and

e. the cistern should be regularly inspected and cleaned internally.

The provision of thermal insulation to a cistern, while protecting the water in the cistern from freezing during winter periods, is not always sufficient to maintain the water temperature to less than the recommended 20°C during summer periods; thus the quality of the water may not be satisfactory when ambient temperatures are elevated. The need for strict control of water temperatures is referred to in detail in Section 4; Clause R9.1.

G27.3

Water that has been softened on site should only be used for drinking purposes when the treated water is wholesome.

R27.3

Softening water alters its chemical composition and may result in non-compliance with the quality requirements for wholesome water. Where a water softener is installed in premises the owner or occupier of the premises is responsible for the operation and maintenance of the softener, and therefore, the quality of the water produced by the softener. If operation and maintenance is not carried out properly the quality of the water may not be satisfactory and may not satisfy the requirements of The Water Supply (Water Quality) Regulations. While commercial and industrial premises may have trained maintenance staff available this is unlikely to be the case in a private dwelling. It is recommended therefore that only water that has been derived from the Water Undertaker's mains and has not been softened on site is used for drinking purposes.

G27.4

Except in a house, all taps that are supplied with cold water that is not wholesome should be labelled 'Not Drinking Water'.

R27.4

In a house the occupier is responsible for maintaining the quality of the water used. Within a commercial or industrial building the responsibility for quality rests with the operators or owners. It is therefore important that all taps that supply drinking water are readily distinguished from those that do not. This can be achieved by labelling either type accordingly.

Baths, sinks, showers and taps

Waste outlets from appliances

G28.1

(Equivalent of Clause G27.5 in DETR Guidance document)

Except for the following appliances listed below, all baths, wash basins, sinks and similar appliances should be provided with a watertight and readily accessible plug or some other device capable of closing the water outlet:

a. *an appliance where the only taps provided are spray taps;*

b. *a washing trough or wash basin where the waste outlet is incapable of accepting a plug and to which water is delivered at a rate not exceeding 0.06 litres per second exclusively from a fitting designed or adapted for that purpose;*

c. *a wash basin or washing trough fitted with self-closing taps;*

d. *a shower bath or shower tray;*

e. *a drinking water fountain or similar facility; or*

f. *an appliance which is used in medical, dental or veterinary premises and is designed or adapted for use with an unplugged outlet.*

R28.1

In the interests of preventing undue consumption and of conserving water it is important that it is not allowed to run to waste during use of an appliance. However, there are cases where water does not need to be retained within the appliance during use and the cases listed within G28.5 are appropriate. In all other instances of sanitary appliances, waste plugs should be provided. Diagrams R28.1a and R28.1b show illustrations of the requirements.

Water supplies to washing troughs must be made through a fitting capable of feeding individual units without, at the same time, discharging to others. Examples of washing troughs are illustrated in Diagrams R28.1c and R28.1d.

Diagram
R28.1a:
Illustrations of the need for waste plugs

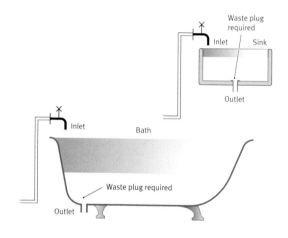

Diagram
R28.1b:
Appliances which are not required to be fitted with a plug

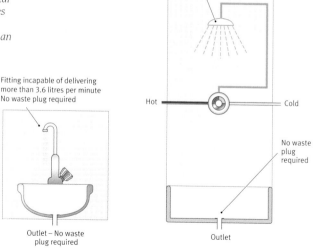

Recommendations

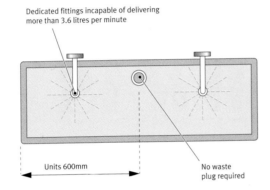

Diagram
R28.1c:
Example of a straight washing trough

Dedicated fittings incapable of delivering more than 3.6 litres per minute

Units 600mm

No waste plug required

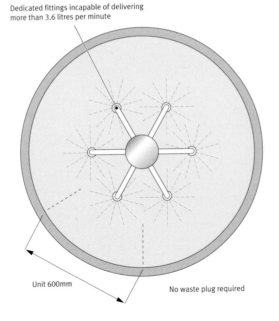

Diagram
R28.1d
Example of a circular washing trough

Dedicated fittings incapable of delivering more than 3.6 litres per minute

Unit 600mm

No waste plug required

Schedule 2

Section 11:
Paragraph 29:
Washing machines, dishwashers and other appliances

Notes

Schedule 2

29.

(1) Subject to paragraph (2), clothes washing machines, clothes washer-driers and dishwashers shall be economical in the use of water.

(2) The requirements of this paragraph shall be deemed to be satisfied in the case of machines having a water consumption per cycle of not greater than the following –

(a) for domestic horizontal axis washing machines, 27 litres per kilogram of washload for a standard 60°C cotton cycle;

(b) for domestic washer-driers, 48 litres per kilogram of washload for a standard 60°C cotton cycle;

(c) for domestic dishwashers, 4.5 litres per place setting.

Washing machines, dishwashers and other appliances

General

G29.1

(Equivalent of Clause G28.1 in DETR Guidance document)

Domestic horizontal axis washing machines should not have a water consumption per cycle greater than 27 litres per kilogram of washload in accordance with Annex 1 of EU Directive 95/12/EC.

G29.2

(Equivalent of Clause G28.2 in DETR Guidance document)

Domestic washer-driers should not have a water consumption per cycle greater than 48 litres per kilogram of washload in accordance with Annex 1 of EU Directive 99/60/EC.

G29.3

(Equivalent of Clause G28.3 in DETR Guidance document)

Domestic dishwashers should not have a water consumption per cycle greater than 4.5 litres per place setting in accordance with Annex 1 of EU Directive 97/17/EC.

R29.1

These requirements limit the volumes of water used in a single cycle of operations of domestic clothes and dishwashing machines and water using tumble driers. Reference should be made to the Water Fittings and Materials Directory published by the Water Regulations Advisory Scheme for appliances satisfying the requirements.

For details of backflow prevention requirements for both domestic and commercial application machines reference should be made to Schedule 2: Section 6.2: Paragraph 15.

Schedule 2
Section 12:
Paragraph 30 & 31:
Water for outside use

Notes

Schedule 2

30.

Every pipe which conveys water to a drinking vessel for animals or poultry shall be fitted with –

(a) a float-operated valve, or some other no less effective device to control the inflow of water, which is –

  (i) protected from damage and contamination; and

  (ii) prevents contamination of the water supply; and

(b) a stopvalve or servicing valve as appropriate.

31.

Every pond, fountain or pool shall have an impervious lining or membrane to prevent the leakage or seepage of water.

Water for outside use

Guidance   **R**ecommendations

Animal drinking troughs or bowls

G30.1

The supply to drinking apparatus for animals or poultry should be fitted with a float-operated valve or other no less effective device to control the inflow of water.

R30.1

The inlet to an animal or poultry drinking trough should be provided with a float operated valve or other no less effective inlet device. The inlet device should be a Type AA or AB air gap installed to prevent backflow from a fluid category 5 risk and prevent any contamination of the supply pipe, see Schedule 2: Section 6.2: Paragraph 15. The inlet device and backflow arrangement should be protected from damage. The general arrangements of the trough will be accepted as being satisfied if the animal watering trough complies with BS 3445: Fixed agricultural water troughs and water fittings (see Diagram R30.1).

Diagram
R30.1:

Typical cattle trough installation

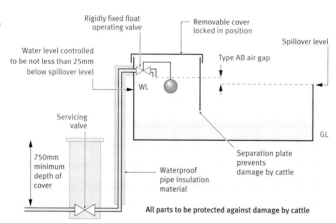

G30.2

A servicing valve should be provided on the inlet pipe adjacent to every drinking appliance for animals or poultry.

R30.2

See Diagram R30.1 for location of the servicing valve which is suitable for underground use.

G u i d a n c e   *R e c o m m e n d a t i o n s*

G30.3

Water supplies to animal drinking bowls should be provided with an appropriate backflow protection device on the inlet pipe or an air gap at the discharge point.

R30.3

Where there are animal drinking troughs which are supplied with water from a single trough the spillover levels of the supplied drinking troughs should be at a higher level than the initial drinking trough in which the water inlet device is located. This is illustrated in Diagram R30.3a where troughs B and C are arranged at such a level that any overflow takes place at A, where trough A is arranged as in Diagram R30.1.

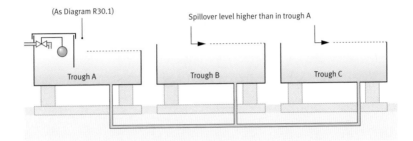

Diagram
R30.3a:

Example of supplying two drinking troughs from another

Where animal drinking bowls are supplied with water the source of the supply will depend on the type of bowl being installed. Examples of the types of animal drinking bowls available are shown below. Diagram R30.3b shows a type of bowl where the inlet valve could become submerged and this type should only be supplied with water from an independent distributing pipe. Diagram R30.3c has an air gap incorporated within the inlet device and this type may be supplied with water from a supply pipe providing that the air gap is equivalent to a Type AA air gap detailed in Schedule 2: Section 6.2: Paragraph 15.

Diagram
R30.3b:

Example of animal drinking bowl with a fluid Category 5 risk (this type of bowl to be supplied from a dedicated cistern or through a Type AA air gap only)

Diagram
R30.3c:

Example of animal drinking bowl which may be supplied with water from a supply pipe

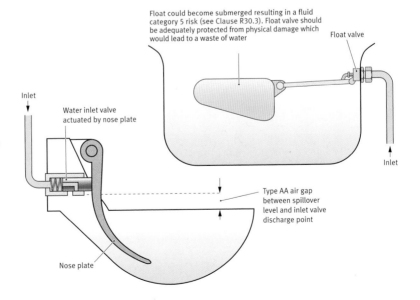

Water for outside use

G30.4
Agricultural water troughs should comply with BS 3445.

G30.5
Water supplies to farm buildings housing pigs should comply with:
BS 5502: Building and structures for agriculture: Part 42: Code of practice for design and construction of pig buildings: Section 7.2 – Drinking arrangements; and, Section 8.3 – Water.

Ponds, fountains and pools

G31.1
Any pond, fountain or pool filled or supplied with water by the Water Undertaker should have an impervious lining and be watertight.

R31.1
Pools etc. constructed of concrete will be accepted if they have been designed, constructed and tested in accordance with BS 8007: 1987: Code of practice for the design of concrete structures for retaining aqueous liquids.

G31.2
No supply or distributing pipe should be permanently or directly connected to a pond, fountain or pool. Where temporary connections are used they should comply with the requirements of Paragraph 15 of Schedule 2.

R31.2
Clause G31.2 is referring to prevention of backflow when stating that no supply or distribution pipe should be permanently or directly connected to a pond, fountain or pool.

In the context of both Regulation (Byelaw) 5 (1); Table; Item 5, and the Guidance, a pond, fountain or pool may be replenished by automatic means providing a method of backflow prevention suitable for a fluid category 5 risk is provided.

Index

Index

Index

Index

Index

Index

Index

Abbreviations and Symbols

GL	Ground level	
WC	Water closet	
WB	Washbasin	
SL	Spill-over level	
WP	Warning/overflow pipe	
SV	Stopvalve	
SgV	Servicing valve	
CV	Appliance control valve or tap	
DT	Drain tap	
T	Tundish with air gap	
SCV	Single check valve	
DCV	Double check valve	
FC	Siphonic or non-siphonic flushing cistern	
PFC	Pressure flushing cistern	
FV	Pressure flushing valve	
PRV	Pressure reducing valve	
TRV	Temperature relief valve	
TPRV	Combined temperature and pressure relief valve	
EV	Expansion valve	
ExVl	Expansion vessel	
S	Strainer	
AVV	Anti-vacuum valve	
PIDC	Pipe interrupter with permanent atmospheric vent	
PIDB	Pipe interrupter with atmospheric vent and moving element	

Water Regulations Advisory Scheme